CW01511788

FOR TOWN AND COUNTRY

The story of the 12 Ipswich Town players
who played for England

FOR TOWN AND COUNTRY

The story of the 12 Ipswich Town players
who played for England

KARL FULLER

Foreword by Terry Butcher
Ipswich Town & England

DB
PUBLISHING

For all those who enjoyed watching those
Ipswich Town and England players who are covered in this book...

First published 2024 by DB Publishing, an imprint of JMD Media Ltd,
Nottingham, United Kingdom.

Copyright © 2024, Karl Fuller

All Rights Reserved. No part of this publication may be reproduced, stored in a
retrieval system, or transmitted in any form, or by any means, electronic, mechanical,
photocopying, recording or otherwise without the prior permission in writing of the
copyright holders, nor be otherwise circulated in any form or binding or cover other
than in which it is published and without a similar condition being imposed on the
subsequent publisher.

Paperback ISBN 9781780916637
ebook ISBN 9781781563571

Printed in the UK

CONTENTS

FOREWORD

by Terry Butcher

EVERY day, as a youngster at Ipswich Town, I was surrounded by my heroes, most of whom were England internationals like Kevin Beattie.

I never believed that I would follow in their footsteps, but fast forward ten years from when I put pen to paper as a professional in 1976 to the World Cup in Mexico, I had unbelievably managed to play more games for England than any other Ipswich Town player, ever.

Karl's wonderful book, *For Town and Country*, rekindles what it was like for me to represent both Ipswich Town and England across the world. Forensically researched, this excellent book has made me understand the huge achievement of reaching football's highest level and the privilege of playing alongside many illustrious colleagues.

It details the opposition teams, substitutes, managers, referee and even the commentators! The glorious era of an England starting 11 containing three Ipswich players, led by two legendary managers, Sir Alf Ramsey and Sir Bobby Robson, may have gone, but Karl manages to bring that history right back into the spotlight, giving all of us Suffolk people a chance to once again be proud of what our small, provincial club did for England.

For Town and Country is a must for not only Ipswich Town fans but for all supporters of the underdogs.

Terry Butcher

Ipswich Town and England

INTRODUCTION

AS someone who discovered football in 1978, aged just six years old, it was a rarity to watch many games live on television at all, let alone live England games.

And to watch them in any capacity back then, you pretty much had to rely on highlights programmes on BBC's *Sportsnight* presented by Harry Carpenter, or ITV's *Midweek Sports Special*, presented by Brian Moore.

I can just about remember snippets of the 1978 World Cup, and England did not qualify for that! My vague recollections are of an Archie Gemmill goal for Scotland against the Netherlands, Peru and their diagonal red stripe on their white kit, and Argentina winning in the final in their own country.

My first memory of an Ipswich Town player playing for England was when Paul Mariner scored the only goal of the game against Hungary in a World Cup qualifier at Wembley in November 1981. The 1-0 win secured England's spot at the 1982 World Cup in Spain when for much of the second half of the qualification period, it looked as if they would not make it.

I can remember that World Cup as if it happened yesterday despite only being ten years old. It was the first time I had collected Panini stickers – I have no idea if I completed that album, or indeed what has happened to it. For England's opening game against France, I had gone crabbing with my friends a couple of hours before kick-off and was desperate to be back in time for the start of such a big match.

I missed nothing more than the first minute. By that time, England were already 1-0 ahead thanks to a goal by Bryan Robson after just 27 seconds. They went on to win 3-1 with Mariner once again on the scoresheet. I had seen an Ipswich player scoring for England at a World Cup.

While I remember nothing about their next two games, against Czechoslovakia which they won 2-0 and Kuwait, a narrow 1-0 victory, I do remember then being in St Mary's Hospital in Colchester (which now no longer exists) and I was on a children's ward with five other children – all girls. I had my adenoids out and grommets fitted at the worst possible time as England faced West Germany in the second group stage.

I asked a nurse if I could watch the game and was wheeled into an old boys' ward as the other kids did not want to watch it on the TV in our ward. That was probably my first experience of armchair experts shouting obscenities at a television screen as the game finished 0-0. It was quite fun I have to say.

I then recuperated for a while at my grandparents' house and remember watching England bow out of the World Cup after another tame goalless draw with Spain.

At the time, we had the magazine *Shoot!* delivered every week to our house. It was wonderful to see so much coverage dedicated to England's World Cup campaign, and plenty of photos of the three Ipswich players who played in that tournament.

In nearly all the England games that took place, it was only Town and Manchester United who were represented by as many as three of their players. And while we had Paul Mariner scoring against France, Terry Butcher was part of a defence that conceded just one goal and kept four clean sheets, and Mick Mills captained the team in all five games.

It is incredible to think of three Ipswich players playing in an England team nowadays at a World Cup and one of them wearing the armband. The magnitude of what I was witnessing back then was lost on my youthful mind. But that was how football was.

England squads were littered with players from many different clubs. Not just the bigger clubs.

And not having access to all the games through live TV meant that when you could watch them, it was always special. This would typically be either major tournaments or the British Home Championship.

The 1986 World Cup, which saw a last appearance by a Town player for 14 years, was another standout moment for obvious reasons pointing towards a certain Diego Maradona.

While watching England and the Ipswich players who played in 108 of those games between them is nothing more than a haze, writing this book has helped piece together those matches that contained at least one Ipswich player. It has brought back lots of memories of the game in general, and non-Ipswich players who I fondly recall from days of collecting those stickers.

I have had so much help with putting this story together. I have been able to personally interview seven of the 12 Ipswich players who played for England, each with thoughts and stories of their time wearing the jersey sporting the three lions.

They took me back to halcyon days. They spoke with pride and brought to life the dream of playing for their country while Town players. A picture of times gone by that perhaps a provincial club like Ipswich will never see again.

From Ray Crawford's first England game in 1961 to Richard Wright's debut in 2000, this is the story of the dozen Ipswich Town players who gave their all for Town and Country.

I hope you enjoy reading this book as much as I did in putting it together.

Karl Fuller

X: @fullerflavour

CHAPTER 1

Ipswich's first England international

IT is November 1961, and by now, England have already played 353 full international matches. Yet, no Ipswich Town player had ever featured for the Three Lions.

A month earlier, England, under the guidance of Sir Walter Winterbottom, beat Portugal 2-0 at Wembley in a World Cup qualifier. Their goals come from Burnley's pairing of John Connelly and Ray Pointer.

This was Pointer's second goal in his third game. But it was also his final England appearance. Winterbottom was in search of a new striker to lead his front line.

Less than halfway through the month, there were two strikers at Portman Road knocking on Winterbottom's door. Ted Phillips had already scored 18 goals, and Ray Crawford was not far behind on 15. This dazzling duo had already amassed 33 goals between them and were in form. They were proving impossible for Winterbottom to ignore.

Ultimately, it would be Crawford who was to receive a first call-up and following a 4-1 win over Manchester United in a league game at Portman Road in which the former Portsmouth man was once again on the scoresheet, he joined up with the England squad.

Crawford had started the season on fire and by this point, England were going through a spell of giving players a chance for their country. But Crawford still wondered if an opportunity would come his way.

That first call-up was for a Home International game at Wembley. The England selectors tried yet another attacking combination altogether, this time pairing Crawford with Johnny Byrne, who was making a name for himself in the Third Division with Crystal Palace. Both were winning their first England caps.

They were never comfortable with each other against an Irish team in which Danny Blanchflower was in imperious form. The game was decorated with a goal each from Bobby Charlton and Jimmy McIlroy, and the Irish could claim to have been unlucky to only get a draw.

England took the lead on 20 minutes through Charlton's right-footed effort following a pass from Crawford. Northern Ireland equalised eight minutes from time thanks to a goal from 18-year-old McIlroy who was assisted by Bill McAdams.

England's forwards too often played like passing strangers, and there was little sign of the confidence with which the team had started the year.

This game saw Danny Blanchflower extend his tally as the record appearance holder for Northern Ireland.

Ipswich had finally seen one of their own representing England. Their next game did not come round until April 1962, when they hosted Austria in a friendly. Once more Crawford was selected to start.

Four days earlier, Ipswich had beaten Wolverhampton Wanderers 3-2 at Portman Road to go to the top of the First Division for the first time in the 1961/62 season. They had just six more games to go on their way to winning the title in their very first season in the top flight, a year after they had won the Second Division. They were the first club to achieve this feat.

Crawford scored his 30th goal of the season in that win over Wolves and was a striker in red-hot form going into his second international appearance.

England avenged the defeat in Vienna of the previous year thanks mainly to the midfield domination of Johnny Haynes, who kept picking holes in the massed Austrian defence with low, angled passes.

Middlesbrough's Alan Peacock was the original chosen centre-forward, but his place went to Crawford three days before this game. Peacock needed surgery on a fractured cheekbone and would miss the rest of the season. Crawford would in fact be making his second and last appearance for his country.

Five goal chances fell to the feet of Liverpool striker Roger Hunt, who was making his debut along with Sunderland's rugged Stan Anderson. Hunt was able to score from only one of the opportunities, and the London press started the Greaves v. Hunt debate that was to last throughout their careers.

It is worth pointing out that Jimmy and Roger had nothing but the highest respect for each other and that the 'bitter rivalry' between them was manufactured by the media.

England opened the scoring in the seventh minute when Crawford turned on the spot and fired home to become the first Ipswich Town player to score for the Three Lions. This would be the only goal that Crawford would score for his country.

A penalty was then scored by Ron Flowers on 37 minutes after John Connelly was brought down. A Roger Hunt header on 67 minutes extended England's lead before Hans Buzek pulled a goal back with a header on 76 minutes.

Crawford's England career was over after just two games. Ten days later, England played Scotland at Hampden Park and his place was taken by Tottenham's Bobby Smith.

Crawford's first knowledge of his call-up to the England squad for that first appearance against Northern Ireland was rather unconventional and certainly in a manner that would be unthinkable nowadays.

'I was doing some shopping in Ipswich for my then wife Eileen, and fellow Ipswich player of the time Reg Pickett was across the street. We shouted hello to one another and then he congratulated me. I thought he was having a joke and wondered what he meant. He told me that just before leaving home, he had heard on the radio that I had been selected for the next England squad.

'I could not believe it until I arrived home. Eileen opened the door with a large smile on her face and told me that someone was indoors waiting to see me.

'When I went into the living room, Ipswich Town chairman Mr John [Cobbold] shook my hand and congratulated me as this was the first time that an Ipswich player had been selected by England. A few seconds later, the champagne cork hit our ceiling, and later in the day, the living room was full of press, cameras, lights, and the full works. Celebrating with Eileen and Mr John was a real highlight.'

A few days later came that victory over Manchester United with Crawford on the scoresheet. England manager Walter Winterbottom was sat in the stands, with Crawford thinking that he must have been in attendance to watch team-mate Ted Phillips.

'It was sad that Ted never played for England. Not just for him, but also for England fans who never saw one of the most exciting players in the game,' said Crawford.

'Ted was flying in those days. We were a good pair together. We knew how one another played and I would never go near Ted when he was near to goal. I knew that he could create an angle and get a shot away. His shot was so hard too. I knew the goalkeeper might drop it, so I was on hand to tuck the loose ball into the net.

12

'We trained well together, and he became a very good friend of mine. He would stay at my house a few times and when we had a few events at Ipswich, him and his wife would stay at mine rather than going back to Colchester where he lived.'

The following Monday morning, Crawford drove to London to join the England squad at the Lancaster Gate Hotel. Players would make their own way to the hotel and got paid petrol money. It was an experience that Crawford was not really anticipating.

'I was expecting more from the setup but that's just how they ran it. We did have two nights in the hotel before playing Northern Ireland on the Wednesday afternoon.'

Before that game, England played a practice match against Fulham at Craven Cottage, which they won 3-0, including a goal from Crawford.

Winterbottom did not relay a pre-match tactical team talk and when it came to Crawford's debut against Northern Ireland the only instruction to Crawford from Winterbottom was, 'Just play like you do for your club.' This left Crawford somewhat unhappy with matters.

'I was very disillusioned with the England setup and the way that Walter Winterbottom was running the team. For my first game, I was expecting more information from the manager to help me play and get through that first game.

'How could I play for England just like I did for Ipswich Town? I was playing with different players, and it was a different setup. '

On creating that goal for Charlton against the Irish, Crawford revealed that it was not all praise that came his way, 'I remember getting told off by Alf Ramsey. He picked me up after the game and said what was I doing going down the wing crossing the ball for Bobby to score? He should have been going down the wing and crossing for me to score! That was the end of the conversation.'

Also included in the England line-up against Northern Ireland was none other than future Ipswich boss Bobby Robson, and Crawford recalled playing in that game with Robson quite fondly.

'Bobby was an out-and-out wing-half. He was a good player, a good controller of the ball, very fit, and I got on quite well with Bobby. Of course, I never knew then that one day he would be my club manager.

'That was strange given that we were a similar age. But he was a very experienced player, and a very nice man.'

Fortunately for Ray, he received a second call-up and that held a happier memory for him, 'I scored in that next game. So, I was very happy with that. We did play much better against Austria and won 3-1.'

Of his goal, he recalled, 'John Connelly ran down the wing and crossed the ball over and I ran into the area and hit the ball into the net. It was exactly the sort of goal that Alf wanted me to score for Ipswich.'

When asked about how the system that England played compared to what Ray was used to in Ramsey's Ipswich side, he was quite bullish in his response.

'Well, there was no system how to play. The manager just said what he stated previously. Each player just had to go out and play like they did for their club. I was a centre-forward, and Bobby Charlton was a left-winger and you expected him to be running down the line and crossing the ball and yet we were a bit ugly. It was not right. When Alf took over as England boss, he sorted all that out.'

When asked if Ray had any hopes to play for England when Ramsey took on the England job, he was quite dismissive of such thoughts.

'No, because I knew what Alf was like. Don't get me wrong, I would have liked to have played for England under him, but I did not think that I probably would do because Alf had a different setup in his mind. He wanted to play his players. He would be handed a team sheet by the selectors before the game and told how to play the game.

'He would thank them very much for taking the time to write that all out for him and tell them to take their seat in the stand, enjoy the football, but leave the selection to him. They had to do that really as he had only just been appointed as manager and there was no way that he was going to be dictated to, because we knew what he was like at Ipswich.

'He picked the side, the tactics, and told them that's what he would do. The selectors were made up of people running different clubs, and they obviously wanted to pick their own players.'

For those two games that Ray played for England, he had plenty of support in the stands watching on.

'My wife Eileen came to the games and Alf brought the Ipswich first team to the games. My dad came too and after the Northern Ireland game, he was interviewed and was asked what he thought of my performance. His response was that it was rather average!'

CHAPTER 2

Johnson & Beattie put Ipswich on England's map

IT would be more than ten and a half years before the second Ipswich player represented England as Mick Mills received the first of his 42 call-ups in October 1972 for a friendly at Wembley against Yugoslavia which finished in a 1-1 draw. There had been 108 England games between Crawford's second and final appearance and this first cap for Mills.

Along with Mills, Frank Lampard (senior, of course), Jeff Blockley, and Mick Channon made their international debuts as Sir Alf Ramsey juggled his squad because of club calls and injuries.

The quartet of newcomers looked set for a winning start when future Ipswich manager Joe Royle scored his first goal for England (the 200th goal under the reign of Sir Alf Ramsey) in the 40th minute. But Yugoslav centre-forward Franjo Vladić snatched an equaliser five minutes after half-time and Peter Shilton had to be at his best as skilful winger Dragan Džajić started to pull the uncertain England defence apart.

The Yugoslavs missed three clear-cut chances in the closing stages. Tough luck on Mills that he had to make his international bow against the famed and feared Džajić, one of the greatest players ever produced by Yugoslavia. It was a baptism of fire, and Mills had to wait four years for his next cap.

This was now four matches at Wembley without victory and saw a new record set, beating the previous record of three from 1947 to 1951, and equalled in 1953.

Before kick-off, the teams were presented to His Grace the Duke of Marlborough, the FA's honorary vice-president.

While it would be a further three years and more before Mills would win his second cap, Kevin Beattie was the third Ipswich player to receive a call-up. It would be two and a half years, and 25 England games after that Mills appearance against Yugoslavia, before Beattie was called upon for a European Championship qualifier against Cyprus at Wembley which England won 5-0.

Prior to that senior call, Beattie had nine under-23 caps to his name, three of which came in the 1972/73 season. His first under-23s game was a 3-0 win against Wales at Vetch Field, home of Swansea City. This was a game that saw a hat-trick from Malcolm Macdonald.

Then, a 3-1 win over the Netherlands played at Arsenal's Highbury saw fellow Ipswich player Trevor Whymark score. The third game of that season saw England under-23s win 2-1 against Scotland at Rugby Park, home of Kilmarnock, with another goal from Whymark.

There were five more under-23 appearances in 1973/74 with three goalless draws against Poland, Wales, and Turkey followed by a 1-0 defeat in Yugoslavia, and a 2-2 draw in France.

Beattie's final under-23s game came in the 1974/75 season when he scored in a 2-0 win in Wales at Wrexham's Racecourse Ground. Ipswich's David Johnson also scored.

A month before that win in Wales, Beattie was due to play in a game in Scotland at Aberdeen. He had caught the train from Ipswich to travel to Scotland via London. But when the train from Euston to Glasgow pulled in at his native Carlisle, he decided to get off and see family.

He felt tired and did not feel like playing so decided to stay in Carlisle. The following day, a not-too-pleased Bobby Robson rang him and ordered Beattie to return to Ipswich.

Yet, despite Beattie believing that he had done his chances of future call-ups severe harm, Don Revie selected him for the next game against Wales. The evening before that match in Swansea, Revie had a chat with Beattie and told him that he understood why he had pulled out and that he would also be in the full England squad if he kept up his form for Ipswich. The discussion worked!

The first of just nine full caps that Beattie won saw Malcolm Macdonald score all five goals – four of them with his head – in an extraordinary display of finishing.

Macdonald became the first player to score five at Wembley and it equalled the five-goal haul by Tottenham's Willie Hall for England against Northern Ireland at Old Trafford in 1938.

He scored his first in the second minute, made it 2-0 in the 35th minute and added two more early in the second half against an outplayed and outclassed Cypriot team. He finished off his one-man spectacular with a brilliantly headed goal in the closing stages, which was the 1,300th goal scored by England. Macdonald's team-mates came off at the end wondering how between them they had managed to miss at least six more goals.

'To be honest,' said Macdonald, 'I should have had eight goals. I managed to miss three easy chances. But I suppose I can't complain!'

This was England's first hat-trick in European Championship qualification. Wembley had to wait a further six years for its next treble – its 11th.

Beattie had a goal disallowed for a foul on goalkeeper Michalakis Alkiviades on 59 minutes; the injury sustained by Alkiviades meant that he could not continue.

For Cyprus, there were two Andreas Konstantinous on the bench. One was a midfielder, and the other a goalkeeper.

A further note for this game was that of the four managers to have sat at Wembley up to this point, Don Revie was the first to have kept four clean sheets in his first four matches.

In their next game less than a month later, England played in Cyprus and had to be content with a sixth-minute winning goal from a Kevin Keegan header in the European Championship qualifying return.

A bumpy pitch led to many of the England passes missing their target in a scrappy match during which goalkeeper Ray Clemence was hardly tested.

Kevin Beattie, winning his second cap, limped off with a groin injury just before half-time, and at the time, he was the youngest starter to be replaced by a substitute. He was 67 days younger than Wilf McGuinness when he was replaced in May 1959.

Dennis Tueart came on as a 73rd-minute substitute for Dave Thomas for his debut, and to be the 60th player to become an England substitute, 25 years after the first.

This was the first match to be played at the new Tsirion Stadium in Limassol, and while the stands were impressive the pitch needed a lot of groundwork!

'Probably the worst pitch any England team has had to play on,' was the terse comment from manager Don Revie.

Injury kept Beattie out of England's next game when six days later, they met Northern Ireland in Belfast and dug out a 0-0 draw in a Home International Championship match. This match did, however, provide a fourth Ipswich player to play for England as Colin Viljoen debuted for the first of his two caps.

England equalled their record of six consecutive clean sheets in a match that provided an emotional return to Belfast for the first time in four years. Security issues meant that Northern Ireland had been unable to stage games at Windsor Park from 1971 to 1975.

The Irish defence, in which Tottenham Hotspur goalkeeper Pat Jennings, Arsenal right-back Pat Rice and Ipswich Town centre-half Allan Hunter were outstanding, allowed the England forwards little time and space in which to work.

'We were given a wonderful welcome by the crowd,' said Revie, 'and we are disappointed that we did not provide them with a better spectacle. All credit to the Irish defenders. They worked their socks off, but we should have had at least two goals to show for our supremacy.'

Viljoen became the 907th player to win a cap for England in a game that also saw Ipswich's Bryan Hamilton feature for the hosts. Hamilton was replaced in the 36th minute having to leave the field of play through injury; in the 29th minute he had been caught on the back of his right heel from behind by Tueart.

He was carried from the field and given treatment on the sidelines. He came back on briefly after five minutes but could not continue and looked a forlorn figure, limping across the field before he was eventually replaced.

It would be only four further days before England were next in action, and this was another Home International Championship match at Wembley that saw them draw 2-2 with Wales. It was a game that had more than one connection to Ipswich Town.

Viljoen made his second and final appearance, while for striker David Johnson, he became the fifth Ipswich player to play for England and marked his debut superbly by scoring both of his country's goals. It was also the first time that an England game had two players who were representing Ipswich.

Prior to that first call-up to the senior side, Johnson had already played seven games for the under-23s. He would play for that team in a total of nine games.

The two matches he played in the under-23s prior to his full debut saw him score his first and only goals at that level. In a 3-2 win over Portugal in Lisbon in November 1974, Johnson scored two of England's goals in a 3-2 win. His strike partner that day was Ipswich's Trevor Whymark.

And in January 1975, Johnson was on the scoresheet again as was Beattie in a 2-0 win over Wales at Wrexham's Racecourse Ground.

Johnson made a memorable debut, scoring both of England's goals including an 85th minute equaliser that stole victory from a spirited Welsh team. It was the first time that an Ipswich player would score two goals in a game for England, and one of only two occasions that this feat occurred at all.

Johnson gave England an eighth-minute lead, but Wales were rewarded for their persistence with two goals ten minutes into the second half. The first was scored by John Toshack, who then laid on a second for Arfon Griffiths.

Aston Villa's Brian Little, sent on as a substitute in the 70th minute for his only England cap, found Johnson with a centre from which he headed the goal that ended Welsh hopes of a first ever win at Wembley.

Ipswich's South African-born Colin Viljoen made his second and final appearance for England.

Little was the ninth England player to make his debut from the substitutes' bench, and the first to not make a second appearance.

Three days later, England were in more Home International action when they took on Scotland and won 5-1. Once again, it was a game that had Ipswich fans purring for Beattie and Johnson both scored a goal apiece.

England scored twice in the first seven minutes, and the opening goal from Gerry Francis was a spectacular shot that rocketed into the net from 25 yards. It was his first senior international goal.

Scotland never recovered from this shattering start despite some superb play by Kenny Dalglish.

Beattie, in his third cap, doubled the lead with his first goal for England, before Colin Bell made it 3-0 five minutes before half-time. Bruce Rioch pulled one back from the penalty spot in the last minute of the half.

Bell, Francis and Alan Ball, in his last game for England, were in unstoppable form, and it was Francis who made it 4-1 in the 63rd minute with a deflected shot after Ball had pushed a free kick through Bell's legs into his path.

Kevin Keegan, a bundle of energy in the England attack, rammed a shot against the bar ten minutes later, and Johnson steered the rebound into the net for his third international goal to complete the rout of a dispirited Scottish side.

'That's as good as it gets,' said Ball, who felt he was cemented into the team as skipper. Of the game, Beattie later said, 'Although my international career was brief, there is no doubt about the highlight. I will always have a vivid memory of this game with me scoring one of the goals.'

FOOTBALL ASSOCIATION INTERNATIONAL

ENGLAND
v
IRELAND

WEDNESDAY, NOVEMBER 22nd, 1961   **KICK-OFF 2.30 p.m.**

EMPIRE STADIUM

WEMBLEY

OFFICIAL PROGRAMME   -   ONE SHILLING

Ray Crawford - H v Northern Ireland - 22 November 1961.

THE FOOTBALL ASSOCIATION
INTERNATIONAL MATCH

ENGLAND

VERSUS

YUGOSLAVIA

Wednesday, 11th October, 1972   Kick-off 7.45 p.m.

Empire **WEMBLEY** Stadium

Official Programme . . . Ten pence

Mick Mills - H v Yugoslavia - 11 October 1972.

EUROPEAN FOOTBALL CHAMPIONSHIP

HENRI
DELAUNAY
CUP

WEDNESDAY, 16th APRIL 1975

GROUP ONE
QUALIFYING
COMPETITION

ENGLAND v CYPRUS

Official
Programme
Fifteen pence

WEMBLEY
STADIUM

Kick
off
7.45 p.m.

Kevin Beattie - H v Cyprus - 16 April 1975.

THE BRITISH CHAMPIONSHIP

NORTHERN IRELAND

VERSUS

ENGLAND   MAY, 17th, 1975
AT 3 O'CLOCK

A N D

20p   MAY, 23rd, 1975
AT 7 O'CLOCK   **WALES**

AT WINDSOR PARK

Colin Viljoen - A v Northern Ireland - 17 May 1975.

FOOTBALL ASSOCIATION INTERNATIONAL
(BRITISH CHAMPIONSHIP)

ENGLAND

versus

WALES

WEDNESDAY, 21st MAY, 1975

Official
Programme
Fifteen pence

WEMBLEY
STADIUM

Kick
off
7.45 p.m.

David Johnson - H v Wales - 21 May 1975.

THE F.I.F.A. WORLD CUP

QUALIFYING TOURNAMENT — GROUP II

WEDNESDAY 30 MARCH 1977 ● Kick-off 8.00 p.m.

ENGLAND
v
LUXEMBOURG

OFFICIAL SOUVENIR PROGRAMME . . . . 20 pence

EMPIRE **WEMBLEY** STADIUM

Paul Mariner - H v Luxembourg - 30 March 1977.

Brian Talbot - A v Northern Ireland - 28 May 1977.

Fédération Luxembourgeoise de Football, a. s. b. l.

COUPE DU MONDE DE LA F. I. F. A.

tour qualificatif — groupe II

mercredi, 12 octobre 1977, 19.15 hrs.

Stade Municipal de Luxembourg

LUXEMBOURG
ANGLETERRE

Programme officiel — prix : 25.— Lfrs

Trevor Whymark - A v Luxembourg - 12 October 1977.

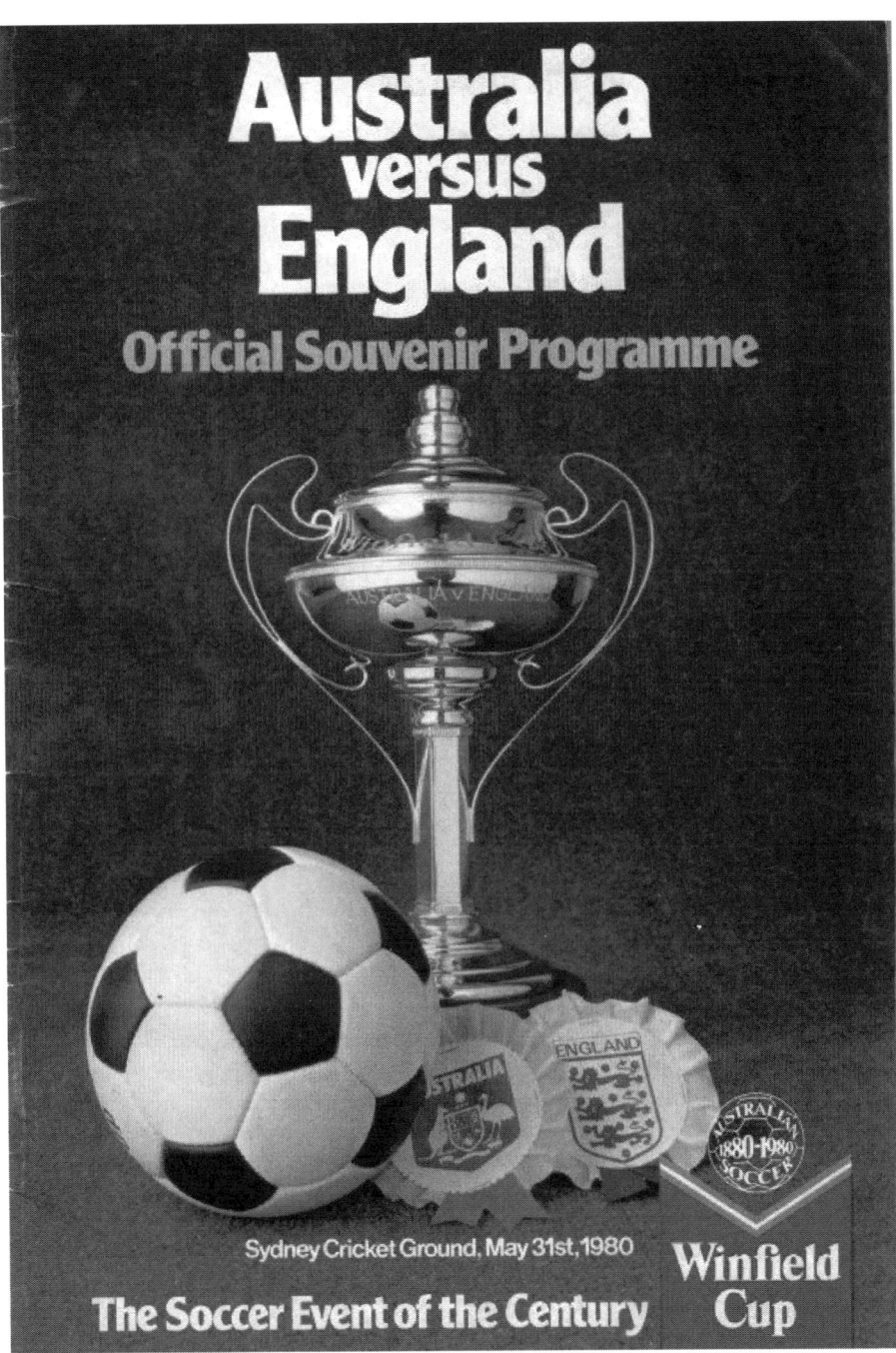

Terry Butcher and Russell Osman - A v Australia - 31 May 1980.

FIFA WORLD CUP
QUALIFYING TOURNAMENT GROUP IV
ENGLAND · HUNGARY · NORWAY · RUMANIA · SWITZERLAND

Wednesday 10th September 1980   Kick off 7.45 pm

England v Norway

Wembley Stadium

Official programme 50p

Eric Gates - H v Norway - 10 September 1980.

28

MALTA vs ENGLAND

INTERNATIONAL "A" FRIENDLY MATCH

Saturday, 3rd June 2000
National Stadium, Ta' Qali
at 16.00

Official
Souvenir
Programme
Lm1.00

MALTACOM plc · Official Sponsors of Malta's National Teams

Richard Wright - A v Malta - 3 June 2000.

29

CHAPTER 3

Mills returns as Beattie says farewell to Wembley

KEVIN Beattie and David Johnson both appeared for England once again, in the first international of the 1975/76 season – a 2-1 friendly win over Switzerland in Basel.

Kevin Keegan scored from close range in the eighth minute and had a penalty saved three minutes later after Colin Bell sent Johnson haring into the penalty area before goalkeeper Erich Burgener brought him down to give Keegan the chance of settling the game after only 12 minutes.

Burgener, diving hard to his right, pushed aside a kick that was firmly struck, though high enough to bring about the possibility of a save.

Johnson then turned creator as he laid on a second goal for Mick Channon in the 19th minute and England looked on course for a comfortable victory.

But they got caught in the clutches of complacency, and the Swiss were allowed back into the game after sloppy marking had allowed Kurt Müller the freedom of the penalty area for a headed goal in the 30th minute.

An England defence which saw Beattie booked in the 63rd minute, at left-back, was often at full stretch in the second half, but the best scoring chances fell to the feet of substitute Malcolm Macdonald who missed the target twice in the closing stages.

Alan Ball was surprised to find himself axed and started a one-man vendetta against Revie's style of management. It was the first sign that all was not well beneath the surface in the Revie empire.

England's next game was against Czechoslovakia in Bratislava, and for the first time in more than a year, there was no Ipswich player present. The match originally kicked off on the Wednesday evening but was abandoned after 17 minutes because of fog. It was played the following evening with the Czechs running out as 2-1 winners.

The next game, against Portugal in November 1975, was also a European Championship qualifier and was played in Lisbon, ultimately ending in a 1-1 draw. The evening before, David Johnson was back in the under-23 side who beat their Portuguese counterparts at Selhurst Park, Crystal Palace.

Beattie returned, however, and won his fifth England cap in a game where they went a goal down in their final European Championship qualifier to a 16th-minute free kick by Rui Rodrigues that swerved viciously on its way into the net from 25 yards.

The Portuguese missed two easy chances before Mick Channon equalised with a free kick that deflected into the net off a defender three minutes before half-time.

England needed a victory to boost their fading chances of reaching the European Championship, but they kept running blindly into an offside trap.

The draw left the Czechs needing only a draw in Cyprus to qualify ahead of England in first place with only the group winners progressing. They beat the Cypriots 3-0 and went on to win Euro '76. England were left kicking themselves.

Beattie was booked in the 40th minute, and four players all made their final appearance for England in this game – Stephen Whitworth, Malcolm Macdonald, Allan Clarke, and Dave Thomas.

Four months later, England returned to action in a friendly against Wales in Wrexham. This game saw the return of Mick Mills to the England setup for his second appearance, some three and a half years after his first. It ended with a 2-1 win for England.

Crystal Palace striker Peter Taylor became the first Third Division player capped since Johnny Byrne, then also with Palace, in 1961. Taylor came on as a substitute for Mick Channon and scored the victory-clinching second goal ten minutes from the end of a match staged to mark the centenary of the Welsh FA.

It was the eighth goal scored by an England substitute and the first to be scored by a debutant. This game marked the first occasion that the two players making a substitute appearance were also making their senior team debuts. It was also the first time since December 1968 that a substitute had debuted in a friendly.

Peter Taylor was the tenth England player to make his debut as a substitute; Dave Clement was the 11th.

It was all part of an experimental England side that included seven other new caps: Trevor Cherry, Phil Neal, Phil Thompson, Mike Doyle, Phil Boyer (only cap), Ray Kennedy, and Dave Clement.

Kennedy, one of five Liverpool players in the team, gave England the lead in the 70th minute after a Trevor Brooking centre had been headed out. Alan Curtis scored for Wales in the last minute. Kevin Keegan captained his country for the first time.

Meanwhile, Don Revie had been notorious during his career as an outstanding club manager for finding excuses to withdraw players from international duty. Now he was on the receiving end of the club v country controversy, as managers continually pulled players out of his squad at the last minute.

This was the first of seven consecutive games that Mills would line up in the England defence, and for a second successive match, they would be back in Wales once more just over a month later in Cardiff. This time, they came away with a 2-1 victory in the Home Championship.

England were fortunate not to be three goals down before Peter Taylor scored the only goal of a scrappy match with a low shot from 20 yards in the 59th minute.

Eight of England's players had just ten caps between them, with Tony Towers, Brian Greenhoff, and Stuart Pearson making their debuts. Only some exceptional goalkeeping by Ray Clemence saved England from defeat, and the player turnover was so great that many people were beginning to question Don Revie's grasp of international management.

Just three days after that game in Wales, Mills once again lined up for another Home International Championship match against Northern Ireland at Wembley.

The Irish side included Mills's Ipswich Town team-mate Allan Hunter, as well as former Ipswich player Bryan Hamilton who was by now playing for Everton.

Mick Channon, dropped against Wales, responded to his recall with two goals. His first came from the penalty spot just 90 seconds after skipper Gerry Francis had opened the scoring with a superbly taken goal in the 35th minute. In scoring, Francis was the first captain to score for over six years since Bobby Charlton did so in April 1970.

Stuart Pearson made it 3-0 with his first goal for his country after the England defence had snuffed out an Irish revival early in the second half, and Channon rounded off an impressive display when he drove the ball wide of goalkeeper Pat Jennings and into the roof of the net following a clever flick pass by Kevin Keegan.

Joe Royle came off the bench in the 75th minute to replace Keegan for England.

Not since 1948/49 had England played at the national stadium just once in a season.

Mills's fifth cap came in England's 500th game, which resulted in a 2-1 defeat to Scotland at Hampden Park.

This match proved to be a skeleton in Ray Clemence's cupboard. He allowed a half-hit shot from Kenny Dalglish to roll through his legs for Scotland's winning goal in the 49th minute.

Mick Channon had given England an 11th-minute lead following enterprising play by Roy McFarland, and Bruce Rioch equalised six minutes later when he headed an Eddie Gray corner powerfully wide of Clemence.

A spectacular 40-yard run by Dalglish ended with Clemence snatching the ball from him in the penalty area, a complete contrast to what was to happen in the second half.

'It was the worst moment of my career,' Clemence said many years later. 'I thought I had the ball covered, but it bobbled and the next thing I knew it was through my legs and into the net. I wanted the Hampden pitch to open and hide me.' This game was to be the last for England for striker Peter Taylor.

Eight days after that defeat in Scotland, Mills was part of an England side that took part in the US Bicentennial Cup in the USA.

A last-minute goal by substitute Roberto gave Brazil a flattering victory in this opening match which condemned England to their 100th loss in all games played. Roberto became only the third substitute to score against England, and the first since May 1968.

England dominated for long periods, but their finishing lacked the accuracy of their approach play. 'It was heartbreaking to have lost so late in the game,' said Don Revie.

'I am sure that any neutral observer would say that England deserved at least a draw.'

It would be just a further five days until Mills took part in England's second Bicentenary Cup game as England beat Italy 3-2 in New York. He was named as a substitute and came on at half-time for Liverpool's Phil Neal.

Jimmy Rimmer was named in goal to win his only cap for England, while Ray Wilkins, Gordon Hill, and Joe Corrigan also won their first caps. Tony Towers of Sunderland played his third and final game.

England had to fight back from going two goals down inside the first 20 minutes and did so superbly to win with three goals in the opening seven minutes of the second half.

The game was played on an unsatisfactory pitch at Yankee Stadium, the home of the New York Yankees – which is a baseball stadium. It was transformed into a football pitch for this match, but still bearing the sand of the baseball diamond, which cut across the middle of the Italian, then England's, half of the pitch. All the goals were scored in the grass half.

Both teams played open and enterprising football. Mick Channon was in inspiring form, captaining his country for the first time, and his two goals sandwiched a headed goal by Phil Thompson – his first for England – from a Hill corner.

Wilkins made an impressive debut, while Corrigan was the 12th player to make his England debut as a substitute, the first goalkeeper sub.

At 3-2, England had the ball in the net in the 62nd minute, but Hill was adjudged to be offside. Italy, likewise, in the 93rd minute saw Giacinto Facchetti's last-gasp equaliser ruled out due to future England manager Fabio Capello's barge into Corrigan.

The 17th England game to feature an Ipswich Town player was the first to be a World Cup qualifier as Mills and England travelled to Finland for a Group Two game.

Kevin Keegan was outstanding as England got off to a flying start in their 1978 qualifying campaign. He laid on the first goal in the 14th minute for Stuart Pearson, who returned the compliment after the Finns had forced an equaliser against the run of play.

Mick Channon made it 3-1 in the 57th minute and Keegan wrapped it up three minutes later with a superb solo goal.

The only downside of the performance was that England missed a procession of simple chances against the whipping boys of their group.

Gerry Francis captained his country for the eighth and final time in what proved to be his final appearance. For Mills, this was the last game in a run of seven successive England appearances as he then missed the first international match of the 1976/77 season, a friendly against the Republic of Ireland at Wembley.

Next up was the return match against Finland at Wembley. After almost a year since his last cap, Ipswich defender Kevin Beattie played his first World Cup qualifier and was later joined by club team-mate Mick Mills who had been named on the bench.

England spurted into the lead with a third-minute goal from Dennis Tueart, his first in international football, but they finished with chants of 'Rubbish' ringing in their ears after they had made a hash of a match in which they needed a resounding win against unrated opponents.

The Finns played above themselves, and equalised early in the second half before Joe Royle headed a 52nd-minute winner from Mick Channon's centre to notch up England's 300th win.

Those close to the camp knew that all was not well between Don Revie and a faction of Football Association officials, who quietly questioned his methods of management and his commercial interests.

While Mills had the honour of being the first Ipswich player to appear as a substitute for England, Beattie became the second to do so in the very next game as their roles in the squad reversed; Beattie dropped to the bench and Mills came into the starting line-up.

This was in yet another Word Cup qualifying game in Rome against Italy, and England were defeated 2-0.

Italy, including six Juventus players, were a class above in this crucial match. Goals in each half by Giancarlo Antognoni and Roberto Bettega were enough to settle it for the hosts, who virtually booked their tickets for the 1978 finals in Argentina.

Just when England needed continuity, quick-change artist Don Revie made six changes plus two positional alterations. He clearly went into this vital game nowhere near knowing what his best side was. The press was beginning to turn against him, and the first of the 'Revie Must Go' newspaper headlines started to appear.

Beattie became the 80th substitute to be used by England when he came off the bench on 80 minutes to replace Dave Clement after the Queens Park Rangers man twisted his ankle as he jumped to try and stop the ball going out of play.

Derby County's Roy McFarland played for England for the 28th and final time. For Italy, Fabio Capello once again featured.

Three months later, and for England's first game of 1977, little did we know at the time that Kevin Beattie was making his penultimate appearance for his country, and his final international appearance at Wembley.

The Netherlands produced what many considered the finest display at Wembley by a visiting team since Hungary beat England 6-3 in 1953.

The two Johans – Cruyff and Neeskens – dictated the pace and pattern of the match, and it was Jan Peters, playing in only his second international, who nipped in for two goals in less than ten minutes in the first half.

Shortly after the first Dutch goal, Manchester United's Brian Greenhoff injured his right elbow. He made his exit from the pitch slowly, and in the time that it took England to prepare and send on his replacement Colin Todd, the visitors took advantage and scored their second. This was the 100th friendly goal that England had conceded at home.

Trevor Francis made his debut for an England team that spent much of the game chasing shadows. The 90,000 crowd were torn between applauding the brilliance of the Netherlands, and slow hand-clapping the woeful home performance.

Four England players – Dave Clement, Mike Doyle, Paul Madeley, and Stan Bowles – all appeared for their country for the final time.

Meanwhile, it was an occasion that Beattie was keen to overlook, 'My last England match at Wembley is one that I wanted to forget. The Dutch rang rings around us that night, and I had a real stinker. I would go as far to say that it was my worst performance of my career. After the game, I cried my eyes out. Johnny Rep, the Dutch winger, gave me a real roasting and I just wanted to get off the pitch.'

CHAPTER 4

Mariner & Talbot debut for England

THE last England game before the regular season of 1976/77 had finished saw Paul Mariner become the sixth Ipswich Town player to play for his country when he came off the bench to replace Joe Royle at half-time at Wembley against Luxembourg.

He was the 13th player to make an England debut as a substitute. For Royle, this would be the last time that he would play for the Three Lions.

Four goals in the last half an hour just about kept alive England's faint hopes of qualifying for the 1978 World Cup finals as they were comfortable 5-0 winners.

Kevin Keegan had given England a tenth-minute lead, but then they became too anxious against the Luxembourg part-timers.

Trevor Francis doubled the lead with his first goal for his country, and then Ray Kennedy added a third.

For Mick Channon's first goal, TV footage showed that his headed effort was cleared off the line by Roger Fandel before the ball wholly crossed. Despite this, the referee awarded a goal.

Channon's second was from the penalty spot before Gilbert Dresch was sent off in the 87th minute for a foul on Channon. He became only the second player to be sent off in a Wembley international, following Argentina's 1966 World Cup skipper Antonio Rattín into the black history book.

On TV commentary, Brian Moore stated that it was for two foul challenges. However, the first yellow card was for kicking the ball away after a foul, and then a second caution for a total hack at Channon.

Aston Villa's John Gidman also made his debut at right-back to win his only England cap.

Mariner recalls the moment that Ron Greenwood put an arm around him before his first training session, and the England manager's words, 'There's one reason you're here and it's because of what you've done at your club. Just do the same and you'll be fine.' That had similar connotations to the words that Ray Crawford received from Walter Winterbottom during his time with the Three Lions.

For that game against Luxembourg, Mariner's room-mate was Manchester United winger Gordon Hill. Mariner said, 'When you played with him, you knew the crosses were coming in, perfect for a centre-forward, but that was a short-lived relationship.

'My half-time appearance as a substitute was one of only three occasions that we were in the same squad together, the final time being in Luxembourg later that year when I scored my first goal for England, and he won his last England cap.'

The 1976/77 season came to an end with Ipswich finishing third in the First Division. With Mills, Beattie and Mariner having already received England recognition, there was then to be a call-up for a fourth player.

For the first summer game of 1977, it was a trip to Belfast to take on Northern Ireland in the Home Championship. And for the first time, Ipswich were represented by three men as Brian Talbot joined Mariner and Mills for his debut and thus became the seventh Ipswich player to play for England.

Northern Ireland had taken a fifth-minute lead through Chris McGrath against an England team weakened by the absence of Liverpool players, who had helped the Merseyside club win the European Cup three days earlier.

Mick Channon equalised in the 27th minute, and then missed two clear-cut chances with headers that were misdirected. Talbot's debut came when replacing Ray Wilkins in the 65th minute and he made an impressive impact with several power-charged runs through the Irish defence.

Dennis Tueart ducked low to head in a Talbot cross in the 86th minute to give England a victory they barely deserved.

After Mariner was the 13th substitute to debut for England in the previous game against Luxembourg, Talbot became the 14th.

Only a brilliant save by Pat Jennings prevented Talbot marking his first England appearance with a goal shortly before Tueart's winning header.

Derby's Colin Todd played his last game for England, while Ipswich's Allan Hunter was captain for the hosts whose line-up also included ex-Ipswich player Bryan Hamilton.

Of his international debut, Talbot recalled, 'Bobby Robson was told that I was under consideration for being called up by England. I then had an official letter sent to me via the club by the FA. There had been a lot of talk at the time about me being selected. People were saying that I was playing well, and I was the type of player that Don Revie liked. You only had to look at the Leeds United team who he managed before England. They were hard-working, tough players on the pitch. So, I knew there was the interest.

'In those days, we did not have international breaks and I remember before the first squad that I was in was announced, it was in the press that they were going to watch me in a game away at Manchester United. On the day, the press named me as the man of the match. Obviously, I done something right as I got picked.

'I remember my debut at Windsor Park. Pat Jennings was in goal for them, and I became very friendly with Pat when I left Ipswich. We won 2-1 and I felt I had a good enough game.'

Three evening's later, England hosted Wales for their next Home Championship game, and Mills was the only surviving Ipswich player to feature as he won his 12th cap. Talbot was an unused substitute. Wales scored their first victory in England for 42 years, and their first at Wembley, thanks to a 1-0 win.

Leighton James netted the only goal from the penalty spot a minute before half-time after Peter Shilton had pulled him down following a mistake by Emlyn Hughes.

The calls for Revie to be replaced were now reaching a crescendo, and the manager seemed to have lost all the confidence and enthusiasm that were such vital ingredients of his days as manager at Leeds.

Unsubstantiated rumours were flying around Fleet Street that Revie was ready to throw in the towel, and it was many months later before it emerged that around about this time, he had been making overtures to the Football Association hierarchy about settlement of his contract.

Talbot returned to the England line-up to win his second cap in their next game, which was their third and final Home Championship match of the summer, against Scotland at Wembley. Mills also started in this fixture.

Goals in each half by Gordon McQueen and Kenny Dalglish pushed England to defeat and for the first time they lost consecutive matches at Wembley.

Mick Channon's consolation goal came from the penalty spot three minutes from the end of a game in which Scotland were always the more productive and enterprising side.

Willie Johnston was sent off for the Scots, while Dennis Tueart came off the bench to win his final England cap. The man he replaced, Ray Kennedy, was the 50th different England player to be replaced by a substitute.

The Scottish fans decided that Wembley belonged to them so invaded the pitch, and started to tear up the hallowed turf, taking huge chunks of it back to Scotland with them. They also wrecked the goals after sitting on a crossbar which broke under the sheer weight.

It brought into question the need for fencing at Wembley and the future of the Home Championship was put in doubt. It all helped fuel Revie's increasing distaste for his job as England manager.

Talbot remembers only too well the day that England were beaten by Scotland and their fans causing problems.

'I remember my full debut well. At Wembley, we lost 2-1 against Scotland and their fans got on the pitch. We got off it when they came on. They caused bedlam. It was a crazy day. When we arrived at the stadium, the Scotch were everywhere in massive numbers, and they were partying before the kick-off.

'Obviously, it was disappointing for us as Scotland won at Wembley. I wore number ten. I don't think I played as a ten, but I had number ten on my back. We did not play particularly brilliantly. It was a disappointing result.'

Talbot played a total of six games for England, five of those caps coming while as an Ipswich player. After those two appearances kicked off the summer of 1977, his other three matches all came in June 1977 as England played three times on a South American tour. Talbot was the only Ipswich representative on the tour.

In the first of those three games, a goalless draw against Brazil in the Maracanã, Rio de Janeiro, England could and should have been three goals clear at half-time if they had taken their chances.

Brazil were equally careless in front of goal in the second half, during which acting manager Les Cocker sent on substitutes Ray Kennedy and Mick Channon to put new life into a tiring team.

A sequence of saves by Ray Clemence and three off-the-line clearances by Trevor Cherry stopped the Brazilians from snatching victory.

Don Revie was not present for this game. He was supposed to be in Helsinki watching Italy beat Finland 3-0, but he was in Dubai negotiating a lucrative deal to become the UAE manager on a £340,000-a-year, four-year contract.

The second of those three games saw England move on to Buenos Aires where they drew once again, this time, 1-1 with Argentina.

Cherry, with two teeth knocked out by a punch, was unluckily sent off with the culprit Daniel Bertoni in the 82nd minute.

The game was heading for a draw when Cherry made a mild challenge from behind on Bertoni, spread his hands palms wide as the Argentinian turned, and received a hit in the mouth.

The referee had his back turned and missed the incident, but a linesman saw and brought the matter to his attention.

His version may not have been totally correct as after Bertoni was sent off, an amazed Cherry, with his mouth starting to bleed, was also dismissed.

It was Bertoni who had equalised a third-minute goal by Stuart Pearson when he scored with a curling free kick in the 15th minute. The game became bogged down in midfield, with England unable to penetrate Argentina's in-depth defence. Emlyn Hughes cleared off the line in the closing moments.

With Bertoni's sending off, he became the seventh player to be shown a red card against England – the second Argentinian.

The final tour match saw a third successive draw and another 0-0 stalemate as Uruguay were the hosts in Montevideo.

This was Talbot's fifth and final England game while still with Ipswich.

Upon signing for Arsenal in January 1979, he would only play for his country on one more occasion – against Australia in May 1980 when, coincidentally, Terry Butcher and Russell Osman would make their debuts alongside another Ipswich player, Paul Mariner.

This game was also the final match in charge of England for Revie, and it was notable in that it marked the completion of England's first undefeated tour of South America. But the match itself was best forgotten.

Uruguay showed interest only in defending their goal, and England's tired players could not work up the energy to find a way through. They finished the tour with only one goal to show for all their efforts in three matches.

Then came the bombshell news that Revie was deserting to the Arabs. He had been manager for 29 matches, of which 14 were won, eight drawn and seven lost.

Enter Ron Greenwood. It was described as like a vicar taking over from a second-hand car salesman.

As for Talbot, he recalled the trip, how he returned to two of those stadiums played at later in life, and with reflection on his England career overall.

'I played in all three games on that tour. It was a fantastic experience for me going to South America. I went back in 2023 to see the Maracanã stadium in Brazil and it has totally changed. Flamengo play there and when I went it was full.

'I have been back to Argentina recently as well to watch football matches and went to the stadium I played at, and it has been nice to go back so many years later to see these places where I played.

'On that tour, I established myself in the team. I did OK, and we got three draws on the trip. It was a year before the World Cup in Argentina. We went to South America to get acclimatised, and maybe to look at it, but unfortunately, we failed to qualify and when we got back from South America, Don Revie resigned. So, it was a change for England.

'I was in each of Don's last four squads, but in the next get-together in September for Ron Greenwood's first game, he picked several Liverpool players. He wanted a club team, he said, and told me that I would be given my opportunity. I never got one. It was disappointing for me, but that's up to the manager in charge. I was kept in the squad for maybe another year until I left Ipswich. I didn't play. I was always a sub.

'It was three years later when I was at Arsenal before I played again in a centenary game in Australia. It was the only game I played for England under Ron Greenwood, but in fact, it was Bobby Robson that took charge of the team over there. Although it was classed as a full international, on paper, at least, it was a select team.

'As for favourite memories, playing at Wembley for England with my parents watching I suppose was the goal. As a young lad growing up in Ipswich, I wanted to be a professional footballer. I wanted to try and get in Ipswich's first team, play in an FA Cup final, and play for England. I achieved those three things that I wanted to do. I was disappointed that I did not get more caps. Maybe that was due to my performances, or maybe the coach for not wanting a player of my style of play.

'You always talk in hindsight, but that was disappointing for me because when Don Revie left, I was in the team, and Ron Greenwood never really picked me. He went with Ray Wilkins and Trevor Brooking. That was the decision of the coach, and you accept it. If you don't get picked, there is nothing that you can do about it. All you can do is do your best on a Saturday for your club team. It's down to the coach at the time to pick the squad. And if he doesn't think that you are good enough to play, that's his decision. No problem. If I had been given two or three games and not played well, then I would have accepted it better.'

CHAPTER 5

The merry month of May for Mariner & Mills

ENGLAND'S first game of the 1977/78 season, a 0-0 friendly draw at home to Switzerland, was bereft of any Ipswich players. It was the first England match in 11 where none of Bobby Robson's men featured.

But for the next game, a World Cup qualifier in Luxembourg, there was plenty of interest for Ipswich fans to ponder.

For the first and only time in an England fixture, two Ipswich players would appear from the bench as Trevor Whymark won his only cap to become the eighth Town man to play for the Three Lions. He came on in the second half as a replacement for Liverpool's Terry McDermott, and Kevin Beattie appeared four minutes later as a replacement for Manchester City's Dave Watson.

It was just the third time that both substitute appearances were provided from the same club, the first since May 1972. In Beattie's case, this proved to be his last cap and but for injury, he would surely have won many more.

With Paul Mariner in the starting line-up, and scoring his first international goal, this was the second time that three Ipswich players were on the field of play for England. They needed a goal avalanche to breathe life into their hopes of qualifying for the 1978 World Cup finals, but they were too anxious and continually snatched at the chances they created.

A 30th-minute goal by Mariner and an injury-time effort by Ray Kennedy lifted England to their first victory in seven but it was too little too late.

Debutant Whymark was sent on in a bid to increase the pressure on the Luxembourg defence, but they were too tense and wasted at least six clear-cut opportunities.

Whymark was the 15th England player to make his debut as a substitute – and the second to never play again.

As well as Beattie, Ian Callaghan and Gordon Hill also won their final caps.

Ipswich's Clive Woods was also named in this squad by Ron Greenwood but did not feature or ever play for England.

Having made nine appearances, there was much for Beattie to reflect upon after his international career was cut short, 'My last appearance in an England shirt came on 12 October 1977, when I was a substitute in a World Cup qualifier in Luxembourg. Ron Greenwood sent me on in the second half to make sure that there were no scares after we had established a 2-0 lead.

'Portman Road was full of international players at the time and there was always a buzz in the dressing room on a Friday morning prior to an England match which was to be played the following Wednesday.

'Because my knee would blow up so often, Bobby Robson would have to ring the FA to tell them that I had to pull out. I joined up with a few squads which was fun, but it never felt the same knowing that I wasn't going to play. I'd rather have stayed at home.'

Watching England many years further down the line, memories would come back for Beattie of his goal against Scotland, 'When somebody scores for England, I still get that tingling feeling despite my goal being all those years ago.

'I always wanted England to do well and am proud that I represented my country, although, of course, it should have been many more times.'

Talbot was an unused substitute in England's next game, which saw them beat Italy 2-0 at Wembley in a World Cup qualifier. It was their final match of 1977.

The first fixture of 1978 was a friendly defeat in Munich against West Germany. Mick Mills returned to the line-up after an eight-month absence to win his 14th cap.

A disputed goal four minutes from the end robbed England of a deserved draw against the World Cup holders. England had led from late in the first half when Stuart Pearson beat goalkeeper Sepp Maier with a looping header from a Steve Coppell cross.

Hamburg-based Kevin Keegan ran himself to the edge of exhaustion in his attempts to make the game safe and had to be replaced by Trevor Francis.

It was Germany's substitute, Ronnie Worm, who equalised shortly after coming on in the 75th minute to become only the fourth substitute to score against England. The previous evening, he had scored after being sent on as a substitute in the 'B' international also against England.

In the closing moments, Dave Watson was adjudged to have fouled Manfred Burgsmüller, and while England were still forming their defensive wall, Rainer Bonhof smacked a free kick low into the net. It was Ron Greenwood's first match as official manager, and with a little luck it would have been a winning start.

'We have the nucleus of an excellent team,' he said. 'If we had not lost our concentration when the free kick was being taken, we would have come away with a deserved draw. That's not bad considering we were playing on the home patch of the world champions.'

Eleven days after beating West Bromwich Albion in the FA Cup semi-final, Mills appeared for England against Brazil in a friendly at Wembley knowing that he would be back at the same venue less than three weeks later to take on Arsenal in the FA Cup Final.

Brazil, a goal up in ten minutes through Gil, abandoned their silky-smooth samba football for uncompromising tactics that led to five of their players being booked.

England missed a hatful of chances to equalise before Kevin Keegan earned a merited draw with a Brazilian-style free kick that he bent around the defensive wall.

The hosts also had a goal disallowed on 30-seven minutes following a push on goalkeeper Émerson Leão by Bob Latchford.

Football purist Ron Greenwood said privately after the match, 'I would much rather to have been beaten by a Brazil team playing the sort of skilled football that is their tradition than holding on to a draw against a side that, let's be honest, was thuggish in their approach. It was very sad to see them resorting to such tactics. That is not the Brazil way.'

A week after winning the FA Cup, Mariner and Mills were back on international duty for their country as they were part of an England side that romped to a 3-1 win in Wales for a Home Championship encounter.

It was a proud moment for Mills as he captained England for the first time. Mariner came off the bench as a first-half substitute.

Two spectacular goals in the last eight minutes – a 35-yard rifle shot from Tony Currie followed by a rising drive from the edge of the penalty area by Peter Barnes, his first international goal – gave England a winning start to the championship.

Currie had come on as a substitute for Trevor Cherry, who was carried off with a fractured collarbone in the 16th minute. Latchford gave England an eighth-minute lead with his first England goal before limping off to be replaced by Mariner.

Wales equalised through Phil Dwyer during a long spell of dominance in the second half before Currie and Barnes stepped on to the scoring stage.

Currie's goal was the ninth scored by an England substitute, and the only one by a substitute in the Home Championship competition at that stage.

This was the first occasion that England had made two first-half substitutes. Of the 99 England substitutes up to and including this game, Leeds United had provided 11 players, and were one behind Manchester City's record of 12. Ipswich had provided eight, equal with QPR, and one behind Manchester United.

Three days after that win in Wales, and ten days after winning the FA Cup, Ipswich skipper Mick Mills returned to Wembley to face a Northern Ireland side that included former Town player Bryan Hamilton who was captaining his country.

Phil Neal scored his first goal for England seconds before half-time to break the resistance of a brave Northern Ireland team for whom Middlesbrough goalkeeper Jim Platt was in outstanding form.

The two best chances of the second half both fell to Dave Watson, who was twice denied goals by the brilliance of Platt. It was Watson who had created the opening for Neal's goal with a clever back-heel, and the Liverpool right back drove through a forest of legs past the unsighted Platt.

Tony Woodcock made his England debut and went close to scoring two goals in the final moments, each time being prevented from getting on the scoresheet by man of the match Platt.

Manchester United's Stuart Pearson made his final appearance for England, who held on to win 1-0 and record a second successive Home Championship win.

Four days later, England were once again in Home Championship action as they travelled to Hampden Park to take on Scotland.

Mills was rejoined in the starting line-up by Mariner. Scotland were given a miserable send-off to the World Cup finals in Argentina with England winning 1-0, although a draw would have been a fairer reflection of the play.

The Scots had long periods of possession but could make little impact against an England defence in which Dave Watson was a tower of strength. Scotland disputed the deciding goal in the 83rd minute. They claimed that goalkeeper Alan Rough was fouled by Trevor Francis when he dropped a cross from Peter Barnes.

Steve Coppell scored his first goal for his country and England's 1,350th overall after firing a loose ball into the net to clinch the Home Championship.

Even in the wake of this defeat, Scottish manager Ally MacLeod persisted with his wildly optimistic forecast that his team could win the World Cup.

Brian Greenhoff came off the bench to replace Emlyn Hughes in the 73rd minute to become the 100th substitute to be used by England, since the first some 28 years previously.

May finished with a third England game in nine days for Mick Mills who saw a third successive win as the Three Lions routed Hungary 4-1 at Wembley. This would also be the first England match in a run of 11 where if an Ipswich player featured, it would just be Mills representing the club.

England, with Kevin Keegan and Trevor Brooking pulling the Hungarian defence apart, rushed into a 3-0 lead inside the first 35 minutes through Peter Barnes, a Phil Neal penalty, and a Trevor Francis header.

Hungary had their best moments immediately after half-time and pulled a goal back through László Nagy before Tony Currie finished them off with a crashing shot from the edge of the area in the 73rd minute.

Ron Greenwood could not disguise his delight at the finest display by England for several months. 'Like anybody from my generation,' he said, 'I always associate Hungary with the [Ferenc] Puskás team of the 1950s, and so a victory like this is particularly special. I have been saying that we have the players to match the best, and tonight it was proved that I am not talking nonsense.'

Currie's goal was his second as an England substitute and made him the first to score twice in two separate matches. After scoring three minutes after replacing Brooking, he also became the quickest substitute to score. It was also just the second time that Wembley had seen an England goal scored by a substitute. Goalkeeper Peter Shilton won his 25th cap in this game.

For Mariner and Mills, their England appearances in May 1978 supplemented winning the FA Cup perfectly. It had certainly been a merry month for the Ipswich duo.

CHAPTER 6

Butcher & Osman debut as Mariner returns

THE first England international game of the 1978/79 season saw Mick Mills win his 20th cap in Copenhagen against Denmark.

Two headed goals from Kevin Keegan from well-directed free kicks saw England ahead, before the Danes were allowed to pull level with two goals inside five minutes against a less-than-disciplined defence.

Bob Latchford directed a header against a post and Keegan also hit the woodwork as both teams played all-out attacking football in what coach Don Howe later described as 'the most exciting international match I've ever seen'.

England regained the lead through a disputed goal by Latchford after the break, and Phil Neal made it 4-2 before the Danes forced a third goal in the dying moments of a pulsating 1980 European Championship qualifying match.

England's second qualifier came at the end of October when they were in Dublin to take on the Republic of Ireland.

Latchford headed an early goal with the help of a deflection, but England became disjointed after centre-half Dave Watson went off with an injury in the 21st minute.

Steve Coppell, continually running the Irish defence into disarray, smacked a shot against the bar and Keegan headed wide when well placed before Gerry Daly hooked in an equaliser.

Mark Lawrenson and David O'Leary were rock solid at the heart of the Irish defence, and Liam Brady was their most creative player as Ireland battled to a deserved draw.

In this game, Trevor Brooking won his 25th England cap, while Tony Woodcock came off the bench to make Nottingham Forest the 25th different club to provide an England substitute – the 60th different player to be used as a sub.

Mick Mills was a notable absentee from England's line-up in their next game – a friendly at home to Czechoslovakia at the end of November – and so it would be the first week of February 1979, before England would play again with Mills restored to the starting line-up as they defeated Northern Ireland in a clinical European Championship qualifying performance.

Keegan was irrepressible after bravely heading England into an early lead in the face of a strong challenge from goalkeeper Pat Jennings.

He then laid on the first of Bob Latchford's two goals with an accurate cross, and back-headed a Trevor Brooking corner on to Dave Watson for the fourth goal, and his first for England.

The victory sent England leapfrogging over the Irish in the group table to top place. Northern Ireland manager Danny Blanchflower fumed, 'I know that football is a game of physical contact, but England took this to extremes. There were times when I was surprised that they wanted a ball to kick.'

The 1978/79 season ended, and Ipswich finished sixth in the First Division to reclaim their place in the UEFA Cup for the following campaign. This was after a season of playing in the Cup Winners' Cup by virtue of winning the FA Cup in 1978. After wins against AZ 67 Alkmaar and SW Innsbruck, Town then beat Barcelona 2-1 at Portman Road before losing the second leg 1-0 in front of a crowd of 100,000 in Camp Nou to go out of the competition on the away goals rule.

The season had seen Mick Mills and Paul Mariner continue to win international caps and before Mills could go away on his summer holidays, there were still four more England games to feature in during May and June.

For the second time in three months, England once again faced Northern Ireland, this time in Belfast, and came away with a 2-0 victory. Mills captained the team for the second time, while the Irish skipper was former Ipswich player Bryan Hamilton.

Dave Watson and Steve Coppell each scored in the first 15 minutes to sink Northern Ireland in this Home Championship match.

England missed the prolific partnership that had been developing between Kevin Keegan and Trevor Brooking, and they lacked the drive and direction that had put them so in command against the Irish at Wembley three months earlier.

The victory gave England a huge psychological advantage with a crucial European Championship match scheduled for the autumn.

Mills missed England's next game four days later against Wales, but he returned a week after that win in Northern Ireland against Scotland at Wembley.

In the visitors' line-up were two Ipswich players in the form of George Burley and John Wark.

Scotland took a 26th-minute lead through Wark as they put England on the rack in the first half and it was against the run of play when Peter Barnes equalised.

A couple of stunning saves by Ray Clemence lifted England's confidence and they bossed the second half, with goals from Steve Coppell and Kevin Keegan giving them the Home Championship.

One of the highlights was a save by Clemence rated as good as any seen at Wembley. Joe Jordan hammered in a first-half shot from 20 yards which took a huge deflection off the head of Dave Watson. Clemence was committed to diving to his left to save the original shot, and somehow managed to twist in mid-air and turn the ball off target with his right fist.

It helped wipe out the memory of his gifted goal to Kenny Dalglish in a previous game against the Scots.

Less than two weeks later, Mills won his 25th cap as England travelled to Bulgaria for their latest qualifier for the 1980 European Championship.

England played with tremendous fervour despite suffocating heatwave conditions. The Bulgarians threatened to take an early lead when Clemence pushed a header by Krasimir Borisov against a post, but then Kevin Keegan scored after combining with Trevor Brooking.

England clinched victory early in the second half with two headed goals in a minute, first by Watson and then Peter Barnes. Ron Greenwood said later, 'Our plan was for Kevin Keegan to play a deeper role than usual. This gave us extra drive in midfield and confused the Bulgarians who had worked out a man-to-man marking policy to try to curb Kevin's freedom of movement.'

Both of England's substitutes were players from Nottingham Forest, making this the fourth occasion that the two replacements were provided from the same club, and the first time since October 1977.

After missing out on playing for England in Sweden for a Swedish FA 75th anniversary celebration match, England and Mills continued their travels when they lost 4-3 to Austria in Vienna.

England had just a Keegan effort to show at half-time in reply to three first-half goals by the Austrians in a match littered with defensive errors.

Goals by Steve Coppell and Ray Wilkins – his first for his country – brought England battling back to 3-3, only for them to lose to a late goal headed past substitute goalkeeper Clemence by Bruno Pezzey following a free kick.

It was England's first setback since the 2-1 defeat by West Germany back in February 1978, and the first time they had conceded more than three goals since the 5-1 defeat by Brazil back in 1964.

West Bromwich Albion's Laurie Cunningham, the second BME player to play for the senior team, was the first to be a substitute when replacing Peter Barnes.

As for that substitute appearance for Clemence, he became only the second goalkeeper to be an official replacement. Discounting the very first swap in 1872, this was the first substitution of a goalkeeper since June 1976.

Since on that occasion Joe Corrigan did not concede a goal (or indeed, no goals were scored in 1872), Clemence was the first substitute goalkeeper to concede a goal. Striker Bob Latchford won his last cap in this game.

Another season of international football ended, during which time Mills had worn the captain's armband again and received his 25th cap.

Mills was once again selected for England in their first fixture of the 1979/80 season.

And with a narrow 1-0 victory over Denmark, they took an important step towards qualifying for the 1980 European Championship finals.

Keegan, shaking off the handicap of a recurring leg injury, scored the only goal of the match with a left-footed volley after a driving right-wing run by Phil Neal in the 18th minute.

Ron Greenwood settled for a 4-3-3 formation, with Terry McDermott joining Ray Wilkins, who was playing his 25th England game, and Trevor Brooking in midfield. They narrowly won the struggle for midfield supremacy, and Brooking found time to push forward to support Keegan in his bustling, trademark runs that made him a constant menace to the Danish defence.

The Danes had an exceptional player in Barcelona forward Allan Simonsen. But luckily for England, his team-mates were not in the same class and squandered several chances that he created.

A month later, England virtually clinched a place in the 1980 Euros with a resounding 5-1 win over Northern Ireland on a soaking-wet Windsor Park pitch.

Trevor Francis and Tony Woodcock (his first goal for England) both scored in each half, and the rout was completed in the 70th minute when Chris Nicholl turned a Phil Neal centre into his own net.

Northern Ireland's goal came midway through the second half from a Vic Moreland penalty. The Irish defence had no answer to the probing runs of Francis and Woodcock, both of whom gave peak-power performances.

As well as the England line-up containing Mills, his Ipswich team-mate Allan Hunter appeared in the Northern Ireland defence in the first half before being replaced at half-time.

This was the second-highest winning margin by England away from home where an Ipswich player featured in their line-up.

Mills missed England's next two qualifying matches against Bulgaria and the Republic of Ireland but returned for a 2-0 friendly win over Spain at Barcelona's Camp Nou.

England ran the Spanish defence to a nervous breakdown, and they might have had three goals before Woodcock opened the scoring in the 16th minute.

Trevor Francis put the seal on a magnificent team performance when he collected a pass from Steve Coppell, outpaced two defenders, and beat oncoming goalkeeper Luis Arconada with a perfectly placed cross shot.

England would have won by at least five goals but for a succession of superb saves by man of the match Arconada. Playing in his 50th international, the ever-effervescent Keegan was again England's outstanding player.

Two points of interest arose from England's substitutions in this game. After 118 substitutions, Real Madrid became the first foreign-based club to provide a substituting player when Laurie Cunningham replaced Trevor Francis.

And then Wolves' Emlyn Hughes replaced Phil Neal to become the oldest substitute used at this point aged 32.

No Ipswich player featured in the first post-1979/80 friendly, which saw England beat Argentina 3-1 at Wembley. Mills would in fact miss seven successive games for his country.

The second game of the summer, however, saw Paul Mariner return to the setup for the first time in two years and he scored England's goal in a heavy 4-1 defeat away to Wales.

Just four days after a triumph over the world champions Argentina, the Three Lions showed their worst side with a loose performance against a Welsh team out to impress their new manager, Mike England.

Larry Lloyd, recalled to the middle of the visitors' defence after eight years, had a nightmare match. He was booked, injured, and substituted after being given a chasing by a lively Welsh forward line in which Leighton James was outstanding. It proved to be Lloyd's last cap for England.

Mariner gave England the lead in the 16th minute, but Wales quickly equalised through Mickey Thomas. Two goals from James and an own goal by Phil Thompson piled on the misery for an England team missing the drive and industry of the injured Keegan.

Phil Neal won his 25th cap for his country, while Lloyd was the 15th player to be substituted and never play for the senior team again. He made his final appearance seven years and 360 days after his previous outing. This was England's first defeat in Wales since 1955.

Mariner had been stuck on five caps and one goal for two years and the timing of his recall to the England squad could not have been better with the European Championship just a month away.

Following that demoralising defeat to Wales, Greenwood made sweeping changes – nine in all – and Alan Devonshire came in for his debut in a Home Championship match against Northern Ireland. Mariner was dropped to the bench.

An undistinguished game seemed set for a goalless draw until former Ipswich player David Johnson forced the ball into the Irish net in the 81st minute.

Northern Ireland equalised just a minute later when substitute Terry Cochrane rammed the ball past the previously redundant Joe Corrigan.

The team play that had been such a feature against Argentina just a week earlier was non-existent against the Irish, who fully deserved their draw in a game that rarely got out of a midfield rut.

Emlyn Hughes captained England for the 23rd and final time.

A third international appearance in eight days for Mariner saw England return to winning ways as they beat Scotland 2-0 in Glasgow in the latest instalment of the Home Championship.

A goal in each half by Brooking and Coppell lifted England to a victory that put them in good heart for the European Championship finals, which were just three weeks away.

Brooking scored after just seven minutes, continuing where he had left off as West Ham's goal hero against Arsenal in their 1-0 win in the 1980 FA Cup Final. He beat Danny McGrain to the ball after Mariner had headed back across goal following a cross from David Johnson

It was a Brooking back-heel that set up Coppell's goal in the 75th minute, the Manchester United winger steering the ball home after goalkeeper Alan Rough had parried his first shot.

England manager Greenwood said, 'Our performances against Argentina and now Scotland prove what we are capable of when we get it right. We must find consistency at the highest level.'

Emlyn Hughes came off the bench to become England's oldest substitute to date aged 32 years, eight months and 26 days, and in the process, to win his last England cap. Meanwhile, Trevor Cherry won his 25th cap, and Ipswich's George Burley came off the bench to replace Iain Munro for Scotland in the second half.

Having played in all three Home Championship games of the summer of 1980, Mariner reflected well on the journey back from Scotland, 'Although I did not score against Scotland, I was feeling optimistic on that journey home that I had done enough to get into Ron Greenwood's squad for the forthcoming European Championship in Italy.

'When the call came a couple of days later, there was a feeling of immense pride. My first major tournament and the chance to represent my country. The first thing I did after speaking to Ron was phone my mum and dad and the three of us dissolved into tears.'

There was one last international friendly for England before the tournament in Italy, which was why at this stage, Greenwood had not named his full Euros squad. It took place on the final day of May – in Australia.

The scheduling was chaotic. The squad left London on the Wednesday, played in Sydney on the Saturday, and returned to England on the Monday.

The game against the Aussies was for the Winfield Cup, celebrating the Australian Soccer Federation centenary. England prevailed 2-1 with Mariner getting on the scoresheet. But it was also a special occasion for two other Ipswich players.

Alongside Mariner were team-mates Terry Butcher and Russell Osman, who were making their England debuts, thus becoming the ninth and tenth Ipswich players to represent the country. This was the third occasion that a Three Lions team had representation from three Town men.

This was labelled as a virtual England 'B' team that had travelled 'down under' to play in a match to celebrate 100 years of football in Australia, although it was credited as a full international by both FAs.

Goals from Mariner and Glenn Hoddle gave England a 2-0 half-time lead, and the Australians managed to pull one back through a second-half penalty.

Ipswich partners Osman and Butcher made their debuts together at the heart of the England defence, and there was also a first cap for future Ipswich player Alan Sunderland, who was substituted by another debutant in Peter Ward. Neither player was selected by England again. Former Ipswich player Brian Talbot also featured.

For the first time in England's substitution history, the three players replaced had never been substituted before.

David Armstrong won the first of his three caps, while Frank Lampard, Talbot, and Brian Greenhoff played for England for the final time.

Of the trip, Mariner said, 'The most pleasing part of the trip for me was full England debuts for my two big pals Terry Butcher and Russell Osman. So, it wasn't a complete waste of time. It was also nice for Bobby Robson, who was part of Ron Greenwood's coaching staff, to take charge of the team in Sydney. That allowed the national team manager to come with us but concentrate on preparations for the Euros.'

Mariner roomed with goalkeeper Joe Corrigan for the trip and had a story to recall, 'I roomed with Joe before we flew out to Sydney and the boys had a proper session that night, resulting in a bumper bar bill. When we were checking out of the room, I asked Joe if he could take care of check-out and I would settle with him on the bus.

'Whilst he was in reception, I tried to persuade Bobby to ask the driver of our bus to move it round the corner so that Joe would think that we had left without him. His look said it all. It is never good when someone raises one eyebrow higher than the other in response to a suggestion.'

Meanwhile, Butcher recalled the moment when he received his first call-up, aged just 21, and that game in Sydney, 'England were in the Euros just after that game in 1980 in Italy. The players that did not make that squad went to Australia at the end of the season. Bobby Robson took the players, and it was going to be a "B" trip. But Ron Greenwood changed it to a full international. So, lots of players went on the trip who would not necessarily have got a full cap otherwise.'

The game was a standout moment from the perspective of Ipswich fans for as well as a goal from Mariner, Butcher had a familiar face called up alongside him.

'Russell played too, and we roomed together which was great. We flew in about two days before the game and out two days afterwards. It was literally a flying visit.

'It was really nice to have Russell and Paul there for my first game.'

Like Ray Crawford nearly 20 years earlier, there was also a less conventional way of finding out how he earned his first selection for the national team.

'I found out through seeing it on Ceefax. You got a letter but that would come about two days after. I remember that you had to forever watch the Ceefax pages scrolling through. If you missed the first page with the squad on it, you might have to wait for it to go through 13 pages back to the beginning. That continued throughout my England career.'

It was Butcher's first trip to Australia, so how did he find the experience?

'It was great. We flew out economy class, which was not great for my legs, but we enjoyed a few beers. I remember with Russell, we used to look at the cricketers when they would fly for the Test matches. The Australians would see how many cans of beer they could drink on the flights coming through when having to stop a couple of times. What was the total number of cans?

'The wicketkeeper Rod Marsh, who had a big moustache, had the record and we were trying to get desperately near it, but we couldn't. I remember getting off the plane and thinking wow! We were a bit worse for wear. It wasn't our typical preparation, but this occasion was like a footballers on tour moment.

'It felt like a tour. It was the end of the season, and it was just one game, and we had an unbelievable time. Really good fun.'

While how he found out about his call-up would seem a bizarre moment today, also would the type of pitch that England played on at the Sydney Cricket Ground for this game as Butcher explains, 'We played on the cricket square at the SCG and at the time, you were thinking of all the great people that had been there. Not football people but cricketers.

'We were in the away dressing room, and you can't help but feel proud and privileged to be there. The inner sanctum at the SCG! The cricket square was about a foot higher than the rest of the pitch and it was brick hard.

'It was their winter and it had been raining. Other parts of the pitch were soddened with rain. We didn't know what studs to wear especially us centre-backs who were in the centre of the pitch anyway. We would run up on to the cricket square and it would be like clip-clop, clip- clop, and then you'd come back down on to the soggy bit of pitch.

'They scored late on in the game as by then, we were knackered. We were suffering with jet-lag.'

Of his first game for England, Russell Osman remembered the call-up and the trip with mixed emotions, 'I recall my first call-up to the England squad being via a letter that came to me via the football club. I had been involved in England setups previously. At under-15s level, I was an England international at rugby. At under-16s, I captained England at rugby, and then under-18s, 21s, and B team at football.

'When I got my full England call-up, it was nice, but the only problem was, it was to go and play in Sydney at the end of the season. A long old trip to travel to the other side of the world just to play one game to get a first cap.'

And as it helped Butcher to have some team-mates on the trip with him, It was a feeling mutually shared by Osman.

'It was great and there were some interesting characters on the trip. Joe Corrigan was always good fun, Trevor Cherry too. Frank Lampard was also there, and Frank was my tailor for the trip because my suit turned up about five sizes too big for me and he had to try and do some adjustments every time I tried to wear it. He would get a couple of pins and tucked it in, fold the sleeves up and made me look half presentable.

'It was strange to play at the SCG as it was very hard in the middle of the pitch because we played straight across a cricket square.

'In that squad, we had Bryan Robson, Glenn Hoddle who I played with at under-18s and under-21s and I was used to being in and around them. It was also strange how it was supposed to be a "B" team squad, but it was classified as a full England cap. So, I'm not going to moan about it too much.'

Ray Crawford.

Mick Mills.

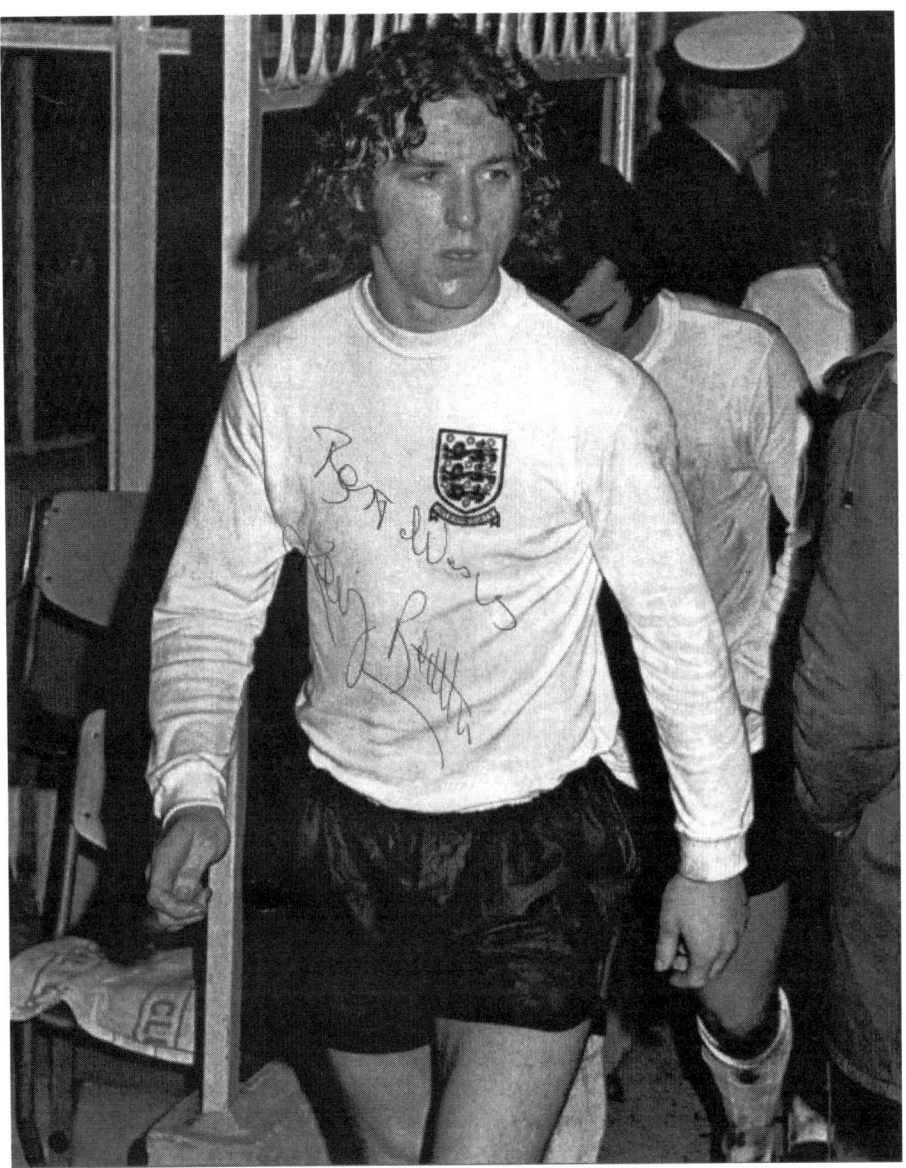

Kevin Beattie.

Colin Viljoen.

David Johnson.

Paul Mariner.

Brian Talbot.

Trevor Whymark.

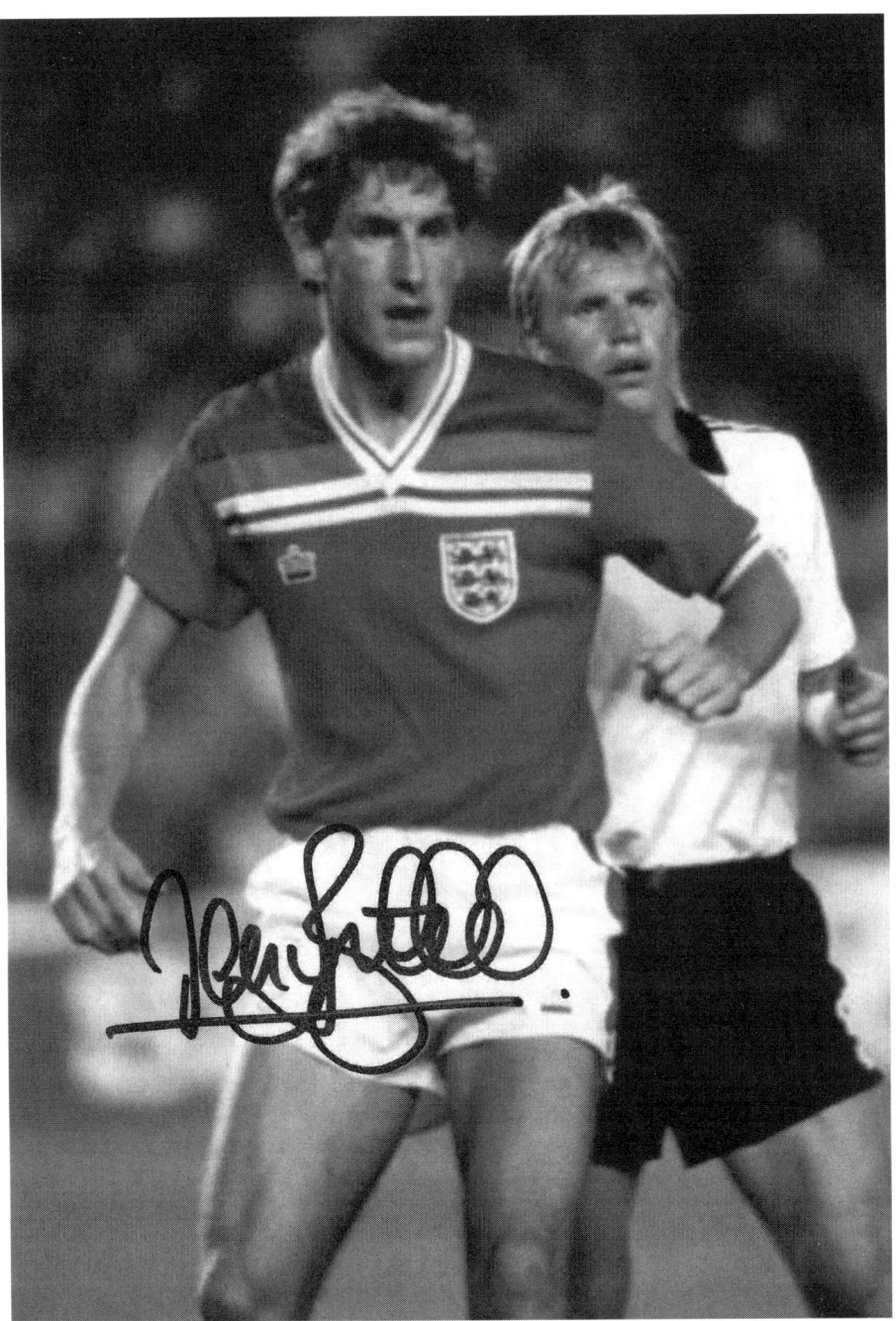

Terry Butcher.

Russell Osman.

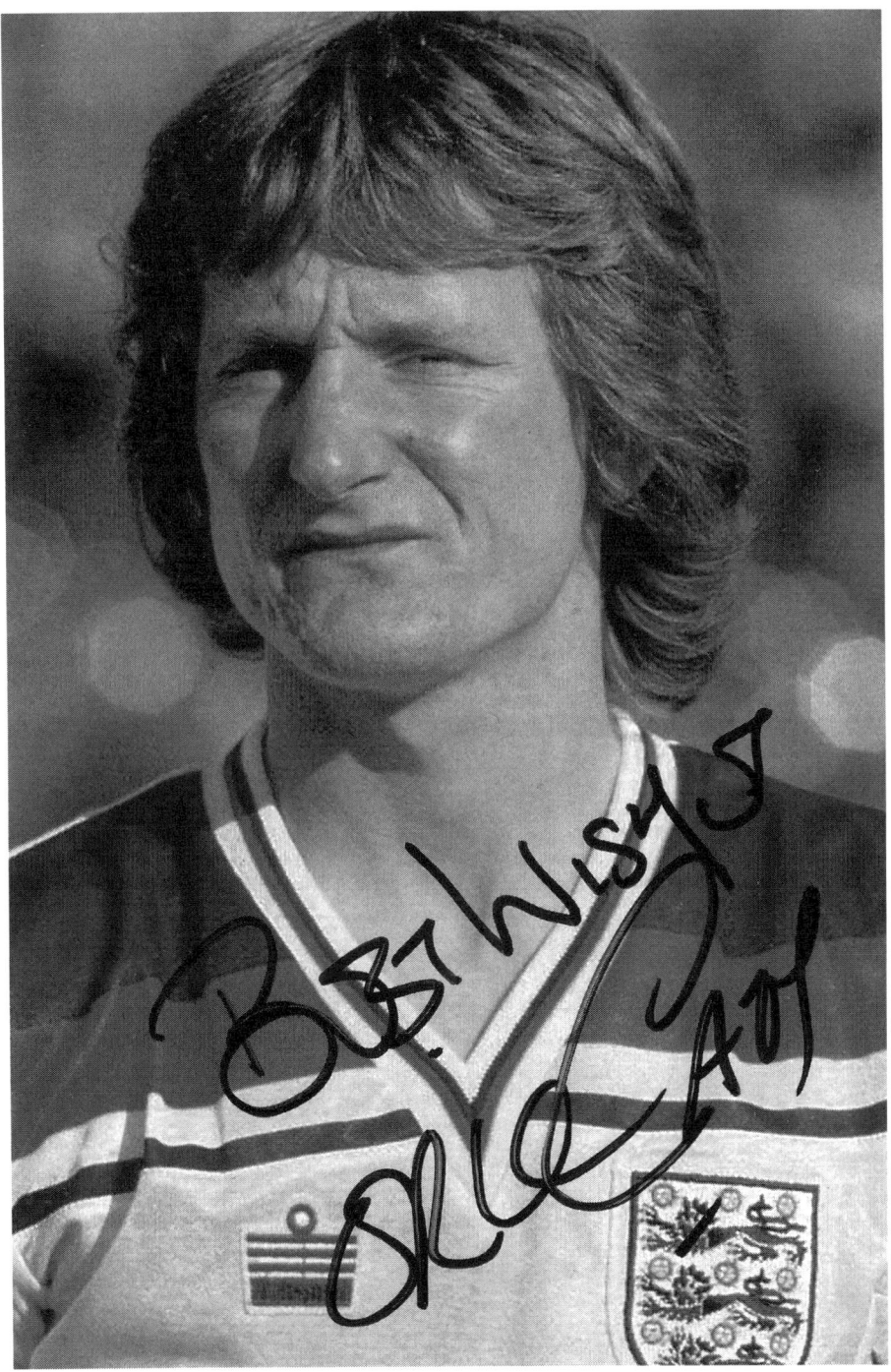

Eric Gates.

Richard Wright.

CHAPTER 7

A first major tournament for a Town player

A 1-1 draw against Belgium in England's opening match of the 1980 European Championship where no Ipswich player featured (Paul Mariner was an unused substitute) was then followed by a 1-0 defeat to Italy thanks to Marco Tardelli's polished finish with one of the goals of the tournament 12 minutes from the end.

Mariner came off the bench to replace Garry Birtles to become the first Ipswich player to play for England at a major tournament.

Francesco Graziani powered past Phil Neal before delivering the ball into the path of Tardelli, who beat Peter Shilton with an unstoppable volley at the near post.

It had class written all over it and was a worthy winner of a game that England often dominated with fast, skilful football that had the disciplined Italian defence stretched near to breaking point.

Ray Kennedy, playing his last match for England, came closest to scoring when he rifled a second-half shot against a post with Dino Zoff beaten.

When Mariner came off the bench, this meant that by now, England had used 17 substitutes throughout 1979/80, beating the record set in 1969/70.

Phil Thompson and Steve Coppell won their 25th caps in this game as England were eliminated from the tournament after just two matches.

Of his appearance, Mariner said, 'I was very proud to make my tournament debut, but the Italians scored the only goal of the game soon after I came on and I hardly got a sniff up the other end.'

The 50th England game to feature an Ipswich Town player was a dead-rubber tie against Spain with the Three Lions unable to qualify for the knockout stages.

They needed a clear two-goal victory over Spain to qualify for the third/fourth place play-off but only managed a 2-1 victory. Spain packed the midfield and made it difficult for a much-changed England team to get any rhythm.

Mariner once again came off the bench to feature while team-mate Mick Mills returned to the starting line-up as Ron Greenwood made six changes.

Trevor Brooking gave England the lead in the 19th minute when he steered the ball over the line from a Ray Wilkins header following a free kick for one of several fouls on dangerman Keegan.

Ray Clemence conceded a disputed penalty early in the second half from which Julio Cardeñosa scored an equaliser. Six minutes later, Spain were awarded a second penalty after a foul by Dave Watson. Dani beat Clemence but was ordered to retake the spot-kick, and this time the Liverpool goalkeeper made a dramatic save.

England lifted their game and had the satisfaction of snatching a deserved victory when the industrious Tony Woodcock steered the ball home after a thumping shot from Terry McDermott had been pushed out.

Mariner's record fifth substitution made him equal with Malcolm Macdonald, Trevor Brooking, and Dave Thomas at the time, while Trevor Cherry played his last game for England.

Mariner had hoped that with so many changes to the starting XI, he would get a start on this occasion.

'Nope, my hopes were dashed. But at least my room-mate Joe Corrigan had a smile on his face after hearing Ron say, "I'm going to put Joe in…" I looked at my big pal and smiled and gave him a wink. But Ron hadn't finished his sentence, "…as the substitute keeper."

'The big man was as frustrated as me. I came on for the last quarter of an hour for Glenn Hoddle, but it wasn't the overall experience I was hoping for as we failed to get out of the group, and I played a total of half an hour in two substitute appearances.

'The knives were out for the manager ahead of the World Cup qualifying. I just wondered if I had done enough to be kept on if he was kept on.'

England's first game of the 1980/81 season saw them beat Norway 4-0 at Wembley in their first qualifying game for the 1982 World Cup.

Paul Mariner not only started, but he was also on the scoresheet. And there was a debut for Eric Gates who became the 11th Ipswich player to play for England.

Without Kevin Keegan, Ray Wilkins, Trevor Brooking, Steve Coppell, and Trevor Francis, a new-look England attack took a long time to get into its stride.

A Terry McDermott goal (his first for England, and the national team's 1,400th goal) in the 35th minute calmed jangling nerves, and the Three lions finally won comfortably with three goals in the last 33 minutes through Tony Woodcock, a McDermott penalty after Mariner had dribbled into the box, past three defenders, and was brought down by Tore Kordahl, and a beautiful creation by Mariner, who skilfully deceived three defenders before firing the ball majestically into the net.

Bryan Robson was a powerhouse in midfield and as well as Gates, Graham Rix also made his debut.

When asked about his memory of his first experiences with England, Gates said, 'I was so proud to have played for England. I still do some after-dinner talks in the north-east and people say to me that I should have won a lot more caps. But I chuck it back and say look, there were probably better players than me that didn't win any England caps. That's the way I look at life. I don't look at it and think I should have won more. I'm just pleased that I won the two.

'I found out about my call-up through a letter that was sent to the club. I never played schoolboys football for England or under-21s. I was not involved with the squad and first knew when the letter arrived at the club. Kevin Keegan was out of the squad, and I got picked. I roomed with Terry [Butcher] for this game. I think he got called up but did not play. I've got a photo in the house of my first squad call-up of Terry and myself with Mick Mills and Paul Mariner.

'I remember playing well against Norway. It was a World Cup qualifier and we had to beat them. There was a lot of Ipswich lads playing and at the time, I was playing well for Ipswich in a great side. I was a different type of player. I was neither a midfield player nor an out-and-out forward. I was like a floater in between and doing what I wanted. And without being big-headed, I was what you call a "flair" player. There wasn't many like me about and Ron Greenwood took a punt on me.

'I was delighted to get picked. A bit embarrassed. I was out of my comfort zone going to England. I was just happy playing for Ipswich. I thought what am I doing here so to speak. I was proud though. I remember being on the pitch when the national anthem was being played and I cried! I was just thinking crikey, tonight, I am one of the best 11 players in England.

'We won 4-0 and I thought I'll win 100 caps here. But it didn't work out like that. But on the night, I thought I did well and just need to carry on like that.'

Gates was the only Town player selected for England's next game, a World Cup qualifying defeat in Romania. He was substituted at half-time and was never selected to play for his country again. Two caps were won in just five weeks.

A controversial penalty decided this match in the 75th minute and dealt a severe blow to England's hopes of qualifying for the 1982 World Cup in Spain.

Kenny Sansom angrily protested his innocence after his tackle on Anghel Iordănescu had been ruled a foul. The Romanian picked himself up and scored the winning goal from the penalty spot.

England had just been getting on top after Tony Woodcock scored in the 66th minute following a neat exchange of passes with Garry Birtles. Romania had their best moments in the first half and scored at the peak of their pressure through Marcel Răducanu in the 36th minute.

As well as Gates playing in his final game for his country, there were also final England appearances for Laurie Cunningham and Birtles, who became the 20th player to be replaced by a substitute and to never play for the senior team again.

So Gates made just the two appearances, and he should not have been anywhere near the game in Romania. He takes up the story, 'Then my next cap was in Romania. I always hated flying. I have never flown since I finished playing football. Obviously, I flew around Europe when I was playing for Ipswich. But I hated it. I was crying, frightened, and I did everything I could. I just didn't like it. Once I finished playing football, I said that's it. I'm not flying any more!

'Before we flew, we turned up at Lilleshall on the Sunday, and then trained on the Monday morning when I was feeling bad. There was something wrong with me like a horrible flu.

'I really should not have travelled to Romania, but I did, and I got picked to play. I had to room on my own over there as I was poorly. I did a bit of training on the morning of the game, but I had a temperature and a fever, yet I thought I hadn't gone all that way not to play and declared myself fit.

'But I had a poor game and got substituted at half-time. It was my own fault. I just shouldn't have played, and we lost 2-1. But when asked if I was fit enough, I wasn't going to say no.

'After that, I got selected for a couple of other squads, but not selected to play for one and for another game, I was injured and couldn't join up with the squad. Ron then named the squad for the 1982 World Cup in Spain, and I was one of the three players out of the 25-man squad that got left behind. I think part of it was that there were a lot of Ipswich lads in the squad and maybe they were thinking that they couldn't take too many Ipswich players.'

Unfortunately for Eric, his chances of playing again for England were not helped when his club manager took over from Greenwood.

'I remember when Bobby Robson took over as manager. When he left Ipswich, we all said our goodbyes to him in the dressing room. I had a good relationship with Bobby. He knew that to get the best out of me was through a good telling off. And I remember shaking hands with him, and he said, "Son, you will be in my first England team." And he never picked me!

'I don't think that he wanted to change the system at England. We played a different system at Ipswich that others were not playing. We had [Alan] Brazil and Mariner up front with me just off them floating around. And maybe Bobby thought that he did not want to change too much with the England squad and the system. And with Mills, Butcher, Osman, and Mariner already with England, maybe he did not want to pick too many Ipswich players either.

'Maybe for that reason, he didn't pick me. But he did well out of it. So, I've got no complaints.'

Paul Mariner and Mick Mills returned to the England line-up for their next game in November 1980 which saw them beat Switzerland 2-1 at Wembley in a World Cup qualifier that had that 'must-win' feel about it. And it proved to be a notable night for the Ipswich duo.

Mariner scored the second goal while Mills captained England for the third time.

England were comfortably leading 2-0 at half-time through goals by Tony Woodcock (a deflected shot) and Mariner, and there was no hint of the way the pendulum of play would swing Switzerland's way in the second half.

Trevor Brooking, who had been dominant in midfield, started feeling the effects of an old injury and when his output dropped, England began to struggle to contain a suddenly lively Swiss side.

A long period of Swiss pressure was finally rewarded when Hans-Jörg Pfister drove a scorching shot wide of Peter Shilton, and England clung on desperately for a victory that revived their World Cup hopes.

By the time that England next played, at the start of the last week of March 1981, a friendly against Spain at Wembley, matters were hotting-up on the domestic front for Ipswich.

A week earlier, Mariner and Butcher had scored for Town in a 3-1 win at home to French side Saint-Étienne in the quarter-final of the UEFA Cup to claim a 7-2 aggregate win after a superb 4-1 win in France. That result and performance is often hailed as one of the best there's ever been by a British team on foreign soil.

And then a few days later, Butcher was on the scoresheet again as Town lost 2-1 at Old Trafford against Manchester United.

For the second time, Butcher, Mariner, and Osman lined up together for what was England's 550th match as they fell to a 2-1 defeat against the Spaniards.

England were on the way to their first home defeat under Ron Greenwood from the moment that Jesús María Satrústegui snatched an early goal following a misunderstanding at the heart of the defence between Butcher and Osman.

A rain-saturated surface seemed to give England greater problems than their opponents, and it was against the run of play when Glenn Hoddle equalised with a blistering volley after a Bryan Robson cross had been blocked in the 27th minute.

Spain quickly regained the lead through Jesús María Zamora, and only their weak finishing prevented them scoring a more emphatic victory.

As hosts of the 1982 World Cup finals, Spain were desperate to find a winning combination and they played with more urgency than a strangely lethargic England side. It was Greenwood's first experience of defeat at Wembley, and sections of the media were now pointing their poison pens at him.

As for Butcher, it would be more than a year before he would play for England again. Meanwhile, Osman recalled the game and playing with one player meant a lot to him, 'We stayed in London for a couple of days before the game. Terry McDermott was one of my usual room partners, but for this game and others where both Terry and I were in the squad, we would room together as we did at Ipswich.

'It was the first time that I played in front of Ray Clemence in a full international game, and that was a real honour. Ray was a great lad. We had a strong side that night with Kevin Keegan, Trevor Francis, and Trevor Brooking among others. How Spain beat us, I don't know.'

Just over a month later, England's next game was again at Wembley and their latest World Cup qualifier against Romania ended in a 0-0 draw.

Osman was the only Ipswich player selected and this match came a week after Town had qualified for the UEFA Cup Final thanks to a 2-0 aggregate win over FC Cologne. It was also four days after a 1-0 win at home to Manchester City. Town had by now played 62 games in the season; Osman had played in them all.

Anxiety anchored the England forwards in front of goal, and they missed vital chances that could have clinched victory against their closest qualifying group rivals.

England's defence generally dominated the Romanian forwards, but there was one amazing escape when Peter Shilton's feet slipped from under him as he reached for a dipping header from Ilie Balaci during a rare raid in the 33rd minute. Shilton was lying on the ground as he scooped the ball clear with two Romanian forwards bearing down on him.

England's players went off to the sound of boos and jeers, and with their prospects of qualifying for the World Cup looking remote.

Trevor Brooking was replaced by a substitute for a record seventh time, equal with Mick Channon and Francis Lee. Southampton's Dave Watson captained England for the first time.

Three Home International Championship games followed but Ipswich players were excused from joining up with the squad after their gruelling season.

We had to wait until a World Cup qualifier in Switzerland at the end of May where we saw the return of Mariner, Mills, and Osman, all fresh from their UEFA Cup Final success over AZ '67 Alkmaar ten days earlier. Osman was playing his 69th match of the season.

Given that the first game of the season had kicked off on 16 August, there had been 287 days between that first day and England's meeting with Switzerland – Osman's last appearance of the season. His 69 games saw him play once every 4.16 days.

Osman had also spent six weeks of the summer of 1980 in Hungary on the *Escape to Victory* film set. That season also saw Town play on Boxing Day when they beat Norwich 2-0 at Portman Road, followed by a 1-1 draw at Arsenal the very next day. Osman's everpresence in all those games without a proper break was truly a phenomenon that will never be seen again.

For nearly 30 minutes, England outplayed the Swiss, and it was totally unexpected when the hosts suddenly swept into the lead with two goals in the space of two minutes.

Ron Greenwood attempted a salvage operation by sending on Terry McDermott for Trevor Francis and pushing Kevin Keegan, captaining England for the 25th time, forward into a striker's role. It was McDermott who at last ended England's run of almost eight hours without a goal when he collected a Steve Coppell pass in the 55th minute and buried a shot in the Swiss net. And for the first time, England's solitary goal was scored by a substitute. This was the 11th goal scored by an England substitute – the first in qualification history.

But Switzerland held out under enormous pressure to record their first victory over England for 34 years. To add to England's despair, the hooligan element among their supporters caused more sickening problems on the terraces. Only a victory in the following match in Hungary could keep alive England's slim hopes of making it into the World Cup finals.

The appalling behaviour of the supporters meant that most neutrals would have been quite happy to see them fail to make it to Spain, and there were whispers that the powers-that-be at FIFA were considering a ban on England.

Osman recalls his last two games of the 1980/81 season, both for England, with memories of changes to the England line-ups as he partnered Dave Watson for the first time against Romania, 'It was a very unsettled time around that era. The likes of Trevor Brooking and Kevin Keegan were getting accused of being a little bit long in the tooth. Their legs had gone maybe, they weren't quite what they had been before.

'Going into those World Cup qualifiers, we had to start getting our act together and start winning a few games. I played with different goalkeepers behind me in Shilton and Clemence. The right-backs changed, as did the left-backs.

'Ray Wilkins and Steve Coppell had come into the side, as did Tony Woodcock against Romania. It was the first time that I had played with Woodcock for England.'

The FC Cologne striker had been an opponent of Osman's in those two UEFA Cup semi-final legs in April. Osman revealed that the pair became good friends.

'Tony went on to become a very good friend of mine. He drove our wedding car. He drove my wife to the church. Tony was a good friend by the time we had played Cologne.'

England's final game of the summer of 1981 saw them get their qualifying hopes back on track with a 3-1 win in Hungary.

Paul Mariner and Mick Mills kept their places from the previous match as England dug deep to come up with one of their finest performances under Greenwood and against all the odds, they breathed life back into their World Cup campaign.

Trevor Brooking gave England an 18th-minute lead which the Hungarians cancelled out seconds before half-time through Imre Garaba.

It was in the second half that England really turned on the pressure, and they got their reward in the shape of a brilliantly taken goal by Brooking, who drove a rising shot so powerfully after accepting a pass from Keegan that the ball jammed in the net behind the stanchion.

Keegan put the result beyond doubt when he scored from the penalty spot in the 73rd minute after being brought down by a desperate tackle.

Brooking and Keegan were devastating together and were the main motivators of one of the greatest displays ever seen from an England team on a foreign field.

Ray Wilkins became the sixth player to have been used as a substitute on five separate occasions, a record that he shared at the time with Malcolm Macdonald, Dave Thomas, Trevor Brooking, Paul Mariner, and Trevor Francis.

Meanwhile, Brooking was the first England player to be replaced eight times. Of the 147 substitutes England had used up to and including this game, Manchester United had provided a record 18 players.

CHAPTER 8

Mariner is in among the goals

FOR England's first game of the 1981/82 season, Paul Mariner and Mick Mills were rejoined by Russell Osman for another World Cup qualifier, against Norway in Oslo.

After hitting the heights against Hungary, England sunk to an all-time low when they lost to Norway's team of part-time professionals – a defeat that seemed certain to end their World Cup hopes.

Bryan Robson scored his first goal for England to give them a 14th-minute lead and a comfortable victory looked well within reach. But the Norwegians battled back to snatch a 34th-minute equaliser that gave them the momentum to go on to what was considered their greatest triumph in a football history that had mostly been about taking part.

Hallvar Thoresen took advantage of dithering in the England defence in the 40th minute to force home what proved to be the match-winning goal. It was a humiliating defeat to rank with the 1950 World Cup loss to the United States. Once again, the knives were out for Ron Greenwood.

The game lives on through the delirious words of Norwegian commentator Bjørge Lillelien, who switched to English as the final whistle blew to tell the world, 'Lord Nelson! Lord Beaverbrook! Sir Winston Churchill! Sir Anthony Eden! Clement Attlee! Henry Cooper! Lady Diana! Maggie Thatcher – can you hear me, Maggie Thatcher! Your boys took one hell of a beating! Your boys took one hell of a beating!'

This result put England's World Cup qualification into some doubt. They still topped the group with seven points, but they had only one game left to play – against Hungary (on five points) who had four fixtures left. Romania and Switzerland (six and four points respectively) both had three to play.

Paul Mariner remembered that defeat only too well, 'The 2-1 defeat in our penultimate qualifying game put our chances of reaching the 1982 World Cup in jeopardy and left us having to rely on other results to qualify. And Ron was under pressure again.

'My son, Dan, who lives in Norway near the Arctic Circle, put me in touch with the Ipswich Town supporters' branch in Oslo. They wanted to talk to me about my time at Ipswich and my international career. But the first thing they did when they called me was put on the recording of that bloody commentary!

'I can watch the highlights again now with a wry smile, knowing we qualified eventually. But we certainly weren't smiling on the journey home after that game. That was a rough Wednesday afternoon for us at the Ullevaal Stadium.'

Meanwhile, Russell Osman remembered the game more for the night out afterwards with a fellow film star, 'Norway were not much of a team back then, and were one of those teams that we were playing where everybody was suddenly thinking that England would walk all over. The same with Austria and stick five in against Switzerland and batter Romania. All these sides were starting to get quite competitive. If you look at our squad then, we had Trevor Brooking and Kevin Keegan who were getting towards the end of their days, and I think that is why we struggled. That and we did not show those sides enough respect. And as such, people were just taking the scorelines on the value that they didn't know anything about these sides. It was a different era then.

'As for Norway, their captain was a lad called Hallvar Thoresen who was part of the *Escape to Victory* team and so I knew him before that game. I had a great night with him after the game. We went out and of course he was lauded for beating England, and I just had a night out with my mate. You could say that we had just a few drinks!'

As mentioned in my introduction to this book, the earliest memory that I have of an Ipswich player scoring for England came in their next game in November 1981, which was just about one of the most crucial qualifying matches I have ever seen the national team play.

A goal by Paul Mariner gave England a 1-0 win against Hungary at Wembley to earn a victory that saw them qualify for the 1982 World Cup.

They had come back from the dead to clinch their place with this nervously constructed victory over the Hungarians.

The door to the finals in Spain was re-opened by group favourites Romania making a mess of their final qualifier, and England needed only a point against Hungary from their last game to book their tickets.

Mariner scored the vital match-winning goal in the 16th minute, scrambling the ball into the net after a mishit shot by Trevor Brooking had confused the Hungarian defenders.

Hungary were already assured of their place in the finals and were content to concentrate on defence and they looked in danger of conceding a second goal only in the final moments when debut-making substitute Tony Morley (England's 150th) had his shot well saved by goalkeeper Ferenc Mészáros.

Rumours of the death of English football were greatly exaggerated following this qualification. In a very straightforward group against middling opposition, England contrived to almost fail to qualify for the third World Cup in a row, but instead they were going to their first finals in 12 years. Just.

Of the Hungary game, his goal, and qualification, Mariner was naturally a very happy man.

'The pre-match warm-up reminded me of the 1978 FA Cup Final. Thousands were already in the stadium with half an hour until kick-off, and that was the first time that I heard them sing, "If you all hate Scotland, clap your hands." I suppose it made a nice change from the Wembley crowd booing us around that time! The weather was miserable, it had rained for most of the day in London, but the atmosphere at kick-off was proper old-school Wembley, noisy and anticipatory.

'With 15 minutes gone, we were awarded a free kick just to the right of centre about 20 yards inside the Hungary half. Terry McDermott floated it long towards me and Alvin Martin at the far side of the penalty box, but the ball was in the air for what seemed like an eternity. So, Hungarian goalkeeper Ferenc Mészáros decided to come off his line to try and collect. Knowing there wasn't enough pace on the ball to reach me, I stood my ground, but the delivery was perfect for Alvin who beat the keeper to the jump and managed to head it back in the direction of Trevor Brooking leaving Mészáros in no man's land.

'As the ball found Trevor, my instinct took over and I started running towards goal. With the ball then coming towards me, I had a split second to sort out my feet and managed to delay my stumble just enough to connect with my right foot and guide it into the back of the net from about six yards out. Instinctive? Yes. Lucky? No.

'When the French referee blew his whistle for full-time, the collective feeling was probably more relief than exaltation. The on-the-field celebrations were enjoyable but relatively low-key.'

With no Ipswich player selected for England's next game, against Northern Ireland in the Home International Championship in February 1982, it would not be until April and the next match that we would see an Ipswich player back in the Three Lions' colours. That was Terry Butcher who returned to the international fold for the first time in over a year, as England visited Wales for the next instalment of the 1981/82 Home International Championship.

A 1-0 win came courtesy of Trevor Francis which gave England their first victory over Wales in five matches when he struck a powerful shot high into the net after Bryan Robson had pushed a short free kick into his path in the 74th minute.

Glenn Hoddle had looked the most inventive player on the pitch, and England lost a lot of their poise and control when he limped off early in the second half.

Wales were always a threat and goalkeeper Joe Corrigan rescued England with three outstanding saves. England played a conventional defence, with Phil Thompson and Butcher proving rock-solid partners.

Terry McDermott became the seventh player to be an England substitute on five separate occasions, a record he shared at the time with Malcolm Macdonald, Dave Thomas, Trevor Brooking, Paul Mariner, Trevor Francis, and Ray Wilkins. Francis won his 25th England cap.

It was Butcher's first game in the Home International Championship. His first involvement was delayed by a serious injury while playing for Ipswich in the FA Cup.

'In 1982, I had a fractured nose at Ipswich after the Luton FA Cup game. I had just got back into the team at Ipswich after two or three months out, and suddenly, I got a call-up from England, straight away. I thought wow, that was a big thing for me because from being in the depths of despair in hospital for five weeks because of the injury, to getting called up.

'We went to Ninian Park in Cardiff and Trevor Francis scored a good goal and we won 1-0. It was a gritty game, and I was delighted that we kept a clean sheet.'

When asked if this tournament should ever be brought back, Butcher said, 'Football has gone past it now. It is something in the past that was great. I enjoyed it very much. But nowadays, it would just get in the way. Especially with the big tournaments.'

Between two Home Championship matches, England squeezed in a friendly as a first warm-up outing ahead of the World Cup against the Netherlands at the back end of May 1982.

Mariner returned to the side for the first time in just over six months and scored to settle this friendly win against a Dutch side with fellow Ipswich player Arnold Mühren in the starting line-up.

The Netherlands' experimental young team were sunk by two goals in five minutes immediately after half-time by Tony Woodcock and Mariner. It was Graham Rix, Bryan Robson, and Ray Wilkins who bossed the midfield, and assured a victory for Ron Greenwood in his last Wembley match as England manager.

He had already decided to stand down at the end of the forthcoming World Cup. Peter Shilton captained England for the first time and became the eighth captain used by Greenwood, creating a new record at the time of different captains used per manager. It was at last clear to see that Shilton was Greenwood's number one choice. This was the last England appearance for Leeds United's Peter Barnes.

Mariner remembered his goal well and made a big statement of it, 'The English public had waited a while to get behind our nation at a World Cup and there was a buzz about the build-up.

'With the feel-good factor returned, more than 69,000 people turned up for the game against the Dutch. Tony Woodcock scored our first goal just before half-time and I scored the second five minutes later with a lovely finish into the top corner. It was probably the best goal that I scored for England.

'I jumped over the advertising boards to celebrate in front of the fans, and it was a nice way for Ron to bid farewell to Wembley in his last game. That didn't stop him from pulling me up in the dressing room after the game and telling me off about my exercise which he had considered to be excessive!'

Before May was out, a trip to Hampden Park for the last Home Championship game of the season was upon England and they beat Scotland 1-0 thanks to yet another goal from Mariner, his scoring for a third appearance in a row. The game had seen a trio of Ipswich players back in the starting XI as Butcher and Mills returned.

It was the seventh occasion that three Ipswich players lined up for England and the Scotland team featured two more in George Burley and Alan Brazil.

Old heroes Tom Finney and George Young led the teams out for this 100th meeting between Scotland and England. Mariner's brave header in the 13th minute clinched the Home Championship for England thanks to a 100 per cent record, and it gave them their third successive victory at Hampden Park. It had also raised their hopes of making a decent challenge for the World Cup.

England exposed flaws in the Scottish tactics that manager Jock Stein knew he had to iron out before they went into a difficult World Cup finals group that included Brazil and Russia.

Trevor Francis became the first England player to make six substitute appearances, and ten minutes later Terry McDermott became the second.

This was Mariner's third and final appearance for England against Scotland, and all three games were played in Glasgow. It was another one that unsurprisingly stands out for Mariner.

'Back in the day, there was no bigger game than England versus Scotland. Whenever I think of that fixture, it makes me smile. It was the most pressurised fixture that I was involved in. Playing against lots of lads who were either club team-mates or you'd butted heads with them in opposition throughout the season.

'And this time, not only would me, Terry Butcher, and Mick Mills be up against our team-mates George Burley and Alan Brazil, but Scotland had also qualified for the World Cup, and they used to love nothing better than putting one over us. Of everything I did in football, all the matches I played and goals I scored, you might be surprised to learn that playing against Scotland in front of more than 80 thousand at Hampden in May 1982 is one of my best moments in the game.

'It was fantastic to score the only goal of the game, don't get me wrong. But the whole occasion was one of the greatest days of my life.'

This was a first experience for Terry Butcher of facing Scotland and when asked about the trip and facing his team-mates, he was just as enthusiastic in his response.

'It was great. Generally, I was marking Alan, and it was a good tussle. We had been to see the Rolling Stones at the Glasgow Apollo on the Thursday night before the game, beat Scotland on the Saturday, and then flew back. What a great trip!'

June 1982 was then upon us, and the month started with two England friendlies on successive nights, the final two warm-up games before their World Cup campaign would kick-off.

Up first was a fixture in Reykjavík which featured Russell Osman who won his sixth cap. Ron Greenwood fielded a second-string team from his World Cup squad, and they struggled in difficult conditions on a frozen pitch to hold an enthusiastic Iceland team.

Future Ipswich player Paul Goddard made his debut as a substitute for the injured Cyrille Regis, and cancelled out Iceland's 23rd-minute lead when he ran on to a precise pass from Glenn Hoddle and steered the ball home in the 69th minute.

It proved to be Goddard's only cap, and he found his way into the record books by becoming the first England player to score while playing less than a full match. He also became the second player (Peter Taylor being the first six years previously) to score a debut goal as a substitute; the 12th goal scored by an England substitute.

This was the second occasion that two substitutes made England debuts (the first time being against Wales in March 1976), but the first instance of them never playing for the senior side again.

Goddard was the 20th player and Steve Perryman the 21st to mark their debuts as a substitute.

Joe Corrigan, Terry McDermott, and Dave Watson all played their last internationals too, and Phil Neal captained England for the one and only time.

The following night, Mariner and Mills featured in a 4-1 win against Finland in Helsinki for England's final warm-up game before the World Cup. Mariner scored twice to take his consecutive games scored in tally to four.

Then Ron Greenwood would face the harshest and most cruel decision of his career as England manager a day later, following his 50th match in charge.

That is when he had to tell ten of his 32 players across these two games with high hopes that their baggage will not be needed on the voyage to Spain for the World Cup.

Those 32 players were sent in two groups of 16 players to matches in Iceland and Finland. Greenwood made a desperate if unconvincing attempt to reassure the half of the party which was sent to Iceland that they were very much more than makeweights.

He had, for instance, insisted to his International Committee that all of those who played should be awarded the velvet reward of a full cap – and that was sure to be agreed. 'A team of such strengths deserves caps,' he said before that last game against Iceland. And with the weight he could throw behind such wishes, there was no doubting they would get them, if only as consolation prizes.

For what would prove to be only the second time and last occasion, an Ipswich player scored two goals in an England game. David Johnson scored twice against Wales in 1975, and then on this occasion it was Mariner. His second goal was his tenth for his country.

While Mariner and Mills started, Terry Butcher was an unused substitute.

Trevor Francis became the first England player to be used seven times as a substitute, while Kevin Keegan was the captain for the 31st and final time.

Of the two games in two nights experience, Russell Osman said, 'The FA had two fixtures that they wanted to fulfil. So, rather than have a full cap and a B cap, both games were classified as full caps even though the team that went to Iceland was probably only worthy of a B cap. So, it was a bit of a mixed side. You had Phil Neal and Viv Anderson and obviously one of those played out of position.'

In goal for England against Iceland was Joe Corrigan, and Russell had a great story to tell of the Manchester City custodian.

'Joe was Paul Mariner's room-mate for England games. He would take the wardrobe for his clothes and Paul would have to put his on a chair in the corner. There was a time when I put some invisible ink on his shirt, and we were on a train when he noticed. He ended up taking his shirt off and throwing it out of the window. He then made us all take our socks off.'

With their final friendlies now behind them, attentions for Butcher, Mariner, and Mills now turned to Spain and the beginning of the 1982 World Cup. Russell Osman had been omitted from Ron Greenwood's final squad selection.

CHAPTER 9

1982 World Cup beckons for Town trio

TERRY Butcher had found out that he had been called up for the England World Cup squad in further unorthodox fashion. He picks up the story, 'I was driving home in my car and had the radio on. The news came on and the last item pricked my attention. "And finally, England manager Ron Greenwood has named his squad of 22 players for the World Cup."

'The newsreader paused, and my heart was pounding with a mixture of fear and anticipation. "Anderson, Brooking, Butcher…" I could hardly believe it. I was in. Three months earlier, I didn't even think that I would play for Ipswich again as I was laying in hospital having a blood transfusion.

'My parents were the first to phone and congratulate me. I could sense how proud they were. I was sad that Russell wasn't included with me.

'We never got told of our selection though until a nice official letter came through, but it came the day after. They posted it on the day of the announcement while it was announced to the press, but we did not find out before.'

Butcher spoke further about the build-up to the tournament including missing the recording of England's World Cup song, 'This Time (We'll Get It Right)', and how he found himself sharing a room at the tournament with Aston Villa's Peter Withe which came as somewhat of a shock, 'I was a relative newcomer to the squad, and I even missed out on the recording of the World Cup record.

'I was paired with Peter Withe. How about that! We didn't get a choice of whom to room with, we were just told. To be fair, Withey was magnificent. He used to go down and get the papers when they first arrived. They would come two or three days after they had been published.

'So, me and him would have a read of all the papers first, and then give them out to all the other players. Honestly, he was like a magpie. You see all the shampoos, soaps, hair nets and combs in the hotel room, and Peter would put them all in his bag. He always used to say, "I have got a mate who'll want them." The bathroom area would always be completely emptied because he rifled everything!

'But how could you have, because we would kick seven bells out of each other during the season, two opposites, two players that were fiercely intense towards each other, then room together? But it worked well.

'We were based in Bilbao, in the heart of the Basque region, where separatists wanted an independent homeland. There had been a series of bombings in support of their campaign and there was strict security around our hotel.

'The guards seemed tense, but the atmosphere around the squad was very relaxed. We had taken over the hotel and before long, a games room was in place with pool tables, space invaders, and a table tennis table.'

I imagined that there might have been cliques within the group in those days, perhaps believing that the Ipswich players would have stuck together for example. But Butcher said that was not the case.

'The senior players like Keegan, Brooking, and Thompson were the ones up the top. They were the ones to be looked at, watch what they did and all that sort of thing. Then you had the players who had a good number of caps, and then it came down to us young ones like Glenn Hoddle, Kenny Sansom, Graham Rix, and me. We were the four younger ones, the new kids on the block. So, we stuck together a lot.

'The wives all came out too for the latter stages of the tournament, but we had to pay for them to come out. They were all on different flights. My son Christopher, who was only 12 weeks old, was brought out by my wife Rita, and I remember that for the Kuwait game, being behind the goal, with Christopher in my arms and I was feeding him with a bottle during the game. That was a lovely surreal moment that happened in those days.'

For the eighth time, an England line-up contained three Ipswich Town players, as they got their World Cup campaign under way in Spain against France. It was the first time that an Ipswich player featured for England at a World Cup, and it proved to be a momentous occasion for Mick Mills who became the first and only Town man to date to captain the Three Lions in this tournament.

Equally as historic was Paul Mariner's goal, England's third, which remains as the only goal scored by an Ipswich player at a World Cup at the time of writing. It was the fifth successive international in which the striker had found the net.

England made a dream start when Bryan Robson scored one of the fastest goals in the history of the tournament. He struck after just 27 seconds, lashing the ball left-footed past a startled French goalkeeper after Butcher had headed on a quickly taken Steve Coppell throw from the right. At the time, it was England's second-fastest goal ever.

France recovered from this shattering start to equalise after 25 minutes, but England raised their pace despite scorching heat in the second half and the switch by Ron Greenwood of Graham Rix to a left-sided role in midfield proved a tactical masterstroke.

Rix, playing in place of the injured Trevor Brooking, enjoyed his new freedom and England took full control when Robson headed in his second goal in the 67th minute. Mariner underlined their supremacy with a close-range shot following a defensive mix-up.

Butcher received a yellow card to become the first Ipswich player to be booked in the World Cup finals.

This was an encouraging start for an England team missing the input of their most famous player, Kevin Keegan, who was suffering a recurrence of an old back injury.

Mariner's goal equalled an England record, one that he was rightly proud of, 'Seven minutes from time, I scored our third to complete a 3-1 win. Trevor Francis tried a shot which deflected off French defender Marius Trésor and fell perfectly for me seven or eight yards from goal. It was a pretty easy finish beyond goalkeeper Jean-Luc Ettori to extend my goals-in-consecutive-games-for-England streak to five and move level with my hero Jimmy Greaves.

'That was a proud moment for me to equal Jimmy's record because it took a lot of hard work to get to that position, 11 goals in 22 appearances for England up to that point was a very decent record.'

Meanwhile, for Terry Butcher, it had been a meteoric rise from where he was at the start of 1982 to be taking part in the World Cup.

'I had gone from in January, being in hospital for five weeks, to playing against Wales and Scotland, and then to be selected for the World Cup. It was fairytale stuff for me. The saddest thing was that Russell wasn't with me. The other centre-half that came with us was Steve Foster. I thought that Russell was better than Steve personally, but obviously Ron didn't see it that way.

'As for the game against France, I played my part in Bryan Robson's first goal after 27 seconds when flicking on Steve Coppell's throw-in. Then I made a mistake for Gérard

Soler to equalise. I got his shirt after the game. There is no name on the back, and it just says World Cup underneath the badge.

'Mick was captain, Marrers played, and I played. Three Ipswich players in the starting line-up. Brilliant isn't it. What a picture that is of us lining-up before the game. Will that ever happen again? I don't know ... wow.

'It was common for three Ipswich players to feature. There was a great picture in the early '80s of me, Gatesy, Millsy, and Marrers. The four of us got selected. Eric and I hadn't made our debut by then, but Millsy and Marrers had.'

Four days later, the Ipswich three were all once again starters for an unchanged England side for their second group game. Mills was once again named as captain.

Two fortunate goals in three minutes midway through the second half booked England's place in the second phase of the finals.

Trevor Francis rammed the ball into the net after Czech goalkeeper Stanislav Seman had dropped a Ray Wilkins corner, and then Czech defender Jozef Barmoš diverted the ball into his own net as Francis raced to meet a pass from Mariner.

A blow for England was that they lost Bryan Robson, who had been their outstanding player, at half-time with a groin strain. Robson joined Kevin Keegan and Trevor Brooking on the injury list.

For the Czechs, Seman completed his unhappy evening by breaking a finger and being replaced by Karel Stromšík.

A further five days on, England played their third game of the tournament against Kuwait, and Ron Greenwood made three changes to his starting line-up. Out went Butcher to be replaced by Brighton & Hove Albion's Steve Foster, but Mills and Mariner retained their places as Mills once again wore the captain's armband.

A gem of a goal by Trevor Francis was the one highlight of England's third victory, 1-0 against a Kuwaiti side that battled bravely and with some eye-catching skill.

The match-winner came in the 27th minute when Mariner back-heeled a Peter Shilton clearance into the path of Francis, who set off on a 30-yard run that he finished by sliding the ball past the oncoming goalkeeper.

Mariner was booked in the 42nd minute. Colombian referee Gilberto Aristizábal had a frustrating habit of getting in the way of play. Prior to brandishing the yellow card to Mariner, he had been in the way of play on three occasions in the first half and later blocked a Hoddle shot in the second.

Mariner was off the ball, ahead of play, when he found Aristizábal wandering in front of him when he was ready to receive a pass from Rix, so he gave him a small shove out of the way. The referee subsequently booked him.

England qualified for the next round, another group stage, with a 100 per cent record.

Mariner was quite rightly frustrated regarding both his booking and the unsatisfactory format of the tournament.

'I was annoyed at the Colombian referee, Gilberto Aristizábal, who had an annoying habit of getting in the way of play. Three times in the first half he failed to get out of the way. On the fourth occasion, I was trying to get on the end of a pass from Graham Rix, I found him [Aristizábal] wandering in front of me, so I gave him a gentle push to get him the hell out of the way. He then booked me!

'Our reward for winning group four and securing a place in the second round, was a spot in Group B alongside West Germany and Spain. Meanwhile, France, the runners-up, got to play Austria and Northern Ireland.

'There was absolutely no advantage given to the initial group winners ahead of the second round. One of the other three – team groups contained Italy, Brazil, and Argentina! It was a daft format having a second group stage with only three teams after the initial groups contained four teams, and it came as no surprise to me to see it ditched for the World Cup in Mexico four years later.'

England then moved on to Madrid for the first of their second phase of group games. Butcher returned to the heart of the defence to make it three Ipswich players in the line-up once again. Only Manchester United could match Town for having three players from one club in the starting XI. For Paul Mariner, this was his 25th international.

England and West Germany have had some classic confrontations on the football field, but this was not one of them as it petered out into a 0-0 draw. The Germans decided on a policy of a suffocating defence, and the game deteriorated into a midfield muddle.

Bryan Robson came closest to scoring with a first-half header that was tipped over the bar by Harald Schumacher, and the subdued, half-fit Karl-Heinz Rummenigge threatened to win the match with one moment of brilliance.

His sniper shot from 25 yards rocked the England crossbar in the closing minutes of a best-forgotten game. England now had to beat Spain by two goals in their next match to qualify for a place in the semi-finals. Of this disappointing draw and what it then meant for England, Butcher said, 'I missed the game against Kuwait as I had been booked against France.

'Two cautions in the first three games got you a ban for one game. So, Ron Greenwood left me out because we had already qualified. We drew with West Germany 0-0 and then West Germany played Spain and beat them 2-1. That meant that we then had to beat Spain by two goals.'

England could only manage a 0-0 draw against Spain – their second of the stage – and went out of the World Cup without losing a game. It ended Ron Greenwood's time as manager.

England were unable to put the vital finishing touches to some excellent approach work that was a good advertisement for the quality football that Greenwood had always believed in. His reign finished with a rare gamble against a Spanish team determined not to be beaten. He sent Kevin Keegan and Trevor Brooking on for their first action of the World Cup, and the double substitution so nearly brought reward.

Keegan headed wide from the best chance of the match, and Brooking had a rasping shot well saved. In the event, it was a final England appearance for both.

It was also a farewell appearance for Ipswich's Mick Mills. His 42nd and final match saw him captain England for the eighth time, and at the time of writing, he was the last Ipswich player to have the honour of skippering the national team. All of his caps were earned as an Ipswich player – the second most-capped Town man for England after Terry Butcher.

There was a solemn reflection from Butcher when asked about the game against the Spanish and the exiting of that tournament.

'The Falklands War had just finished, and Spain had sided with Argentina. Anyone associated with the England team got absolute pelters. Honestly, I thought that there was going to be a riot after the game, I really did.

'Trevor and Kevin came on after about an hour and Kevin missed a great chance to score. But we played the tournament without them. We conceded one goal, never lost a game, and yet we were out of the tournament. How could that be? It was devastating really.'

Paul Mariner was equally as scathing about the format that had seen England cruelly eliminated, 'Our record at that World Cup – played five, won three, drew two, lost none, scored six and conceded one. We did not lose a game and only let in one goal but that still wasn't good enough.

'Yes, the format was poor, with no advantage whatsoever to the initial group winners. But we knew what we had to do in our last game against Spain and the bottom line is we didn't get the job done. That was on us.

'It's easy to question Ron Greenwood's tactics or team selections, but he was not the one who couldn't put the ball in the back of the net.

'I started every game, scored once in the opener against France, and provided a couple of assists. Could I have done more? If we're talking practically, then no. I gave everything I had. Can't change things now.

'Overall, I look back on the tournament with great joy and I think we gave a good account of ourselves. There was camaraderie and togetherness among the lads, and I have some incredible memories. The team spirit was fantastic, despite injuries to Kevin Keegan and Trevor Brooking, and if they'd both been fully fit, I think we would have gone very close indeed to winning the whole thing.

'The game against Spain was an end of an era. It was the last time Keegan, Brooking and Mick Mills played for England, while Ron Greenwood's time as manager was over and he'd be replaced by Bobby Robson. It was also the last tournament I would be involved in. I only played nine more games for my country [seven of those while still at Ipswich]. The times they were a-changin'.

Exit Ron Greenwood after 55 matches (won 33, drew 12 and lost ten) and enter Ipswich Town's Bobby Robson, who had been named as England's next manager during the World Cup finals.

CHAPTER 10

Bobby swaps Town for Country

THE first England game of the 1982/83 season was a trip to Copenhagen and they came away with a 2-2 draw against Denmark.

It was the first time that a third successive England match contained three Ipswich Town players as Bobby Robson took charge of his first international.

Former club stalwarts Terry Butcher, Paul Mariner, and Russell Osman all lined up in Robson's inaugural starting XI with Ipswich being the only club that featured three of their players.

For Osman, this was his first England appearance since missing out on Ron Greenwood's World Cup squad.

Jesper Olsen stopped Robson from celebrating a victory in his first match when he conjured a spectacular last-minute goal that gave Denmark a thoroughly deserved draw in this European Championship qualifier.

Olsen outwitted three England defenders in a jinking run before guiding the ball wide of Peter Shilton, who had performed minor miracles keeping out the talented Danish forwards.

Trevor Francis had given England a seventh-minute lead, but they were then forced on the defensive and it was thanks mainly to the acrobatics of Shilton that the Danes had to wait more than an hour before they finally got an equaliser through an Allan Hansen penalty after Osman had fouled Olsen.

Francis scored his second goal ten minutes from the final whistle with a hooked shot that restored England's lead and looked like being the winner until Olsen's moment of magic.

Luton Town's Ricky Hill became Robson's first new cap when he came on as a substitute for Tony Morley in the 83rd minute.

Two of Robson's Ipswich prodigies recalled that first game in charge well.

Butcher said, 'The Danes had a striker called Preben Elkjær who was like trying to grab a slippery fish. He was everywhere. He wasn't particularly quick, but sharp. I'd never met him before, and he caused us no end of problems. Somehow though, it looked like we were going to win the game and then Jesper Olsen scored a late equaliser. We did then realise that Denmark were a force to be reckoned with, and they were for the next five or six years.'

Osman added, 'This is when we went from Ron Greenwood's era of being too old and changes were needed, to Bobby Robson looking at players through the "B" team's schedule and that Iceland game, and you could see the changes he made for the Denmark game. Peter Shilton was in goal, but Ray Clemence was the better goalkeeper. He was better on crosses, and the better footballer.'

At this point, I asked Russell if he thought that all three England goalkeepers at that time were better than our own Paul Cooper.

'No. No I don't. I think that for shot stopping, Shilton was good. Clemence for me was better all round. But Paul Cooper was probably the best footballer out of the three of them, and I would say that Paul Cooper was better than Joe Corrigan.

'Maybe he wasn't as big as them, but he was a good footballer.'

Robson's second game in charge in October would be his first at Wembley as England faced old foes West Germany in a friendly and fell to a 2-1 defeat. Osman was left out of the squad and indeed would not return until after the 1982/83 season had come to an end. Meanwhile, Butcher and Mariner retained their places in the starting line-up.

England had the better of the first half during which new cap Gary Mabbutt of Tottenham Hotspur hit a post with a fierce cross-shot. But the Germans took control when Pierre Littbarski came on as substitute just 24 hours after helping Germany beat England 3-2 in an under-21 international in Bremen.

Karl-Heinz Rummenigge ended brave resistance by England's overworked defence in the 72nd minute when he delicately chipped the ball over Shilton, and shortly after, he held off a tackle from Butcher as he swept the ball into the net from a Littbarski cross.

Tony Woodcock, playing in his 25th international game, scored for England four minutes from the end with a shot that went in off the bar. Watford's Luther Blissett came on as a substitute in the 80th minute for his first taste of international football.

'Germany are always strong,' reflected Butcher. 'We were just finding our feet really with Bobby and the group. We trained at Bisham Abbey and would stay in their accommodation which was ultra basic. There is a good picture of me and Marrers in the room and it was like a little box. Then we would go and play at Wembley. Bobby was just finding out what was the best solution for the players with accommodation and training wise.'

A trip to Greece a month later next saw Paul Mariner as the sole player to represent Ipswich as Bobby Robson rang the changes for his third game in charge.

Woodcock, playing in borrowed boots, put England on the way to a first victory under Robson with a goal in the second minute, and he made it 2-0 in the 64th minute of this European Championship qualifier.

Five minutes later, Liverpool's Sammy Lee made his debut memorable when he crashed the ball into the net after Bryan Robson had transferred a Woodcock free kick into his path.

Lee and Mabbutt were exceptional in midfield in place of the injured Ray Wilkins and Glenn Hoddle in a hard-fought game played on a difficult, rain-saturated surface.

Phil Thompson and Tony Morley played their last games for England, while Bryan Robson won his 25th cap and captained the team for the first time.

In mid-December, Butcher returned as Mariner was omitted for Luxembourg's visit to Wembley. With a 9-0 victory, it was the biggest England win that has featured an Ipswich player to date.

England struggled to find their rhythm in the goalless first 20 minutes of this European Championship qualifier, but the floodgates opened with a Luxembourg own goal.

A minute later, Steve Coppell headed in a Robson cross, then Woodcock and Blissett made it 4-0 by half-time.

The first 20 minutes of the second half were, as in the first half, barren. But then England stepped up the pace and Blissett completed his hat-trick, the 12th hat-trick to be scored at Wembley. And then substitutes Mark Chamberlain, winning his first cap, and Glenn Hoddle found the net. Chamberlain became the third England player to score on debut, and his club side, Stoke City, were the 31st different club to provide an England substitute.

In the final seconds, Phil Neal netted the ninth goal to equal the haul when England – including Bobby Robson – beat Luxembourg in 1960.

Wembley also witnessed its fourth and fifth goals by a substitute. This was the first time that two goals had been scored in a match by two different substitutes.

For Chamberlain's goal, it was a moment of excitement for Butcher, who recalled, 'I was on the left wing somehow and I crossed the ball and Mark ran off the other way. He never even came over and said thanks.

'I spoke to him in the dressing room after the game. I said hey you, you could have said thanks!'

For their first match of 1983, England returned to Home International Championship action at Wembley against Wales, and Paul Mariner returned to the line-up, joining team-mate Butcher who scored his first goal for his country in this game and became the fifth Ipswich player to score for England.

Phil Neal scored from the penalty spot in the 78th minute to end a bold victory bid by Wales on an ice-bound pitch. Neal's penalty was the seventh successive converted kick scored, equalling a record set in 1955.

Ian Rush had given Wales a 14th-minute lead and they were just a coat of paint away from making it 2-0 nine minutes later when his shot struck a post.

Butcher equalised six minutes before half-time following a quickly taken free kick by Gordon Cowans who, along with Derek Statham, was making his debut.

Neal slotted his penalty home just four days after missing a vital spot-kick for Liverpool in an FA Cup tie. Of his first game with a goal for England, Butcher said, 'The pitch was frozen down one side. And right down the middle of the pitch was a line that defined a frozen pitch and a soft pitch. So, in the first half, we were kicking towards the tunnel end, and I played on the left side and therefore on the frozen side.

'I was wearing pimple boots, and I was up for a free kick. The ball came to me on the edge of the box and just bounced up in front of me. I hit it as sweet as a nut like a volley and it flew past the goalkeeper.'

The following month, it was back to European Championship qualifying action as England hosted Greece at Wembley. Butcher was Ipswich's sole representative in this game.

England were frustrated by a Greek team that came only to defend in this return match. Trevor Francis was the one England forward to play with any penetration, and he might have had a hat-trick before he was subdued by some spiteful tackles.

The night was a sad milestone for Steve Coppell, whose international career ended after 42 caps because of a serious knee injury. After-match quotes by Bobby Robson about Alan Devonshire were taken out of context, and he had to contact the West Ham player to tell him that he had not meant to make him the so-called 'scapegoat' for England's dismal performance.

And Butcher was once again the only Ipswich player involved in England's next game in April – another Euro qualifier at home to Hungary which was won 2-0.

Goals in each half from Trevor Francis and Peter Withe, his first in internationals, sank a skilful Hungarian team and strengthened England's position at the top of their European Championship qualifying group.

Francis was always a handful for the Hungarian defence and his goal was the 1,450th scored by England. Withe topped a powerhouse performance with a cracking goal in the 70th minute when he chested down a long pass from Sammy Lee and rifled in an unstoppable cross shot.

Action man Withe had to go to hospital for treatment to a fractured cheekbone and a broken thumb. There was the rare sight of two goalkeeping captains tossing the coin at the pre-match ritual.

A 0-0 draw followed in England's first game following the culmination of 1982/83, in which Ipswich finished ninth in their first season without Bobby Robson in charge.

Butcher once more featured as attentions turned back to the Home Championship. An unused substitute for this game was Russell Osman.

John Barnes, making his debut as a substitute for Watford team-mate Luther Blissett, threatened to end the deadlock in the final seconds but goalkeeper Pat Jennings managed to block his close-range shot. Barnes was also the first teenage England substitute, and the youngest since Ray Wilkins in September 1977. He was the 25th England player to make his debut as a substitute.

Bobby Robson also introduced Graham Roberts to international football, and he almost turned the ball into his own net in the 28th minute, Peter Shilton saving the day by diving across goal to punch the ball against a post.

Glenn Hoddle had his first full game for Robson after a succession of injuries. Jimmy McIlroy and Martin O'Neill bossed the midfield for long periods, and England were fortunate to escape with a draw.

Just four days later, England played their final game in the 1982/83 Home Championship against Scotland with Butcher remaining at the heart of the defence.

Skipper Bryan Robson gave England the lead in the 13th minute with a carbon copy of the goal he scored in the opening seconds of the 1982 World Cup, forcing the ball into the net from close range after Butcher headed on a Kenny Sansom throw.

Robson limped off with a groin injury ten minutes later, but England continued to dominate in midfield and schemer Gordon Cowans turned scorer in the 54th minute for his first international goal to clinch victory and the Home Championship.

Sammy Lee and Trevor Francis each had goals disallowed. Goalkeeper Shilton marked his 50th international appearance with a wonderful diving save that prevented Scotland's best player, Gordon Strachan, from pulling a goal back.

For Scotland, the Ipswich pairing of Alan Brazil and John Wark both came on as second-half substitutes for Eamonn Bannon and Charlie Nicholas.

To finish off the summer of 1983, England then went on tour to Australia, and it was back to where international football life all started for Butcher and Osman.

The first of three games on the tour saw the pair return to the Sydney Cricket Ground where they had made their England debuts some three years earlier.

It was the first of three friendly games in eight days against the Aussies, and the Town duo were paired together for all three.

The game ground out to a 0-0 draw with Bobby Robson making several changes in this new-look side. Handed their first caps were Danny Thomas of Coventry City, Steve Williams of Southampton, Norwich City's Mark Barham, and John Gregory of QPR.

Meanwhile, Luton Town's Paul Walsh came off the bench to replace Luther Blissett to become England's 26th player to debut as a substitute.

Barham's inclusion in the side meant that this was the first time that a Norwich player had featured for England with at least one Ipswich Town player.

This was also the first clean sheet kept for Butcher and Osman when playing together for England.

Robson then made three changes to his starting line-up for the second game of this tour, with Phil Neal returning at right-back in place of Danny Thomas, John Barnes coming in for Luther Blissett, and Paul Walsh making his first starting appearance as

Steve Williams was placed on the bench. Walsh marked the occasion by scoring the only goal of the game to give England a narrow win.

Statham and Barham played their last games for England, winning three and two caps in total respectively. It was another clean sheet on the board for Butcher and Osman.

The third and final match of the tour ended all-square thanks to a 1-1 draw. Trevor Francis missed a 73rd-minute penalty after Butcher had been fouled, failing to take the chance to give England a second victory.

Francis had to take the penalty twice. First time around, he scored but the referee disallowed the goal because he had not blown the whistle. He then carded Francis and the re-take was hit over the bar.

Robson had inherited this 'down under' tour and went there reluctantly with what was virtually an England B team; it was a controversial issue that full caps were awarded.

Australia missed the chance to turn the games into a soccer showpiece and defended grimly and often brutally in all three matches. A crowd of 14,000 saw England struggle through a goalless first match in Sydney, and there were just 10,000 to watch Paul Walsh score the only goal of the second one three days later in Brisbane.

In this final game, a Phil Neal own goal cancelled out a Francis goal in front of 20,000 spectators in Melbourne, and the fixture was described by Robson as 'of little value to anybody, and nothing like the sort of preparation we needed for the European Championship'.

Barham, Williams, Thomas, John Gregory, Nick Pickering, and Nigel Spink were, along with Walsh, the new full caps, and not one of them was still in the frame for England when the 1986 World Cup build-up started.

Back to that first time where Butcher played for England with a player from Norwich in the shape of Mark Barham. How did that make Terry feel? Did he give Barham any stick?

'No, I didn't. Because when the younger players, as Mark was, came into the England camp, they left their club badges at the door. We all wanted that. You could sit on any table. In some squads, it would be maybe Manchester United players at a table or Liverpool players at another table. But with England, you could sit anywhere. If you went into a room, and a seat was empty, you would sit there. It was a nice comfortable feeling, there was no pressure, or, "Why did you not save me a spot?"'

There was also a familiar presence lining up alongside Terry in each of the matches.

'Russell and I played in all three games, and we roomed together. They were three dreadful games. Australia just spoiled them. They hardly bothered to attack. They were poor as a football team.

'Our team was vastly different to our normal team, and we hadn't played much together. It should have been classed as a "B" game.'

And for Osman, he confirms the friendlier nature of teaming up with a Norwich player for England and summarises the feeling of that trip.

'I know Mark very well. I knew his wife very well too before she died. Mark's a good lad. It was the end of the season, we'd played close to 50 games again, and then you go on a trip to Australia. You look at the consistency of the squads that I played with over that period and it's surreal. There was quite a few!'

Mariner, Butcher, and Osman lining up for England.

Mick Mills in England training.

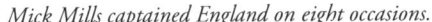

Ipswich quartet of Mariner, Gates, Mills and Butcher.

Mick Mills captained England on eight occasions.

Colin Viljoen in action.

Ipswich four with manager Ron Greenwood.

Gates and Mariner in discussion.

CHAPTER 11

Final caps for Mariner & Osman

ENGLAND'S first game of the 1983/84 season saw them return to European Championship qualifying action at Wembley against Denmark. This match was ultimately a final England appearance for Russell Osman.

A first-half Allan Simonsen penalty decided things on a soaking-wet pitch and gave Bobby Robson what he described as 'the blackest day of my career'.

England disputed the penalty, which was awarded when the ball bounced up and struck Phil Neal on the hand. The midfield trio of Sammy Lee, John Gregory and Ray Wilkins failed to function together, and England did not deserve to take a point from the Danes, who were always the more inventive and industrious team.

The home players were jeered off and a section of the crowd turned on Robson as he made the long, lonely walk back to the dressing room. The tabloid press were unmerciful with their criticism and poured scorn on Robson, who said privately, 'Even the prime minister does not get the pressure and criticism of an England manager. Some of the things written and said are completely out of order, but you just must bite your tongue and take it.'

When John Barnes was replaced by Mark Chamberlain in the 70th minute, he became the first teenager, and therefore the youngest of the 187 players, to have been replaced by a substitute at this time.

Also playing for the last time for his country was Neal who also earned his 50th cap.

As time was called on Russell Osman's England career, he looked back with mixed feelings.

'I saw a press cutting recently from just after that second trip to Australia. It was an interview from Bobby Robson after the last of those games, saying how well he thought I played in that game.

'And then that coupled with what he said after the next game against Denmark which we lost 1-0, where he told me I had played my best-ever game for my country, I had gone from those two comments, to never playing for England again!

'It was strange. When you look at how many changes were made in the squad, five different left-backs, five different right-backs, and three different goalkeepers for example, it doesn't make for a settled team. In the space of three years from my debut to my last game, there were only three players who played in both games and that was myself, Terry, and Marrers.

'My outstanding moment though was probably playing at Wembley for the first time against Spain. There was always something a little bit special about playing at Wembley when you go out there for a full international.

'The style of football was not really any different to what we were playing at Ipswich, it was just a case of getting on with the personnel there. There were a few big hitters, older statesman, like Kevin Keegan, Trevor Francis, Trevor Brooking, Phil Neal, Ray Clemence, and Peter Shilton. It was just a case of getting in and around players that had not only done it in the league but on the European stage too.

'Bobby got a lot of stick for playing too many Ipswich players which is maybe a reason why I not selected any more. Nobody would say anything these days though. The managers these days would just say to the press what's it got to do with you. You're just selling newspapers! The whole press thing is different these days.

'Liverpool, Aston Villa, and Ipswich were the dominant clubs of the time, but it was not reflected in the selections. There were a lot of clubs supplying players for England. We were playing European football. So, when you're playing international matches against European sides, and you're used to playing against European players, you've got half a chance. And a better chance than those that played say for a club like Brighton and just playing league football.

'It all baffled me to the extent where I just gave up predicting it and trying to make any sense of it. It drove me mad at times. I still think that Terry and I were the best English centre-half partnership for a good four or five years and would have been the case for longer if we hadn't had to leave Ipswich.

'I had already missed out on the 1982 World Cup because Ron Greenwood took Steve Foster of Brighton instead of me even though he only played once, and I had six caps. I thought that I would have gone along with Terry. I didn't really watch much of that tournament. I was very disappointed.

'To then miss out again in 1986 … I thought I was still good enough to go to that World Cup, but I was bombed out by Bobby.

'The thing that was really disappointing there was because of what Bobby had said to me about my last game against Denmark. He said he was very pleased for me as it had been my best-ever game. Not only did he never pick me again, but he never gave me a reason why.

'The following game against Hungary, I was in the squad, and we were away from home. He didn't name the side until about an hour and a half before kick-off. So, we were all sat in the changing room in our club suits, and he names the side and substitutes and I'm not even on the bench. Yet a month before, I'd had my best-ever game.

'He never told me why, no explanation, and never mentioned again. I was a bit stubborn in those days. I never asked him why. In my eyes, I thought how he'd known me since I was 15 years old, and I would have thought that he would have had a little bit more respect for me than leaving me out in front of everybody.

'Don Howe, England's coach at the time, came up to me and asked why I wasn't playing. I said to him that I didn't know why. He asked if I'd spoken to Bobby, and I told him that the game was kicking off in an hour and I thought that Bobby would have done the decent thing and spoken to me before the announcement. And that was that. The end of my England career.

'At the end of the day, I'm still very thankful for what Bobby did for me. He gave me the opportunity to play for Ipswich and if you don't get that opportunity to start with, then my whole career wouldn't have existed.

'But he disappointed me in the manner that he left me out of the England side.'

Back to that defeat by Denmark at Wembley, it was a game that Terry Butcher recalled, 'We never got going that day. Allan Simonsen scored from the penalty spot. It wasn't me that gave the penalty away. It was Phil Neal! The crowd and press were starting to turn on Bobby. We were struggling to qualify for the 1984 Euros in France.'

Three weeks later, England travelled to Budapest for their next qualifier against Hungary.

In his penultimate game for England as an Ipswich player, Paul Mariner found himself on the scoresheet and in the referee's notebook after receiving a yellow card in the 71st minute.

Bryan Robson and Glenn Hoddle were recalled to the midfield, and they were the tandem team that gave England a decided edge over the Hungarians.

Hoddle scored an early goal to settle England down and made the third goal for Mariner after Sammy Lee had made it 2-0 with a 20-yard drive.

This victory meant that England were still just about breathing in the qualifying stages of the European Championship.

Just over a month later, England were once more in Euro qualifier action, in Luxembourg, and this proved a noteworthy game for Ipswich Town fans. Paul Mariner made his last appearance for England as an Ipswich player prior to his move to Arsenal three months later. He also scored for the second successive England game and not only was this his last goal too as an Ipswich player, but it was his final goal for England.

Mariner played a total of 33 games for England as an Ipswich player and would add just two more caps to that tally as an Arsenal player. One of England's other three goals in this game came from Terry Butcher – his first in a Euro qualifier. This was the last time that more than one Ipswich player would play in the same game for England.

Just before the kick-off, England heard the news that Denmark had beaten Greece 2-0 to clinch the place in the European Championship finals. With only the top team in the group stage going through, England had failed to qualify for the tournament in France.

So, it was something of an anti-climax as they went into action against Luxembourg. Skipper Bryan Robson refused to allow chins to drop, and he was the main motivator as England cruised to a comfortable four-goal victory.

Robson scored two of the goals, with Bobby Robson's former Ipswich faithfuls Butcher and Mariner netting their goals. Manchester United right-back Mike Duxbury made his debut in an England defence that was rarely troubled by the shot-shy Luxembourg forwards.

Butcher recalls the feeling of not qualifying for his second major tournament, 'We had to beat Hungary in our penultimate qualifier which we did before heading to Luxembourg for our final game. In the changing room before the game, we were listening to the Greece v Denmark game and Denmark coasted to a 2-0 win.

'By playing before us, we knew that we had failed to qualify before we went out for our game. It was the worst feeling ever knowing that we hadn't qualified for a tournament, yet we still had to play this stupid game, a dead rubber. We won 4-0 and I scored from a yard with my right foot, and I didn't even celebrate. I just ran back to the halfway line and wanted the game to be over.'

For Mariner, his time as an England player while at Ipswich came to an end and he bowed out with this failure to qualify for the Euros. Looking back on his last game and England career overall, Mariner said, 'Thirty-three of my 35 England caps were won during my time at Ipswich. This was also the game that I scored the last of my 13 England goals. But was it my goal? It was scruffy to say the least. Sammy Lee sent a hanging cross over for me to attack but I honestly don't know how much contact I made with the ball. It hit an arm, maybe mine or the defenders. That flummoxed their goalkeeper who did not even bother to attempt to make a save.

'I did not really know what happened at the time and never did get closer to the truth. It was either an own goal or it went in off my arm. The Dutch referee allowed it to stand, and nobody ever tried to take it away from me.

'Overall, I look back on my international career with nothing but joy. Thirty-five caps for England, some people would say that's not too many, but for me, it's 35 more than I thought I would get. I'm a humble type of bloke, I was as proud as punch to play for my country and whenever I got called up, I was absolutely elated.'

Next up was a friendly in France in February 1984 which started a run of 23 games where each time an England match featured an Ipswich player, it would just be Terry Butcher.

Two second-half goals by Michel Platini gave France a victory that was earned in midfield where they were always a thought and a deed ahead of an experimental England side for whom Luton partners Brian Stein and Paul Walsh failed to find their club form. This was Stein's only game for England.

France went on to win the European Championship in the summer, so there was no disgrace for the England team. The disgrace came off the pitch where hooligans among England's followers again ran riot. Hooliganism had become known as 'the English disease'.

When manager at Ipswich, Bobby Robson had landed himself in trouble by saying that the way to deal with hooligans was 'to turn a flamethrower on them'. Asked what he thought of the hooligans who had poisoned the atmosphere in Paris, he shrugged and said, 'You know my feelings. I honestly do not know what the solution is, but I do know it needs to be sorted out before there is a tragedy.' The Heysel Stadium disaster was just over a year away.

Tony Woodcock became the first player to be used as a substitute on eight separate occasions.

This was a game that sparked Butcher's memory for more than one reason, 'I remember this well. It was in the Parc des Princes stadium, Platini scored two unbelievable free kicks past Peter Shilton, and the England fans rioted that night.

'I was coming off the pitch and I heard this voice behind me saying "Bouchere, Bouchere" and I looked round, and it was Michel Platini. He's saying "maillot, maillot, maillot" which is French for jersey. I was looking around thinking well he's not talking to me, who's he talking to.

'And it was me. He wanted to change jerseys with me, so I changed jerseys with him. I've got his jersey. He probably remembered me from the game that Ipswich had against Saint-Étienne in the 1981 UEFA Cup. He remembered my name anyway! That was quite nice. It's nice to hear "Butcher" being said in French.'

England's next game, Butcher's final international of the 1983/84 season, was the first of three encounters within the final Home International Championship.

A Woodcock goal won the match for England, and Northern Ireland might easily have got at least a draw if the central strikers had made more of the many chances created for them by winger Ian Stewart.

Alan Kennedy won the first of his two caps at left-back, while Graham Rix played his last England game.

After the victory over Northern Ireland, Butcher did not appear in the next two matches, as England lost 1-0 against Wales with Mark Wright and Terry Fenwick making their debuts in central defence in the Town man's absence, and Alan Kennedy, John Gregory and David Armstrong make their final appearances.

Then a 1-1 draw in Scotland followed where Gary Lineker and Steve Hunt made debuts. Former Ipswich midfielder John Wark played, and was by now a Liverpool player.

The 1983/84 British Home Championship was the 100th anniversary and the final football tournament between the Home Nations to be held, with both England and Scotland announcing their withdrawal from future competition, citing waning interest in the matches, crowded international fixture lists, and a sharp rise in hooliganism. Although the football competition was instituted in 1884, it was only the 87th tournament to be completed due to a five-year hiatus during the first world war, a seven-year gap in the second world war, and the cancellation of the 1981 competition following threats of violence during the Troubles in Northern Ireland.

All four nations finished this tournament on three points each, with Northern Ireland finishing first thanks to a goal difference of +1. England finished third.

CHAPTER 12

Butcher makes World Cup qualifier debut

BUTCHER missed the next four England games – a summer friendly defeat at home to USSR, and summer tour matches in Brazil, Uruguay, and Chile.

He returned to the heart of the defence for the first international of the 1984/85 season to win his 25th cap, as England beat East Germany 1-0 at Wembley.

Bobby Robson made a double substitution in the second half when he sent on Mark Hateley and Trevor Francis for Paul Mariner and Tony Woodcock, and within a minute, England at last broke down the massed East German defence.

The goal was scored by Bryan Robson who volleyed in a cross from former club-mate Ray Wilkins for his tenth England goal.

In a match that was a warm-up for the start of the 1986 World Cup qualifying campaign, England had one scare when East German striker Joachim Streich, playing his 100th international, smacked a 25-yard shot against a post. There was an attendance of just 23,951, and the tabloids blamed Bobby Robson!

Butcher's 26th cap was won in his first World Cup qualifier as England took on Finland at Wembley in what was Bobby Robson's 25th match in charge.

Mark Hateley excited the crowd with an exhibition of old-fashioned centre-forward play, powering his way through the Finnish defence for two goals in this opening 1986 qualifier.

Bryan Robson and Tony Woodcock were also on the mark, and in the closing moments, Kenny Sansom made it 5-0 with his one and only goal in 86 international appearances.

Tottenham's Gary Stevens made his debut as a substitute for the injured Mike Duxbury who played for the last time for his country. Stoke City's Mark Chamberlain was also making his final appearance.

The Wembley floodlights temporarily failed while the Finnish players were on the pitch for a pre-match warm-up, and they seemed to be in the dark for the rest of the evening.

England might easily have reached double figures with more accurate finishing. Tony Hateley, Mark's father who knew a thing or three about centre-forward play, was a proud spectator.

After scoring five goals against Finland, England went three better in their next match, a World Cup qualifier in Turkey.

Bryan Robson became the first England captain since Vivian Woodward back in 1909 to score a hat-trick as Turkey were steam-rolled 8-0. He was the third different captain to score a hat-trick with Gilbert Smith being the other to do so. Woodward managed the feat four times, the last in 1909, making this the sixth hat-trick by a captain.

John Barnes and Tony Woodcock collected two goals apiece, and Viv Anderson scored the first of his two goals for England.

It was England's most emphatic overseas victory since the 10-0 tanking of the United States in 1964. Even Bobby Robson escaped criticism.

In coming off the bench, Trevor Francis became the second player, after Tony Woodcock, to make a record nine appearances as an England substitute. At the same time, the player he replaced, Woodcock, equalled Trevor Brooking's record of being replaced by a substitute on nine separate occasions.

Southampton's Steve Williams became the 25th England player to be replaced by a substitute and never play for the senior side again. Also playing his last game for England was striker Peter Withe.

Of his first two World Cup qualifying appearances Butcher said, 'The 5-0 win over Finland was a comfortable win, and then I remember the win over Turkey quite well as the Turkish fans were outside our hotel all night. But we were at the back of the hotel, so we never heard anything. So, that was great.

'And we went to a bazaar in Istanbul before the game, and it was lovely. It was good to see some foreign culture. We then got to the stadium about an hour and a half before kick-off and it was full of Turkish fans. They turned up early and were singing. The noise and the atmosphere was hostile but was brilliant to see. They were baying for our blood. I assisted our second goal for Tony Woodcock. I won the ball in the Turkish half with a challenge which played it through for Woodcock to score. I didn't get a hand in too many goals, so it's nice to remember that one. In the end, the Turkish fans applauded us off the pitch.'

England's first game of 1985 was in Northern Ireland, and they took another step towards the 1986 World Cup finals with a narrow but well-merited 1-0 victory churned out in the mud of Windsor Park.

Mick Quinn headed against the English crossbar and Butcher cleared off the goal line from both Norman Whiteside and Gerry Armstrong.

Mark Hateley settled the issue with a second-half goal after Butcher had hammered a Pat Jennings clearance into his path. Everton's Trevor Steven won the first of his 30 caps and became the 40th different player to be capped by Bobby Robson.

Meanwhile, Trevor Francis became the first England player to make ten substitute appearances, and at the same time, the player he replaced, Tony Woodcock, became the first player to be replaced ten times by a substitute.

A Wembley friendly against the Republic of Ireland was up next for Butcher as Gary Lineker scored the first of his international goals and Trevor Steven got his name on the England scoresheet for the first time against an Irish team that battled every inch of the way. This 2-1 win was England's 350th victory.

Their reward for all their industry came in the closing stages when Liam Brady became the first player to score against England in nearly nine hours following an error by goalkeeper Gary Bailey in his debut match. Chris Waddle and Peter Davenport were also introduced to international football for the first time. For Davenport, this would be his only cap.

There were former Ipswich players on both benches. Paul Mariner was an unused substitute for England, while Kevin O'Callaghan came on in the 70th minute to replace Ronnie Whelan of Liverpool.

Also in the Irish line-up was future Ipswich manager Mick McCarthy.

This was England's fifth successive victory at Wembley and at long last the press were off Bobby Robson's back. It was also a game that saw Butcher lining up against McCarthy. Butcher recalled the 2-1 win and McCarthy's appearance with humour, 'That's why we won! I never saw him. He was down the other end. I did play against him later when I was at Rangers, and he was at Celtic.

'He was very tough, but he was slower than me I think, if anybody could be.'

It was back on the road for England at the start of May 1985 as a World Cup qualifier in Romania beckoned.

And after a 0-0 draw, they retained top place in their World Cup qualifying group, although it might easily have been a victory if Bryan Robson's header from a John Barnes free kick had not hit a post, and if Paul Mariner had steadied himself before missing the best chance of the match.

Peter Shilton, Viv Anderson, Mark Wright, and Terry Butcher were outstanding in the hard-worked defence, as was Kenny Sansom, who won his 50th cap and gave a polished performance that added to the legend he was building as one of England's greatest left backs.

As for Mariner, this was his final appearance. He won a total of 35 caps and scored 13 goals from 1977 to 1985. Thirty-three of those caps and all 13 of his goals came while a player for Ipswich Town.

Butcher remembers the game for a reason that had potential ramifications with Ipswich rather than that of England.

'That was a tough game in Bucharest. An agent spoke to me after the game and said that there was an Italian club that would like to sign me. "We saw you in the game, and we liked what you did," and I then thought that he was going to contact Ipswich. Whether he did or not, I did not hear anything else.

'Italy was the place to be. Serie A was the place to be back then. Mark Hateley and Ray Wilkins were with AC Milan, and Trevor Francis was with Sampdoria.'

Three weeks later, it was a second successive World Cup qualifying stalemate as England drew 1-1 with Finland in Helsinki.

The hosts shocked England with an early goal and might have gone 2-0 up but for Butcher clearing the ball off the goal line with Peter Shilton beaten.

Mark Hateley equalised five minutes into the second half, but England were unable to force a winner against a spirited Finnish team that hung on for a deserved World Cup point.

England now needed just three points from their three home qualifying games to qualify for the 1986 World Cup finals, which had been switched from financially strapped Colombia to Mexico.

'Qualifying in 1985 for the 1986 World Cup was quite straightforward. When you don't qualify for a tournament like we didn't in '84, you're desperate to get to the next tournament. So, everybody was on their toes for that,' said Butcher.

Three days later, England played their 600th game, against the 'Auld Enemy' Scotland in Glasgow.

Graeme Souness got the better of Bryan Robson in the battle for midfield supremacy, and he inspired Scotland to their first victory over England at Hampden Park since 1976.

There were 34 goal attempts in all, 20 of them coming from England, but the only one that found its way into the net came from full-back Richard Gough in the 68th minute of this first contest for the Sir Stanley Rous Cup.

It was England's first defeat in nine matches, but the *Daily Mirror* ran a front-page headline that screamed 'Robson Must Go!' The vultures were back.

The trophy was presented to Souness by Sir Stanley Rous. The match was originally scheduled to take place at Wembley, but it was switched to Hampden Park by the FA under pressure from the prime minister, police, and transport authorities.

Fear of disorder from an expected bank holiday weekend invasion of London by 50,000 Scots was stated as the reason behind the unprecedented change of venue. For Butcher, there was an even worse experience to endure following this defeat, 'Richard Gough scored with a header. I wasn't marking him! I was marking Alex McLeish. It came from a corner and Gough rose to smash a header past Peter Shilton.

'I always remember going to Glasgow airport after the game and all the baggage handlers etc. were laughing their heads off at us. That was a really humbling experience. Not nice at all, and there was nothing you could do about it. We just had to take it.'

England next moved on to a summer trip to Mexico and the opening match in a 'Little World Cup' tournament involving Mexico and Italy was staged in the wake of the Heysel Stadium tragedy in which 39 spectators died during rioting before the Liverpool-Juventus European Cup Final.

Instead of the usual line-up of two teams either side of the officials, the two teams lined up together, side-by-side to show unity after that tragedy of the week before. England wore black armbands as a mark of respect to those who died in the Bradford City Valley Parade fire, and the Juventus supporters who perished in the Heysel disaster.

Players from both sides showed tremendous character in what was a difficult game for everybody involved, and a 1-1 draw looked the likely satisfactory outcome until the Mexican referee amazed even the Italians by awarding them an 88th-minute penalty from which Alessandro Altobelli scored the winning goal.

Peter Shilton was beaten by a shot that swerved in the thin air for Italy's first goal, scored by Salvatore Bagni, which was quickly cancelled out by Mark Hateley.

In the last seconds, England had an obvious penalty turned down when Gary Lineker was brought down when shaping to shoot. Gary Stevens made his debut at right-back while Trevor Francis won his 50th cap in a game that raised little excitement in Ciudad de México. There were just 8,000 spectators dotted around the Azteca Stadium, which would be the venue for the World Cup Final a year later.

Butcher was rested for the next game against Mexico and three days later England took on West Germany in the Azteca 2000 tournament that had overlapped the Copa Ciudad de México, this time involving Mexico and West Germany.

The Germans made the mistake of not getting themselves properly acclimatised, and they were run to the edge of exhaustion in the second half as England stepped up the pace.

Kerry Dixon had an exceptional first full game in an England shirt, scoring twice in the second half after laying on the first goal for Bryan Robson in the first half.

Four minutes before half-time, Peter Shilton played a vital part in an outstanding team display when he saved an Andreas Brehme penalty. The Germans arrived in Mexico only two days before the match, and their players were huffing and puffing in less than an hour of running around in the rarified air.

Everton's Paul Bracewell came off the bench for his England debut. He was the 37th player to mark his England debut as a substitute. He was also the 22nd substitute England had used in the 1984/85 season, beating the previous record of 21 set in 1981/82.

England's final game of the summer of 1985 took them to Los Angeles for a friendly against the USA. This was Terry Butcher's 35th cap, and Bobby Robson's 35th match in charge.

Kerry Dixon and Gary Lineker scored two goals apiece against a gallant but outclassed United States team.

Lineker's first goal was memorable. He chested down a pass from Glenn Hoddle, then swivelled round and volleyed an unstoppable right-foot shot into the net. Hoddle, winning his 25th cap, had a penalty saved, and Trevor Steven scored the fifth and final goal after his Everton club-mate Paul Bracewell had acrobatically knocked the ball into his path.

Bracewell was getting his first full outing after playing as a substitute against West Germany, and Bobby Robson awarded a first cap to Norwich City goalkeeper Chris Woods.

England had already broken the record for most substitutes used in a single season, and using four in this game – the first time four had been made in a single match – took the tally up to 26.

Of this tour, Butcher said, 'We had to play Italy in Mexico because of the Heysel disaster. We were already due to be playing Italy in a friendly. Because of that disaster, we had to wear black armbands and play them. Everybody was watching and it had to be such a sporty occasion.

'And then in my next game against West Germany, I laid on a goal for Kerry Dixon because I won the ball from an Augenthaler pass, and then somehow carved my way through the German defence, space then opened and I was faced with goalkeeper Harald Schumacher. I jinked to my left, took the ball on my right foot and was then thinking how am I going to score with my right foot and then Kerry Dixon ran alongside me and just tapped it into an open goal. Then he ran away to the corner flag, and I was just standing there after all the hard work I'd done.

'The Germans had only flown in a day or two before the game. They thought that they could get away without having to acclimatise, keep on European time, and play.

'It was played at altitude as well and they were just gasping. The last 20 minutes was terrible for them.

'Then, the 5-0 win over the USA was brilliant. It was a really hot day and we were staying on Ocean Boulevard. It was a great trip.'

CHAPTER 13

A second World Cup for Butcher

TERRY Butcher missed out on England's next four matches and returned to the side at the end of February 1986 for a friendly in Israel.

England won 2-1 and 'Captain Courageous' Bryan Robson, back following his hamstring injury, scored both goals including a penalty after Israel had taken a shock early lead.

His first goal was a right-footed volley after 50 minutes following a perfect pass by Glenn Hoddle, and he scored the winner from the penalty spot in the closing minutes after former Liverpool player Avi Cohen had punched his header off the goal line.

It was a fitting way for Robson to celebrate his 50th cap, of which 26 of those had seen him as captain. John Barnes made his 25th England appearance, while Tony Woodcock ended his England career when coming off the bench to replace Kerry Dixon. At the time, he was the country's most used substitute, two ahead of Trevor Francis.

Peter Shilton, for the second match running, became the oldest player to be replaced by a substitute. This was a trip that Butcher remembers fondly, 'Going to Israel was beautiful. We stayed in Tel Aviv in a gorgeous hotel. It was nice. I roomed with Alvin Martin which was good.

'But on the pitch, we went 1-0 down, but came back to win 2-1 which we were disappointed with. But overall, it was a great trip.'

With this latest game in his England career, Butcher had certainly been clocking up the air miles. And there was more to come. Following trips to Turkey, Northern Ireland, Romania, Finland, Scotland, Mexico, USA, and Israel, his next appearance, exactly one month later, was in Tbilisi for a friendly against USSR.

The Russians missed a first-half penalty and were beaten for the first time in 18 matches by a classic 67th-minute strike by Chris Waddle.

It was a goal created in Newcastle, with Peter Beardsley chasing a long ball to the corner by his fellow Geordie Waddle, who raced into the middle to meet the return pass at the far post and hammer it into the net.

The Bulgarian referee Velitchko Tzonchev awarded the Soviets a penalty when Viv Anderson caught Sergey Gotsmanov as he burst into the area. Aleksandre Chivadze's kick was well struck but rebounded from Peter Shilton's left-hand post.

Steve Hodge came on for the first of his 24 caps and was the 39th England player to make his debut as a substitute.

Reporters who had been pouring oil on Bobby Robson suddenly started wondering aloud if he had started to put together a team capable of winning the World Cup. Meanwhile, Butcher said, 'We had to wait at passport control when we got to Tbilisi because Peter Shilton had forgotten his passport. When we boarded the plane, we did not need to show our passports because we were on the team bus which took us straight out to the plane that had been chartered for us. So, we didn't need our passports when we left, but we needed them at the other end.

'We had about a three- or four-hour wait at the airport when we arrived. The British Embassy had to come and sort everything out for him. Flipping goalkeepers!'

Shortly before the end of the regular 1985/86 season, England's next game, at home to Scotland, was the 100th match to feature an Ipswich Town player as Butcher made his 38th appearance.

He marked the occasion by scoring his third goal for England. This was the last goal scored by an Ipswich player for England, and this was also the last appearance by a Town player at Wembley for the Three Lions.

First-half goals from Butcher and Glenn Hoddle gave England the edge in a fiercely fought match for the Sir Stanley Rous Cup.

Scotland got back into the game when Graeme Souness scored from the penalty spot after Butcher had upended Charlie Nicholas, who was then carried off with a suspected dislocated shoulder as a result.

The England defence held out for a confidence-boosting victory to win the one-game tournament before their World Cup journey to Mexico. England had stretched their unbeaten run to nine matches, while Trevor Francis won his final cap.

Butcher said, 'I scored in this game, and I also dived in on Charlie Nicholas to give away a penalty. We were 2-0 up at the time … It was also my last goal for England both as an Ipswich player and period.'

Less than two weeks later, Butcher played his last game for Ipswich in a 1-0 defeat at Sheffield Wednesday. After 18 seasons in the top flight, Town were relegated to the Second Division.

But before Butcher's Ipswich contract had expired and he joined Scottish giants Glasgow Rangers, he still had the small matter of a World Cup to look forward to. Ahead of that, there were two friendlies as firstly England travelled to Los Angeles and won 3-0 in a convincing victory over World Cup hosts Mexico.

This warm-up match was spoiled by the sight of skipper Bryan Robson going off with a dislocated shoulder. He was replaced by a substitute for a record-equalling tenth occasion, equal with Tony Woodcock.

Mark Hateley gave England an early 2-0 lead with two magnificent headers, and the victory-clinching goal was Peter Beardsley's first for England.

England used four substitutions in one match for just the second occasion. And it was in the same stadium that the first occasion happened 11 months earlier. Both teams used their squad numbers for the World Cup.

A week later, England moved on to British Columbia for another friendly game, this time, against Canada.

Gary Lineker damaged a wrist so badly in this final tuning-up game that it was feared he would miss the World Cup. Lineker fell awkwardly in a tackle with Randy Samuel 20 minutes from time and had to leave the field clutching his left wrist. X-rays showed it was nothing more than a bad sprain, but he had to have his arm in plaster for the World Cup.

Mark Hateley scored the only goal of a scrappy game against opponents who were out of their depth but determined not to let England get into any sort of rhythm.

The Canadians had also qualified for the finals and were as keen as England for a full-blooded warm-up match, but the action was rarely better than mediocre on what was a dull, depressing, rain-hammered day.

Steve Hodge was the pick of the England players, and with luck he might have had a hat-trick. Peter Shilton broke his own record in becoming the oldest player to be replaced by a substitute when Chris Woods came on for him.

This was the third match in which England had used four substitutions. However, this was the first time that they had done it for two matches in a row, and therefore, for the first time twice in one season.

Butcher recalls those two friendlies which ended in perhaps sometimes typical footballer fashion in those days, 'For the game against Mexico in Los Angeles, this was a pitch that was in the LA Coliseum. And all the way down the left side was a line which had a long jump pit on it. You had a rubber surface which meant that it was grass, rubber, grass.

'I was playing on the left side of central defence, so I got down this part quite regularly and you had to keep waiting for the ball to come off like a rubber runway. It was the Olympic stadium and that was part of it. Something else you would never see nowadays.

'And then moving on to that game against Canada, we stayed at Colorado Springs which is like *Top Gun* in America. It's where all the air cadets are and that was our training camp. We then flew up to Canada.

'We played at noon that day and after the game, we went to the World Expo, but we didn't see anything except three bierkellers and we must have had a 12-hour session. We then had to fly down to Mexico for the World Cup and every England player was asleep because we had drunk so much beer. We were sparked out for the whole journey. It was great!'

Butcher became the first and only Ipswich Town player to date to appear in two World Cup finals tournaments as England kicked off their campaign in Mexico with a 1-0 defeat to Portugal.

A rare defensive blunder by Kenny Sansom led to Carlos Manuel scoring the winning goal in the second half of a disappointing opener.

Butcher received a yellow card in the 79th minute for unsporting behaviour for lunging into the back of Paulo Futre's legs, just within the Portugal half. It was the third yellow card for an Ipswich player in World Cups as Butcher had also been cautioned in the 1982 tournament along with Paul Mariner.

Gary Lineker played with his sprained wrist strapped, and Bryan Robson came off after 75 minutes to protect his shoulder for a record-breaking 11th occasion, one more than Tony Woodcock. Since the very first England substitute on 18 May 1950, they had now used a replacement 250 times.

England created enough chances to have won comfortably, but they lacked finishing finesse. 'A shocking start,' admitted a grim-faced Bobby Robson, knowing that the vultures were ready to swoop at the first opportunity.

A couple of days following this match, Portugal's Manuel Bento would break his leg in a training session. He would never play for his country again.

Aside from having a chuckle when recalling launching himself into the back of Futre for his yellow card, Butcher also remembered the unusualness of the stadium for this opening World Cup game for England.

'They had this privet hedge around the pitch in that stadium in Monterrey. It was a tweed hedge that should not have been at a football pitch. It wasn't a football stadium. It was very open with nice terraces but without stand roofs. It wasn't a stadium for the World Cup. We played at the same stadium for the Morocco game, and then for the Poland game we played in a real proper stadium where we felt more at home.'

England's second group game came just three days later, and their World Cup turned into a nightmare in the space of five minutes just before half-time.

Firstly, Bryan Robson was taken off with a recurrence of his shoulder injury. He was initially injured on 38 minutes after he was running on to a Mark Hateley headed pass in the penalty area. He was bundled over by Mustapha El Biyaz, dislocating his shoulder, and was taken off the field a minute later for treatment.

Morocco restarted with a goal kick. Wilkins then picked up a stray pass, only to be unceremoniously hacked down by the loser of the ball, Abderrazak Khairi, three yards in front of the referee. Although a free kick was awarded, Wilkins soon received a caution for a tussle with Mohamed Timoumi.

Lineker's deflected strike hit the post, and as the corner was being set up, Steve Hodge had entered the field for Robson who was substituted for a record-breaking 12th occasion, two more than Tony Woodcock. He played no further part in the tournament.

Wilkins then picked up a forward pass from Hoddle, only to be considered in an offside position and another free kick awarded against him. Having picked up the ball, believing he had been awarded the free kick, he threw the ball at referee Gabriel González, landing at his feet. He was shown the red card four seconds later, a minute after receiving the yellow card.

The ten men of England battled with enormous energy and spirit in the second half and could feel satisfied with their point as they drew 0-0.

Temperatures on the pitch soared above 100 degrees, and players on both sides were reduced to walking pace. The ten men of England played boldly and bravely, and the defence – with Butcher like a colossus – stifled any hopes the Moroccans had of making capital of their extra man.

Butcher had a wry smile on his face regarding one report that stated that he had been a colossus in the heart of the defence as ten-man England fought boldly and bravely to avoid defeat.

'Ray Wilkins got sent-off, and Bryan Robson did his shoulder. The papers were going bananas at us, but we didn't get them until three days later in any case. I think my uncle must have written about me being colossus!'

Five days later, England faced Poland in a must-win game to qualify for the knockout stage.

Gary Lineker scored all three goals in the first half to put England on the way to an exhilarating victory and into the second round.

Bobby Robson was forced to make changes – both tactical and in personnel – because of injuries and the Ray Wilkins suspension, and Lineker looked more comfortable playing in a 4-2-4 formation.

'People can say what they like about me,' said a triumphant Robson. 'But never ever accuse my players of lacking character. This was a phenomenal performance given the pressure they were under. Phenomenal!'

Lineker's hat-trick, his second of the season, was only England's second in a World Cup, the first being in the 1966 final. He was substituted and replaced by Kerry Dixon, making him the first player to score a hat-trick and then be replaced.

When Chris Waddle came off the bench for Peter Beardsley in the 75th minute, he was carrying several plastic pouches with water in them for his thirsty team-mates. He did not get a chance to distribute them properly and instead dumped them in the centre circle.

England finished second in their group with three points, a point behind Morocco. They were level on points with Poland but had a better goal difference of four goals, while Portugal finished bottom with two points. Butcher remembers a cheeky request from one of the Polish strikers.

'Gary scored a first-half hat-trick and at half-time, we went into the dressing room and had some ice towels which was nice because we were playing at altitude. I remember walking out to start the second half and the Polish striker Jan Furtok comes up to me and says, "Butcher, please, England three, Poland one. I score one. Please, let me score one." I then muttered some unpleasantries towards him. There was no way I was going to let that happen!'

A week later, England played their last-16 tie against Paraguay and came out on top in a 3-0 win.

After surviving some early scares, England took command with a first-half goal by Lineker.

Beardsley netted the second goal with a right-footed strike after Roberto Fernández failed to hold on to Butcher's 15-yard strike from a Glenn Hoddle corner.

When this goal went in, Lineker was off the pitch receiving treatment after being elbowed in the throat, and it was then Lineker who clinched England's place in the quarter-finals with his fifth goal of the tournament after combining with Tottenham team-mates Hoddle and Gary Stevens.

The two substitutions in took England's substituting tally for the season to a record 28. Tottenham Hotspur had by now also supplied a record-equalling 18 players for England substitutes, equal with Manchester United. And one of their own, Gary Stevens, won his final cap in this game.

Waiting for England in the quarter-finals were Argentina and Maradona. It would be the first meeting between the two countries since the Falklands War of 1982.

Of the part that Butcher played in England's second goal against Morocco, once again, his efforts were not recognised by the eventual goalscorer.

He said, 'Then we moved up to Mexico City where we had been the year before on a previous trip when we played Italy and West Germany. We won again 3-0, and I had a hand in the second goal. It was from a corner on the right-hand side. I had gone up into the box, the corner came to the edge of the box and the ball then came to me and I controlled it beautifully with my left foot which wasn't the norm, and smashed a right-footed shot that the keeper couldn't hold, and Beardsley banged in the rebound.

'Again, there was no thanks for my effort. He ran away. I didn't get many assists but what I did provide, the scorers just kept running away from me.'

For the 45th and final time, Terry Butcher played for England as an Ipswich Town player. At the time of writing, this made him the most-picked Ipswich player for England with three caps more than Mick Mills.

Butcher would go on to play a further 32 games for England as a Glasgow Rangers player, including playing in a third World Cup in 1990. His final game came in the semi-final defeat to West Germany, 4-3 on penalties after a 1-1 draw.

Back to this game against Argentina, watched by a crowd of 114,580 spectators in Ciudad de México's Azteca Stadium, and the match was heavy with tension because of the overspill of feeling from the Falklands War. Squads of military police brandishing white batons patrolled the ground, but apart from a few isolated skirmishes, the rival supporters gave all their attention to a game that was electric with action and atmosphere.

All eyes were on Diego Maradona, who was in the form of his life and forcing good judges to reassess whether Pelé really was the greatest footballer of all time. He might have been the shortest man on the field at 5ft 4in, but the chunky, wide-shouldered Argentine captain paraded across the pitch with the assured air of a giant among pygmies.

England's defenders noticeably quivered every time he took possession, which was often because he was continually demanding the ball the moment it reached the feet of any team-mate. When he had the ball on his left foot, he would glide past tackles with the ease of a Rolls-Royce overtaking a Reliant Robin; when he did not have the ball, he was still a menace because of the speed with which he ran into areas of space to make himself available for a pass.

England defender Terry Fenwick, out of the retaliate-first school of football, decided that a physical assault might be the best way to keep Maradona quiet. Wrong! All he got for his clumsy effort was a booking and a cold stare from the Master that could be interpreted as meaning that he would eventually pay for his attempted ambush. He would pick his moment to provide action to go with that look.

England might have fared better in a goalless first 45 minutes had they been more adventurous, but they were so conscious of Maradona's match-winning ability that they cautiously kept players back in defence. They would have been better employed supporting raids against an Argentine back line that looked vulnerable under attack.

The second half belonged almost entirely to Maradona, and his two goals became the major talking point of the entire tournament. The first will always be remembered for its controversy – many would say cheating – and the second for its quite astounding quality.

Six minutes had gone of the second half when Maradona swept the ball to the feet of Jorge Valdano and raced into the penalty area for the return. As he made his break, some England defenders were appealing for offside. But the linesman's flag stayed down as Valdano's centre was deflected across the face of the goal by Steve Hodge. Peter Shilton came off his line prepared to punch clear.

There seemed no way the stocky Maradona, dwarfed by the powerfully built England goalkeeper, could outjump Shilton. Spectators looked on in amazement as the ball cannoned into the net off Maradona with the airborne Shilton stretching out to thrash empty air.

All eyes in the press box swivelled towards the action replay on the television screen for confirmation of what they thought they had just seen, and there was the instant evidence. No doubt about it, Maradona had pushed the ball into the net with his left hand.

The outraged Shilton led a posse of protesting players trying to persuade referee Ali Ben Nasser that the goal had been illegal but, from the angle that the Tunisian saw it, Maradona appeared to have scored with his head. He pointed to the centre circle and the little man from Buenos Aires went on a dance of celebration that should have been a skulk of shame.

Four minutes later, with the aggrieved England players trying to regain their composure, the Jeykll and Hyde character that was Maradona unveiled the genius in his game. He produced the sort of magic that had prompted Napoli to buy him from Barcelona for a world record £6.9m in 1984.

To say he ran rings round England would be too simple a description of a goal that stands comparison with the very best scored anywhere and at any time. Indeed, it was voted Goal of the Century in 1999.

Running with the ball at his feet from close to the halfway line, Maradona drew defenders to him like a spider luring its prey. Kenny Sansom, Terry Butcher and then Terry Fenwick – he who tried a physical assault in the first half – all came into the Maradona web and were left in a tangle behind him as he accelerated past their attempted tackles.

Again, it was Maradona versus Shilton, this time on the ground. Maradona did not have to cheat his way past the England goalkeeper. He sold him an outrageous dummy that left Shilton scrambling for a shot that was never made, and then nonchalantly prodded the ball into the empty net for a goal of breathtaking beauty. It was a moment of magnificence that sweetened the sour taste left by Maradona's first goal. Well, almost.

England, to their credit, battled back and substitute John Barnes laid on a goal for the razor-sharp Gary Lineker in the 80th minute, making Lineker the tournament's top marksman with six goals. But it was Argentina who went through to the semi-finals.

As they walked exhausted off the bakehouse of a pitch after their 2-1 defeat, the England players – led by Shilton – found the energy to continue their complaints to the referee about the first Maradona goal. But most of the capacity crowd were talking only about his second goal as they filed out of the ground at the end of an eventful quarter-final that would always be remembered as 'Maradona's match'.

The little man had a mix between a smile and a smirk on his face as he said later, 'Yes, the ball did go into the England net off my hand. It was the hand of God. It was not deliberate and so I do not in any way feel guilty claiming it as a goal. Would an England player have gone to the referee and said, "Don't award the goal. The ball hit my hand?" Of course not. Anyway, why all the controversy? Surely my second goal ended all arguments.'

Bobby Robson summed up the feelings of most England followers when he said, 'There is no room in football for cheating. Maradona is a magnificent footballer, but he should be thoroughly ashamed of himself. Yes, his second goal was a thing of wonder, but that should have counted as Argentina's first goal.'

England were knocked out of the World Cup, and for Butcher, it was a sad way to add to a summer that had seen his beloved Ipswich Town also relegated. His first international as a Rangers player would also be Bobby Robson's 50th match in charge.

Butcher's feelings about Maradona following that game are well known and the summer of 1986 was one of Butcher's low points of his career, for not only did the forward's actions cost England of potential World Cup glory, but it was at club level where he was hurting too.

'It was the most iconic England game that I played in while at Ipswich. The other iconic game was obviously the head injury game and the blood in Sweden, but I was at Rangers then.

'That was just an awful time as Ipswich had also been relegated at the end of the season before we went out to the World Cup. I was trying to get my head together after that relegation. It was horrible. To be fair to the England players, they were very good to me. They never took the mickey or anything like that. They were just sympathetic. Mind you, if they were taking the mickey, I probably would have just smashed them one!'

When asked about what his most memorable moments were as an England player, Butcher looked back with immense pride.

'There were many moments really. Captaining England in the World Cup semi-final in 1990 against West Germany was probably the best moment. To be captain in a World Cup semi-final at the time, I was literally following in only one person's footsteps to do that, and that was the great Bobby Moore who was my hero.

'But while with Ipswich, every game really. It did not matter who we were playing. Whether it was against Luxembourg or whoever. Just to line up with the jersey on and represent your country was the biggest thrill that you could ever have as a professional footballer.

'To have Russell, Millsy, Marrers, and sometimes Gatesy with me just capped it all. They were very special times indeed.'

SHOOT! GOAL ALL STARS

KEVIN BEATTIE

SHOOT! GOAL ALL STARS

KEVIN BEATTIE

ENGLAND ★ DEFENDER

INTERNATIONAL TEAM

ENGLAND

PAUL MARINER

DAVID JOHNSON
Age 28: Married: Children, Jackie & Katy: Football League Clubs, Everton, Ipswich, Liverpool: Number of Full International Caps, 6: Number of England Goals: Full, 3, U 23 or U 21, 3: Most difficult International team to play against. Czechoslovakia.

1.7.80

ERIC GATES

K. BEATTIE (England)

T. WHYMARK (England)

B. TALBOT (England)

SUN SOCCERCARD No 125

P. MARINER (England)

SUN SOCCERCARD No 128

M. MILLS (England)

SUN SOCCERCARD No 189

C. VILJOEN (England)

CHAPTER 14

A 14-year wait for Town's next Lion

SOME 13 years, 11 months, and 12 days after Terry Butcher was the last Ipswich player to represent England, goalkeeper Richard Wright won a call-up to the senior squad from the under-21s after helping guide Ipswich Town to the Premier League with a play-off final win over Barnsley.

Five days after that Wembley victory, Wright made his England debut in a friendly win in Malta. He became the 1,101st player to appear for England, and the 100th goalkeeper. He was the sixth Suffolkian to represent the Three Lions – the second goalkeeper after Gary Bailey. His first appearance was not without incident!

Emile Heskey's first international goal was enough to give England a deserved if uninspired win in the heat of the Mediterranean – but it took two late saves from debutant Wright to seal the win.

Having already conceded a first-half penalty, Wright gave away a second spot-kick at the death but made a sprawling stop before blocking an even better chance seconds before the final whistle.

Despite dominating possession, Kevin Keegan's men were unable to end their Euro 2000 build-up with a confidence-boosting sackful of goals. Paul Scholes, Sol Campbell, Paul Ince – winning his 50th cap – and Heskey all spurned good chances as Malta, with a team made up mainly of part-timers, tired in the afternoon heat.

Heskey side-footed home the winner on 76 minutes after excellent work from Nicky Barmby left him with an open goal five yards out. In their last match before Euro 2000, England had taken the lead from that most obvious yet dangerous of sources, a David Beckham free kick from the right.

With the Maltese defence in disarray, Martin Keown stooped unmarked to head in at the far post. Barmby, looking lively throughout, came close to making it two moments later. Gary Neville overlapped down the right and looped in a cross that the Everton midfielder put too close to the keeper.

Then, to the delight of the enthusiastic crowd, Malta were level. Wright came tentatively to meet a long through ball, flapped, and only succeeded in bringing David Carabott down. Carabott dusted himself off, scored, was ordered to retake, and duly dispatched the ball again – albeit off the post and the back of Wright's head.

After his diamond of a cameo against Ukraine in England's previous game, Barmby again did his case for inclusion on the left of midfield a power of good. Always looking to switch with Dennis Wise in the centre, his movement created space against a team who frequently put 11 men behind the ball.

Under such conditions, Barmby's ability to spot a late run and slip a pass through became even more valuable. Only a stretch and tip over from keeper Ernest Barry denied him a goal after a clever chip midway through the second half.

In the February, Barmby had been nowhere near the England squad. Now, having arrived with a vengeance, he was close to guaranteeing himself a place in Keegan's starting 11. More worryingly for England, the centre-back pairing of Keown and Campbell looked anything but solid.

No England game has since featured an Ipswich player and it could be a while yet before we see this again.

Wright would make one further appearance for England in August 2001 when he was an Arsenal player. Nigel Martyn had started in a friendly against the Netherlands at White Hart Lane and was replaced by David James at half-time. Two minutes after the restart, James was injured and replaced by Wright.

For Wright, his first England call-up coming off the back of Ipswich getting promoted to the Premier League was a whirlwind moment in his career.

'I remember the letter from the FA was sent to the club which said that I was going to be with the England squad, and I had been selected for the first time. Also, George Burley would have spoken to me along with Malcolm Webster [Ipswich goalkeeper coach at the time], and he talked about the letter coming and what was going to happen.

'At that stage, I was already a regular with the under-21s as I was playing every game for them. I was expecting to get called up, but to get an official letter to say that I was going with the first team was amazing.

'I had already been training with the first team. I used to go with the under-21s, then train with the first team for a couple of days, and then go back to the under-21s. So, that gave me a little bit of exposure with the first team. I got the best of both worlds which was great.'

Wright had played 15 under-21 games before his full debut came around and when he was informed of the fact that he was the 100th goalkeeper to debut, he was pleasantly surprised, 'I never knew that. Wow, that's nice to know.'

And Wright recalled a very hectic time prior to making his bow, 'It was a strange scenario with the whole build up and everything around that game. And linking it to Ipswich, it was incredible. We had the play-off games which started against Bolton and all the emotion around those two games. Then we had a bit of spare time with the build-up to the play-off final against Barnsley at Wembley.

'We then played that final game and I gave away a penalty but was fortunate enough to save that as well. I scored the first goal of that game too. Craig Hignett's shot hit the bar and rebounded in off the back of my head. So, I'm claiming that I have saved a penalty and scored a goal at the old Wembley! Now, I can laugh about it looking back.

'I remember knowing after that game that I was meeting up with England in preparation for the Euro 2000 tournament. And I knew that I was going to get a game prior to the Euros.

'After winning the play-offs on the Monday, we got on the bus back to Ipswich and all the way back, everyone is celebrating and having a great time. The next day was an event at the Suffolk Showground and all the lads were letting their hair down, but I was having to take it easy knowing that I was about to be joining up with England. I just kept a low profile.

'The next morning, I got picked up at 6am and we went straight to our hotel at Burnham Beeches, and then on the Saturday, we played the game against Malta.

'The emotions of that week were incredible. The achievements of winning at Wembley for the football club and everyone involved, and our team was incredible, was amazing. It's not a regret, because there is never a regret because I had an opportunity to play for England, but the biggest thing that I am gutted to have missed out on was the club's bus tour around Ipswich.

'It was only myself and Tony Mowbray who had to go off and do his coaching licence that missed the tour around my hometown. I never had the opportunity to go on to the balcony at the town hall in front of all our fans.

'When you're a local lad and you achieve what we achieved for your hometown club with an amazing team, I look back and feel gutted about missing that.'

If a play-off semi-final and then a final ahead of playing for England was not enough in that merry month of May in 2000 for Wright, then there was an even more special moment that was thrown into the mix.

'I got married in between the second leg of the play offs and the final. The reason I got married then was because we had planned to get married in the summer of 2000. And then I got the nod that I was going to be in the Euro squad. I was told around January/February time that I was going to be the third-choice goalkeeper going to the Euros.

'They planned to take three younger players and along with myself, they took Gareth Barry and Steven Gerrard. As I knew that was happening, we organised the wedding and got married locally in Ipswich in between those two play-off games.

'It was a massively eventful time, but great memories with just loads going on.'

Then it was on to that debut in Malta which proved just as eventful for Wright as those weeks leading up to it.

'I knew I was going to play in that game in Malta. And that was eventful to say the least! I don't think that there are many people that can say that they gave away two penalties on their England debut.

'The first penalty hit me on the head again. I got a touch to it. The ball hits the post and then rebounds off me to go in. So, maybe I scored again! Questionable I guess, and then I saved another penalty.

'I gave it away in the first place, but to save it, it was an amazing feeling, to save a penalty for England. My personality at that stage though was that I beat myself up a little bit that I had given away two penalties. I was a bit disappointed with myself.

'But I played in a game where I had put the England shirt on. I had put the three lions on my chest. So, there is no one that can take that away from me now. I am proud to have achieved that.'

Unlike in earlier years where other Ipswich players who had played for England had roomed with another player, these were different times as an international. And it was also a game that the scoreline was not reflected in England's dominance.

'Everyone roomed on their own. Everything was done on your own. I remember flying over to Malta, it was a beautiful hot day, and a wonderful place. We absolutely hammered Malta that day. We hit the post a few times, their goalkeeper made a few saves, and they pretty much had two counterattacks which provided them with the only two opportunities that they had in the whole game.

'My judgement that day probably wasn't where it should have been. It was hot and dry and nowadays, pitches are watered and much better to play on.'

There was one moment for Wright to reflect on that could have made the occasion perfect for him, and that would have been to have had his family present. But he still had his club family to fall back on.

' I didn't get the chance to get any family over there unfortunately. I remember that David Sheepshanks was there though. So, there was that connection with Ipswich, and I am sure that there would have been some more club delegates there with David. When I came back to Ipswich for pre-season at the end of that summer, David presented me with a plaque that he had got given for that game. And all the other stuff that he had been given, memorabilia of the game, he presented to me. Not in a big way. Just a private moment between the two of us. I really appreciated that.'

The England line-up against Malta included some big names such as Phil and Gary Neville, Sol Campbell, David Beckham, Paul Scholes, and Alan Shearer. So, what was it like for Wright to be training and playing with that calibre of team-mates?

'As I said before, I was lucky to train with the first team. I had been around the group. These were people that I created friendships with. When you are in a team and everyone wants to help you do well, it is a great place to be involved in. As you say, the calibre of player was incredible. What they had achieved individually, at their clubs, and with playing for England was amazing.

'To be able to say that I put on an England shirt with some of those players in those times is great.'

Wright did make that one further appearance for England with his second cap coming as a substitute against the Netherlands while as a player at Arsenal. How does he sum up the experience of playing for his country?

'I'm just pleased that I got two caps. There are lots of players that get just the one opportunity to play and to then get another one, however that comes about, I don't care. An opportunity to put the shirt on twice is special. I'm nearly 47, I'm getting in a position where I can look back at things. Obviously, we all learn things in life and look at what we should have or could have done etc. But I have real pride. I'm lucky to have played for my country at pretty much every level.

'It's not until you look back at things that how amazing them opportunities and times were. They were proud moments of my life.'

CHAPTER 15

Town thoughts from Joe Corrigan

GOALKEEPER Joe Corrigan played nine games for England in an era where he battled for the number one jersey along with Peter Shilton and Ray Clemence.

Joe was the first England goalkeeper to be used as a substitute when he came on at half-time to replace Jimmy Rimmer on 28 May 1976, in Yankee Stadium, New York, against Italy in a USA Bicentennial Cup tie. Italy led 2-0 at that stage, but England came back to win 3-2.

He was also the first goalkeeper to make his England debut as a substitute, and was the 90th goalkeeper to appear for the Three Lions, meaning that between his debut and when Richard Wright made his bow in May 2000, there were only nine other custodians to debut in between the pair.

Corrigan and Rimmer, then at Arsenal, were the only two goalkeepers to be picked first by Don Revie. Six of Joe's England appearances saw him line-up with at least one Ipswich player including that debut where he featured behind a defence that contained Mick Mills with both coming off the bench at half-time.

It would be almost two years later, and just over two weeks before Ipswich won the FA Cup in 1978, that Corrigan and Mills featured again for England in a 1-1 draw against Brazil at Wembley.

Then, it would be another two years to pass before Corrigan once again played with an Ipswich player for his country when Paul Mariner came off the bench in another game at Wembley, as this time England drew 1-1 with Northern Ireland.

Eleven days later, and as Terry Butcher and Russell Osman made their debuts in Australia alongside Mariner, it was Corrigan who was the custodian on that day and then his last two appearances, with Ipswich players in the same side, came in April and June of 1982.

The first of those games was with Butcher in a 1-0 win over Wales in Cardiff, and then with Osman in Reykjavík as England drew 1-1 with Iceland.

Speaking to Corrigan about his memories of playing with those Ipswich players for England, and Town players in general, he had nothing but praise and huge respect for what he labelled as great men on and off the pitch.

'I am not saying it just because of the Ipswich players that I played with, but in that era, they were all phenomenal players.

'The one thing about the Ipswich lads is that they were all good lads. They were not only good professionals, but they were good people as well.'

Of his debut game against Italy where he appeared with Mick Mills, Corrigan said, 'Millsy was up there with one of the best. You could very much see a future captain of England there with him which of course he did in the 1982 World Cup in Spain. In those days, the word "respect" not just for fans and referees that it gave itself, but for fellow players as well, you respected everything they did in those days.

'And Millsy could play left-back, right-back or in midfield and was one of those players that would give 100 per cent every time he put any shirt on. He was very well respected.'

When Corrigan next appeared with Mills for England just before Town's FA Cup triumph in 1978, it got us swiftly talking of their next semi-final appearance in 1981 which saw them defeated in extra time by Manchester City where Joe was in goal. He continued with his glowing praise of Town players following that victory for his side.

'That was a phenomenal Ipswich team in 1981 and they had an equally phenomenal player in Kevin Beattie who was another Ipswich player to play for England of course. He was unfortunate to suffer with so many major injuries. He would have played a lot more games if it wasn't for being so unfortunate with injuries.

'He played the same number of games for England as me [nine]. He should have played a lot more. But that's the way football is.

'Everybody talks about the Beckham era for England, but in those days, in the 1981, and 1982 era, and I look at the England World Cup squad then, and some of those players back then, you would struggle to afford some of them now.'

Corrigan's fourth game for England, against Northern Ireland at Wembley in May 1980, was the first occasion that he played in the same team as Paul Mariner after the Town player came off the bench in the 70th minute to replace Joe's club team-mate Kevin Reeves. And the pair developed a friendship for life that ultimately led to a poignant moment for Corrigan.

'Me and Marrers were great, great friends. I was so honoured, and in a sad way as an honour, I was asked to be one of his pallbearers at his funeral in Ipswich. I was so proud to do this. I loved him dearly.

'He was one of my dearest friends in football and we had so many great laughs. We got up to some mischief too which cannot go into print! One thing I must say though is that we had a great time off the field as well as being great mates on the field. We just gelled. He was such a funny man.'

Corrigan then featured as England's goalkeeper in Australia when both Terry Butcher and Russell Osman made their debuts. He echoes the earlier thoughts shared by Butcher and Osman of playing a football match in a cricket ground.

'We flew out on the Wednesday night and Ipswich's Bobby Robson was the manager of that game, although Ron Greenwood came as well.

'We really played well that day even though it was me that apparently got the man of the match award. It was amazing that we were allowed to play a soccer match on a cricket square. There were one or two questions written in the press as to why we could play "soccer" as it was called over there on the hallowed turf of the Sydney Cricket Ground.

'But we did, and we won, and we made a great account of ourselves. As well as Terry, Russell and Paul, there was another player with an Ipswich connection playing in that game and that was Brian Talbot who was another great player.

'You look back at all those players and every one of them could play in today's Premier League.'

Corrigan's final England appearance came in the team's penultimate warm-up match in Iceland just two weeks before their 1982 World Cup campaign got under way. In front of him in central defence was Town's Russell Osman.

'The FA in their wisdom arranged a friendly against Iceland and then of course the World Cup cropped up. England had a "B" team in those days and the game in Iceland was a mixture of the "B" team and the first-team squads, and the rest went to Finland for a game the following night.

'All the memories come back for that trip. We landed in Reykjavík and then went by road to the hotel, and it was like going to the moon I would imagine. I have never been to the moon, but it was just like it. Bare rock all over the place.

'It was a phenomenal experience, and it was the first time I had ever experienced being able to buy duty free going into a country through the airport. This we did because the price of a drink over there at that time was very expensive.

'Looking back, they were great experiences, and it was an honour to play with so many truly great players. The Ipswich lads included. They were quality players, and quality people. In those days, yes, you had one or two players that you did not get on with, but they were just great lads.

'It is a testimony to Ipswich Town that they were up there in those days as one of the best teams in the country. Most of the Ipswich players in those 1980/81 and 1981/82 seasons would walk into any Premiership team today. I truly mean that.'

It was lovely to hear Joe's tales and words about not only the Ipswich players he played with for England, but others too. It highlights how we had some true greats playing for us that were respected by so many of their peers.

It remains to be seen when Ipswich Town will next have a player representing them in pulling on the shirt with the three lions on it. But we can all look back with great satisfaction at the very thought of 12 players from our club have played for England.

We have had one of our own captaining England at a World Cup, one of our own has scored in a World Cup, and our 12 players have a combined total of 156 caps between them.

I would say that for a small, provincial town club, we have done very well to have provided some great players for England. Sometimes, as many as three in one game. Football was different in those days. Clubs like Ipswich could provide players who were good enough to play for England. We may never see the like again.

For Town and Country, we remember those who gave their all for both with immense pride.

Ray Crawford, middle, bottom row, at a reunion.

Ray's England shirt worn in his second game against Austria on 4 April, 1962.

Ray in his Ipswich shirt.

Ray, bottom row, third from the left, at England training.

No. 1 – Ray Crawford

England 1 v 1 Northern Ireland [1-0]

Wednesday, 22 November 1961, kick-off: 2.30pm
Home International Championship 1961/62
Empire Stadium, Wembley, London, Att: 30,000
Scorers: England: Bobby Charlton (20), **Northern Ireland:** Jimmy McIlroy (82)
Live on BBC: (UK), **Commentator:** Kenneth Wolstenholme
Referee: Leo Callaghan (Wales)
England
Ron Springett (*Sheffield Wednesday*), **Jimmy Armfield** (*Blackpool*), **Ray Wilson** (*Huddersfield Town*), **Bobby Robson** (*West Bromwich Albion*), **Peter Swan** (Sheffield Wednesday), **Ron Flowers** (*Wolverhampton Wanderers*), **Bryan Douglas** (*Blackburn Rovers*), **John Byrne** (*Crystal Palace*), **Ray Crawford** (*Ipswich Town*), **Johnny Haynes (C)** (*Fulham*), **Bobby Charlton** (*Manchester United*)
Northern Ireland
Victor Hunter, James Magill, Alex Elder, Danny Blanchflower (C), Terry Neill, Jim Nicholson, Billy Bingham, Hubert Barr, Bill McAdams, Jimmy, McIlroy, Jim McLaughlin

No. 2 – Ray Crawford

England 3 v 1 Austria [2-0]

Wednesday, 4 April 1962, kick-off: 3pm
International Friendly Match
Empire Stadium, Wembley, London, Att: 50,000
Scorers: England: Ray Crawford (7), Ron Flowers (pen 37), Roger Hunt (67), **Austria:** Hans Buzek (76)
Live on BBC: (England & Ireland), **Commentator:** Kenneth Wolstenholme
Referee: Pierre Schwinte (France)
England (*Manager: Sir Walter Winterbottom*)
Ron Springett (*Sheffield Wednesday*), **Jimmy Armfield** (*Blackpool*), **Ray Wilson** (*Huddersfield Town*), **Stan Anderson** (*Sunderland*), **Peter Swan** (Sheffield Wednesday), **Ron Flowers** (*Wolverhampton Wanderers*), **John Connelly** (*Burnley*), **Roger Hunt** (*Liverpool*), **Ray Crawford** (*Ipswich Town*), **Johnny Haynes (C)** (*Fulham*), **Bobby Charlton** (*Manchester United*)
Austria (*Manager: Karl Decker*)
Gernot Fraydl, Heribert Trubrig, Erich Hasenkopf, Rudolf Oslansky, Karl Stotz, Karl Koller (C), Adolf Knoll, Erich Hof, Johann Buzek, Ernst Fiala, Friedrich Rafreider
Substitution: Rudolf Flögel (for Fiala 40)

Match No. 3 – Mick Mills

England 1 v 1 Yugoslavia [1-0]

Wednesday, 11 October 1972, kick-off: 7.45pm

International Friendly Match

Empire Stadium, Wembley, London, Att: 50,000

Scorers: England: Joe Royle (39), **Yugoslavia:** Franjo Vladić (49)

Referee: Aurelio Angonese (Italy)

England (*Manager: Sir Alf Ramsey*)

Peter Shilton (*Leicester City*), **Mick Mills** (*Ipswich Town*), **Frank Lampard** (*West Ham United*), **Peter Storey** (*Arsenal*), **Jeff Blockley** (*Arsenal*), **Bobby Moore (C)** (*West Ham United*), **Alan Ball** (*Arsenal*), **Mick Channon** (*Southampton*), **Joe Royle** (*Everton*), **Colin Bell** (*Manchester City*), **Rodney Marsh** (*Manchester City*)

Yugoslavia (*Manager: Vujadin Boškov*)

Enver Marić, Petar Krivokuća, Dragoslav Stepanović, Miroslav Pavlović, Josip Katalinski, Blagoje Paunović, Ilija Petković, Jovan Aćimović, Dušan Bajević, Franjo Vladić, Dragan Džajić (C)

Substitutions: Dragan Holcer (for Katalinski 46), Ljubiša Rajković (for Pavlović 60)

Match No. 4 – Kevin Beattie

England 5 v 0 Cyprus [2-0]

Wednesday, 16 April 1975, kick-off: 7.45pm

European Championship 1976 Qualifier

Wembley Stadium, London, Att: 68,245

Scorer: England: Malcolm Macdonald (3, 32, 52, 56, 87)

Referee: Martti Hirviniemi (Finland)

England (*Manager: Don Revie*)

Peter Shilton (*Stoke City*), **Paul Madeley** (*Leeds United*), **Kevin Beattie** (*Ipswich Town*), **Colin Bell** (*Manchester City*), **Dave Watson** (*Sunderland*), **Colin Todd** (*Derby County*), **Alan Ball (C)** (*Arsenal*), **Mick Channon** (*Southampton*), **Malcolm Macdonald** (*Newcastle United*), **Alan Hudson** (*Stoke City*), **Kevin Keegan** (*Liverpool*)

Substitution: Dave Thomas (*QPR*) (for Channon 65)

Cyprus (*Manager: Panicos Iacovou*)

Makis Alkiviadis, Christakis Kovis, Demetris Kizas, Nicos Pantziaras, Kyriakos Koureas, Gregory Savva, Lakis Theodorou, Stefanis Mihail, Markos Markou, Nicos Charalambous, Andreas Stylianou (C)

Substitutions: Andreas Konstantinou (for Charalambous 46), Andreas Konstantinou (for Akliviades 60)

Match No. 5 – Kevin Beattie

Cyprus 0 v 1 England [0-1]

Sunday, 11 May 1975, kick-off: 4.45pm (local)
European Championship 1976 Qualifier
Tsirion Athletic Centre, Lemesos, Att: 15,708
Scorer: England: Kevin Keegan (6)
Referee: Tzwetan Petrov Stanev (Bulgaria)
Cyprus (*Manager: Panicos Iacovou*)
Andreas Konstantinou, Christakis Kovis, Demetris Kizas, Andreas Stylianou (C), Nicos Pantziaras, Stefanis Mihail, Andreas Konstantinou, Andros Miamiliotis, Gregory Savva, Nicos Charalambous, Demetris Panayiotou
Substitutions: Kokos Antoniou (for Panayiotou 57), Takis Papettas (for Miamiliotis 78)
England (*Manager: Don Revie*)
Ray Clemence (*Liverpool*), **Stephen Whitworth** (*Leicester City*), **Kevin Beattie** (*Ipswich Town*), **Colin Bell** (*Manchester City*), **Dave Watson** (*Sunderland*), **Colin Todd** (*Derby County*), **Alan Ball (C)** (*Arsenal*), **Mick Channon** (*Southampton*), **Malcolm Macdonald** (*Newcastle United*), **Kevin Keegan** (*Liverpool*), **Dave Thomas** (*QPR*)
Substitutions: Emlyn Hughes (*Liverpool*) (for Beattie 41), **Dennis Tueart** (*Manchester City*) (for Keegan 73)

Match No. 6 – Colin Viljoen

Northern Ireland 0 v 0 England [0-0]

Saturday, 17 May 1975, kick-off: 3pm
Home International Championship 1974/75
Windsor Park, Belfast, Att: 36,500
Scorer: None
Referee: Thomas Reynolds (Wales)
Northern Ireland (*Player-Manager: David Clements*)
Pat Jennings, Pat Rice, William O'Kane, Chris Nicholl, Allan Hunter, Dave Clements (C), Bryan Hamilton, Martin O'Neill, Derek Spence, Sammy McIlroy, Thomas Jackson
Substitution: Thomas Finney (for Hamilton 36)
England (*Manager: Don Revie*)
Ray Clemence (*Liverpool*), **Stephen Whitworth** (*Leicester City*), **Emlyn Hughes** (*Liverpool*), **Colin Bell** (*Manchester City*), **Dave Watson** (*Sunderland*), **Colin Todd** (*Derby County*), **Alan Ball (C)** (*Arsenal*), **Colin Viljoen** (*Ipswich Town*), **Malcolm Macdonald** (*Newcastle United*), **Kevin Keegan** (*Liverpool*), **Dennis Tueart** (*Manchester City*)
Substitution: Mick Channon (*Southampton*) (for Macdonald 62)

Match No. 7 – Colin Viljoen and David Johnson

England 2 v 2 Wales [1-0]

Wednesday, May 21, 1975, kick-off: 7.45pm
Home International Championship 1974/75
Wembley Stadium, London, Att: 53,000
Scorers: England: David Johnson (8, 85), **Wales:** John Toshack (55), Arfon Griffiths (56)
Referee: John Paterson (Scotland)
England (*Manager: Don Revie*)
Ray Clemence (*Liverpool*), **Stephen Whitworth** (*Leicester City*), **Ian Gillard** (*QPR*), **Gerry Francis** (*QPR*), **Dave Watson** (*Sunderland*), **Colin Todd** (*Derby County*), **Alan Ball (C)** (*Arsenal*), **Mick Channon** (*Southampton*), **David Johnson** (*Ipswich Town*), **Colin Viljoen** (*Ipswich Town*), **Dave Thomas** (*QPR*)
Substitution: Brian Little (*Aston Villa*) (for Channon 73)
Wales (*Manager: Michael Smith*)
Dai Davies, Rod Thomas, Malcolm Page, John Mahoney, John Roberts, Leighton Phillips, Arfon Griffiths, Brian Flynn, David Smallman, John Toshack (C), Leighton James
Substitution: Derek Showers (for Smallman 60)

Match No. 8 – Kevin Beattie & David Johnson

England 5 v 1 Scotland [3-1]

Saturday, May 24, 1975, kick-off: 3pm
Home International Championship 1974/75
Wembley Stadium, London, Att: 98,241
Scorers: England: Gerry Francis (5, 64), Kevin Beattie (7), Colin Bell (40), David Johnson (90), **Scotland:** Bruce Rioch (pen 44)
Live on BBC: (UK), **Commentator:** David Coleman
Live on ITV: (LWT, Tyne Tees, Westward & Channel), **Commentator:** Brian Moore
Referee: John Paterson (Scotland)
England (*Manager: Don Revie*)
Ray Clemence (*Liverpool*), **Stephen Whitworth** (*Leicester City*), **Kevin Beattie** (*Ipswich Town*), **Colin Bell** (*Manchester City*), **Dave Watson** (*Sunderland*), **Colin Todd** (*Derby County*), **Alan Ball (C)** (*Arsenal*), **Mick Channon** (*Southampton*), **David Johnson** (*Ipswich Town*), **Gerry Francis** (*QPR*), **Kevin Keegan** (*Liverpool*)
Substitution: Dave Thomas (*QPR*) (for Keegan 85)
Scotland (*Manager: Willie Ormond*)
Stewart Kennedy, Sandy Jardine (C), Danny McGrain, Francis Munro, Gordon McQueen, Bruce Rioch, Kenny Dalglish, Alfie Conn, Derek Parlane, Ted MacDougall, Arthur Duncan.
Substitutions: Tommy Hutchison (for Duncan 61), Lou Macari (for MacDougall 71)

Match No. 9 – Kevin Beattie & David Johnson

Switzerland 1 v 2 England [1-2]

Wednesday, 3 September 1975, kick-off: 8pm (local)

International Friendly Match

St. Jakob Stadium, Basel, Att: 25,000

Scorers: Switzerland: Kudi Müller (29), **England:** Kevin Keegan (8), Mick Channon (19)

Referee: Walter Eschweiler (West Germany)

Switzerland (*Manager: René Hüssy*)

Erich Burgener, Jörg Stohler, Serge Trinchero, Gilbert Guyot, Pius Fischbach, Hanspeter Schild, Réne Hasler, Bobo Botteron, Hans-Jörg Pfister, Kudi Müller, Daniel Jeandupeux

Substitution: Rudolf Elsener (for Schild 63)

England (*Manager: Don Revie*)

Ray Clemence (*Liverpool*), **Stephen Whitworth** (*Leicester City*), **Dave Watson** (*Manchester City*), **Colin Todd** (*Derby County*), **Kevin Beattie** (*Ipswich Town*), **Colin Bell** (*Manchester City*), **Tony Currie** (*Sheffield United*), **Gerry Francis (C)** (*QPR*), **Mick Channon** (*Southampton*), **David Johnson** (*Ipswich Town*), **Kevin Keegan** (*Liverpool*)

Substitution: Malcolm Macdonald (*Newcastle United*) (for Johnson 57)

Match No. 10 – Kevin Beattie

Portugal 1 v 1 England [1-1]

Wednesday, 19 November 1975, kick-off: 9pm (local)

European Championship 1976 Qualifier

Estádio José Alvalade, Lisbon, Att: 13,912

Scorers: Portugal: Rui Rodrigues (16), **England:** Mick Channon (42)

Referee: Erich Linemayr (Austria)

Portugal (*Manager: José Maria Pedroto*)

Vitor Damas, Francisco Rebelo, Rui Rodrigues, Fernando Freitas, Artur Correia, Octávio Machado, João Alves, Toni (C), Nené, João Batista da Silva, Mário Moinhos

Substitutions: António Taí (for Rebelo 46), Álvaro Carolino (for Rodrigues 50)

England (*Manager: Don Revie*)

Ray Clemence (*Liverpool*), **Stephen Whitworth** (*Leicester City*), **Kevin Beattie** (*Ipswich Town*), **Paul Madeley** (*Leeds United*), **Dave Watson** (*Manchester City*), **Colin Todd** (*Derby County*), **Kevin Keegan** (*Liverpool*), **Mick Channon** (*Southampton*), **Malcolm Macdonald** (*Newcastle United*), **Gerry Francis (C)** (*QPR*), **Trevor Brooking** (*West Ham United*)

Substitutions: Dave Thomas (*QPR*) (for Madeley 64), **Allan Clarke** (*Leeds United*) (for Macdonald 76)

Match No. 11 – Mick Mills

Wales 1 v 2 England [0-0]

Wednesday, 24 March 1976, kick-off: 7.30pm

FA of Wales Centenary Celebration Match

Racecourse Ground, Wrexham, Att: 20,927

Scorers: Wales: Alan Curtis (90), **England:** Ray Kennedy (70), Peter Taylor (80)

Referee: Ian Foote (Scotland)

Wales (*Manager: Mike Smith*)

Brian Lloyd, Malcolm Page, Joey Jones, Terry Yorath (C), Leighton Phillips, Ian Evans, Carl Harris, Brian Flynn, Alan Curtis, John Roberts, Arfon Griffiths

England (*Manager: Don Revie*)

Ray Clemence (*Liverpool*), **Trevor Cherry** (*Leeds United*), **Phil Neal** (*Liverpool*), **Mike Doyle** (*Manchester City*), **Phil Thompson** (*Liverpool*), **Mick Mills** (*Ipswich Town*), **Kevin Keegan (C)** (*Liverpool*), **Phil Boyer** (*Norwich City*), **Mick Channon** (*Southampton*), **Ray Kennedy** (*Liverpool*), **Trevor Brooking** (*West Ham United*)

Substitutions: Peter Taylor (*Crystal Palace*) (for Channon 46), **Dave Clement** (*QPR*) (for Cherry 46)

Match No. 12 – Mick Mills

Wales 0 v 1 England [0-0]

Saturday, 8 May 1976, kick-off: 3pm

Home International Championship 1975/76

Ninian Park, Cardiff, Att: 24,592

Scorer: England: Peter Taylor (59)

Referee: Bobby Davidson (Scotland)

Wales (*Manager: Mike Smith*)

Dai Davies, Malcolm Page, Rod Thomas, John Mahoney, Ian Evans, Leighton Phillips, Terry Yorath (C), Brian Flynn, Alan Curtis, John Toshack, Leighton James

Substitutions: David Jones (for Thomas), Arfon Griffiths (for Curtis)

England (*Manager: Don Revie*)

Ray Clemence (*Liverpool*), **David Clement** (*QPR*), **Mick Mills** (*Ipswich Town*), **Tony Towers** (*Sunderland*), **Brian Greenhoff** (*Manchester United*), **Phil Thompson** (*Liverpool*), **Kevin Keegan** (*Liverpool*), **Gerry Francis (C)** (*QPR*), **Stuart Pearson** (*Manchester United*), **Ray Kennedy** (*Liverpool*), **Peter Taylor** (*Crystal Palace*)

Match No. 13 – Mick Mills

England 4 v 0 Northern Ireland [2-0]

Tuesday, 11 May 1976, kick-off: 7.45pm
Home International Championship 1975/76
Wembley Stadium, London, Att: 48,000
Scorers: England: Gerry Francis (35), Mick Channon (pen 36, 75), Stuart Pearson (60)
Referee: Clive Thomas (Wales)
England (*Manager: Don Revie*)
Ray Clemence (*Liverpool*), **Colin Todd** (*Derby County*), **Mick Mills** (*Ipswich Town*), **Phil Thompson** (*Liverpool*), **Brian Greenhoff** (*Manchester United*), **Ray Kennedy** (*Liverpool*), **Kevin Keegan** (*Liverpool*), **Mick Channon** (*Southampton*), **Stuart Pearson** (*Manchester United*), **Gerry Francis (C)** (*QPR*), **Peter Taylor** (*Crystal Palace*)
Substitutions: Tony Towers (*Sunderland*) (for Taylor 65), **Joe Royle** (*Manchester City*) (for Keegan 75)
Northern Ireland (*Manager: Dave Clements*)
Pat Jennings, Pat Rice, Sammy Nelson, Dave Clements (C), Allan Hunter, Chris Nicholl, Bryan Hamilton, Sammy McIlroy, Tommy Cassidy, David McCreery, Derek Spence
Substitution: Peter Scott (for Nelson 61)

Match No. 14 – Mick Mills

Scotland 2 v 1 England [1-1]

Saturday, 15 May 1976, kick-off: 3pm
Home International Championship 1975/76
Hampden Park, Glasgow, Att: 85,167
Scorers: Scotland: Don Masson (17), Kenny Dalglish (49), **England:** Mick Channon (11)
Live on BBC: (UK), **Commentator:** David Coleman
Live on ITV: (UK), **Commentators:** Brian Moore and Jack Charlton
Referee: Károly Palotai (Hungary)
Scotland (*Manager: Willie Ormond*)
Alan Rough, Danny McGrain, Willie Donachie, Tom Forsyth, Colin Jackson, Bruce Rioch, Kenny Dalglish, Don Masson, Joe Jordan, Archie Gemmill (C), Eddie Gray
Substitutions: Derek Johnstone (for Gray 78)
England (*Manager: Don Revie*)
Ray Clemence (*Liverpool*), **Colin Todd** (*Derby County*), **Mick Mills** (*Ipswich Town*), **Phil Thompson** (*Liverpool*), **Roy McFarland** (*Derby County*), **Ray Kennedy** (*Liverpool*), **Kevin Keegan** (*Liverpool*), **Mick Channon** (*Southampton*), **Stuart Pearson** (*Manchester United*), **Gerry Francis (C)** (*QPR*), **Peter Taylor** (*Crystal Palace*)
Substitutions: Trevor Cherry (*Leeds United*) (for Pearson 46), **Mike Doyle** (*Manchester City*) (for McFarland 70)

Match No. 15 – Mick Mills

Brazil 1 v 0 England [0-0]

Sunday, 23 May 1976, kick-off: 2.30pm (local)
USA Bicentennial Cup Tournament, match two
Memorial Coliseum, Los Angeles, Att: 32,495
Scorer: Brazil: Roberto Dinamite (89)
Live on BBC1: Commentator: David Coleman
Referee: Hans-Joachim Weiland (West Germany)
Brazil (*Manager: Osvaldo Brandão*)
Émerson Leão, Orlando Pereira, Miguel Ferreira Pereira, Beto Fuscão, Marco Antônio Feliciano, Paulo Falcão, Gil, Zico, Neca, Rivellino (C), Lula
Substitutions: Roberto Dinamite (for Neca 46), Marinho Chagas (for Antônio Feliciano 52)
England (*Manager: Don Revie*)
Ray Clemence (*Liverpool*), **Colin Todd** (*Derby County*), **Mick Mills** (*Ipswich Town*), **Phil Thompson** (*Liverpool*), **Mike Doyle** (*Manchester City*), **Trevor Cherry** (*Leeds United*), **Kevin Keegan** (*Liverpool*), **Mick Channon** (*Southampton*), **Stuart Pearson** (*Manchester United*), **Trevor Brooking** (*West Ham United*), **Gerry Francis (C)** (*QPR*)

Match No. 16 – Mick Mills

England 3 v 2 Italy [0-2]

Friday, 28 May 1976, kick-off: 8pm
Home International Championship 1975/76
Wembley Stadium, London, Att: 48,000
Scorers: England: Mick Channon (46, 53), Phil Thompson (48), **Italy:** Francesco Graziani (15, 18)
Referee: Hans-Joachim Weiland (West Germany)
England (*Manager: Don Revie*)
Jimmy Rimmer (*Arsenal*), **Dave Clement** (*QPR*), **Phil Neal** (*Liverpool*), **Phil Thompson** (*Liverpool*), **Mike Doyle** (*Manchester City*), **Tony Towers** (*Sunderland*), **Ray Wilkins** (*Chelsea*), **Mick Channon (C)** (*Southampton*), **Joe Royle** (*Manchester City*), **Trevor Brooking** (*West Ham United*), **Gordon Hill** (*Manchester United*)
Substitutions: Joe Corrigan (*Manchester City*) (for Rimmer 46), **Mick Mills** (*Ipswich Town*) (for Neal 46)
Italy (*Managers: Enzo Bearzot and Fulvio Bernardini*)
Dino Zoff, Moreno Roggi, Francesco Rocca, Romeo Benetti, Mauro Bellugi, Giacinto Facchetti (C), Franco Causio, Fabio Capello, Francesco Graziani, Giancarlo Antognoni, Paolo Pulici
Substitutions: Claudio Sala (for Causio 57), Renato Zaccarelli (for Benetti 57), Aldo Maldera (for Roggi 57)

Match No. 17 – Mick Mills

Finland 1 v 4 England [1-2]

Sunday, 13 June 1976, kick-off: 7.30pm (local)
World Cup 1978 Qualifier, Group Two
Olympiastadion, Helsinki, Att: 24,336
Scorers: Finland: Matti Paatelainen (27), **England:** Stuart Pearson (14), Kevin Keegan (30, 60), Mick Channon (57)
Live on BBC (UK): **Commentator:** David Coleman
Referee: Alfred Delcourt (Belgium)
Finland (*Manager: Aulis Rytkönen*)
Göran Enckelman, Erkki Vihtilä, Ari Mäkynen, Arto Tolsa, Esko Ranta, Pertti Jantunen, Jouko Suomalainen, Esa Heiskanen, Aki Heiskanen, Olavi Rissanen, Matti Paatelainen (C)
Substitution: Seppo Pyykkö (for Suomalainen 65)
England (*Manager: Don Revie*)
Ray Clemence (*Liverpool*), **Colin Todd** (*Derby County*), **Mick Mills** (*Ipswich Town*), **Phil Thompson** (*Liverpool*), **Paul Madeley** (*Leeds United*), **Trevor Cherry** (*Leeds United*), **Kevin Keegan** (*Liverpool*), **Mick Channon** (*Southampton*), **Stuart Pearson** (*Manchester United*), **Trevor Brooking** (*West Ham United*), **Gerry Francis (C)** (*QPR*)

Match No. 18 – Kevin Beattie and Mick Mills

England 2 v 1 Finland [1-0]

Wednesday, 13 October 1976, kick-off: 8pm
World Cup 1978 Qualifier, Group Two
Wembley Stadium, London, Att: 92,000
Scorers: England: Dennis Tueart (4), Joe Royle (53), **Finland:** Kalle Nieminen (48)
Referee: Ulf Eriksson (Sweden)
England (*Manager: Don Revie*)
Ray Clemence (*Liverpool*), **Colin Todd** (*Derby County*), **Kevin Beattie** (*Ipswich Town*), **Phil Thompson** (*Liverpool*), **Brian Greenhoff** (*Manchester United*), **Ray Wilkins** (*Chelsea*), **Kevin Keegan (C)** (*Liverpool*), **Mick Channon** (*Southampton*), **Joe Royle** (*Manchester City*), **Trevor Brooking** (*West Ham United*), **Dennis Tueart** (*Manchester City*)
Substitutions: Gordon Hill (*Manchester United*) (for Brooking 73), **Mick Mills** (*Ipswich Town*) (for Tueart 75)
Finland (*Manager: Aulis Rytkönen*)
Göran Enckelman, Teppo Heikkinen, Erkki Vihtilä, Ari Mäkynen, Esko Ranta, Pertti Jantunen, Jouko Suomalainen, Miikka Toivola, Kalle Nieminen, Aki Heiskanen, Matti Paatelainen (C)
Substitutions: Esa Heiskanen (for Jantunen 61), Seppo Pyykkö (for Suomalainen 67)

Match No. 19 – Kevin Beattie and Mick Mills

Italy 2 v 0 England [1-0]

Wednesday, 17 November 1976,
kick-off: 2.30pm (local)
World Cup 1978 Qualifier, Group Two
Stadio Olimpico, Rome, Att: 70,718
Scorers: Italy: Giancarlo Antognoni (37), Roberto Bettega (78)
Referee: Abraham Klein (Israel)
Italy (*Manager: Enzo Bearzot*)
Dino Zoff, Antonello Cuccureddu, Marco Tardelli, Romeo Benetti, Claudio Gentile, Giacinto Facchetti (C), Franco Causio, Fabio Capello, Francesco Graziani, Giancarlo Antognoni, Roberto Bettega
Substitution: Seppo Pyykkö (for Suomalainen 65)
England (*Manager: Don Revie*)
Ray Clemence (*Liverpool*), **Dave Clement** (*QPR*), **Mick Mills** (*Ipswich Town*), **Brian Greenhoff** (*Manchester United*), **Roy McFarland** (*Derby County*), **Emlyn Hughes** (*Liverpool*), **Kevin Keegan (C)** (*Liverpool*), **Mick Channon** (*Southampton*), **Stan Bowles** (*QPR*), **Trevor Cherry** (*Leeds United*), **Trevor Brooking** (*West Ham United*)
Substitution: Kevin Beattie (*Ipswich Town*) (for Clement 80)

Match No. 20 – Kevin Beattie

England 0 v 2 Netherlands [0-2]

Wednesday, 9 February 1977, kick-off: 8pm
International Friendly Match
Wembley Stadium, London, Att: 90,260
Scorer: Netherlands: Jan Peters (29, 37)
Referee: Walter Eschweiler (West Germany)
England (*Manager: Don Revie*)
Ray Clemence (*Liverpool*), **Dave Clement** (*QPR*), **Kevin Beattie** (*Ipswich Town*), **Mike Doyle** (*Manchester City*), **Dave Watson** (*Manchester City*), **Paul Madeley** (*Leeds United*), **Kevin Keegan (C)** (*Liverpool*), **Trevor Francis** (*Birmingham City*), **Brian Greenhoff** (*Manchester United*), **Stan Bowles** (*QPR*), **Trevor Brooking** (*West Ham United*)
Substitutions: Colin Todd (*Derby County*) (for Greenhoff 38), **Stuart Pearson** (*Manchester United*) (for Madeley 62)
Netherlands (*Manager: Jan Zwartkruis*)
Pieter Schrijvers, Wim Suurbier, Ruud Krol, Wim Rijsbergen, Hugo Hovenkamp, Johan Neeskens, Willy van der Kerkhof, Johan Cruyff (C), Johnny Rep, Rob Rensenbrink
Substitution: Kees Kist (for Rep 75)

Match No. 21 – Paul Mariner

England 5 v 0 Luxembourg [1-0]

Wednesday, 30 March 1977, kick-off: 8pm
World Cup 1978 Qualifier, Group Two
Wembley Stadium, London, Att: 81,718
Scorers: England: Kevin Keegan (11), Trevor Francis (58), Ray Kennedy (65), Mick Channon 69, pen 81)
Referee: Paul Bonett (Malta)
England (*Manager: Don Revie*)
Ray Clemence (*Liverpool*), **John Gidman** (*Aston Villa*), **Trevor Cherry** (*Leeds United*), **Ray Kennedy** (*Liverpool*), **Dave Watson** (*Manchester City*), **Emlyn Hughes** (*Liverpool*), **Kevin Keegan (C)** (*Liverpool*), **Mick Channon** (*Southampton*), **Joe Royle** (*Manchester City*), **Trevor Francis** (*Birmingham City*), **Gordon Hill** (*Manchester United*)
Substitution: Paul Mariner (*Ipswich Town*) (for Royle 46)
Luxembourg (*Manager: Gilbert Legrand*)
Raymond Zender, Roger Fandel, Jean-Louis Margue, Léon Mond, Louis Pilot (C), Jean Zuang, Marcel Di Domenico, Gilbert Dresch, Nico Braun, Paul Philipp, Gilbert Dussier
Substitution: Nibio Orioli (for Di Domenico 76)

Match No. 22 – Paul Mariner, Mick Mills, and Brian Talbot

Northern Ireland 1 v 2 England [1-1]

Saturday, 28 May 1977, kick-off: 3pm
Home International Championship 1976/77
Windsor Park, Belfast, Att: 35,000
Scorers: Northern Ireland: Chris McGrath (4), **England:** Mick Channon (27), Dennis Tueart (86)
Referee: Brian McGinlay (Scotland)
Northern Ireland (*Manager: Danny Blanchflower*)
Pat Jennings, Jimmy Nicholl, Pat Rice, Tommy Jackson, Allan Hunter (C), Bryan Hamilton, Chris McGrath, Sammy McIlroy, Gerry Armstrong, David McCreery, Trevor Anderson
Substitutions: Martin O'Neill (for Armstrong 38), Derek Spence (for Anderson 75)
England (*Manager: Don Revie*)
Peter Shilton (*Stoke City*), **Trevor Cherry** (*Leeds United*), **Mick Mills** (*Ipswich Town*), **Brian Greenhoff** (*Manchester United*), **Dave Watson** (*Manchester City*), **Colin Todd** (*Derby County*), **Ray Wilkins** (*Chelsea*), **Mick Channon (C)** (*Southampton*), **Paul Mariner** (*Ipswich Town*), **Trevor Brooking** (*West Ham United*), **Dennis Tueart** (*Manchester City*)
Substitution: Brian Talbot (*Ipswich Town*) (for Wilkins 65)

Match No. 23 – Mick Mills

England 0 v 1 Wales [0-1]

Tuesday, 31 May 1977, kick-off: 8pm

Home International Championship 1976/77

Wembley Stadium, London, Att: 48,000

Scorer: Wales: Leighton James (pen 44)

Referee: John Robertson Gordon (Scotland)

England (*Manager: Don Revie*)

Peter Shilton (*Stoke City*), **Phil Neal** (*Liverpool*), **Mick Mills** (*Ipswich Town*), **Brian Greenhoff** (*Manchester United*), **Dave Watson** (*Manchester City*), **Emlyn Hughes** (*Liverpool*), **Kevin Keegan (C)** (*Liverpool*), **Mick Channon** (*Southampton*), **Stuart Pearson** (*Manchester United*), **Trevor Brooking** (*West Ham United*), **Ray Kennedy** (*Liverpool*)

Substitution: Dennis Tueart (*Manchester City*) (for Brooking 79)

Wales (*Manager: Mike Smith*)

Dai Davies, Rod Thomas, Joey Jones, John Mahoney, Leighton Phillips, Ian Evans, Peter Sayer, Brian Flynn, Terry Yorath (C), Nick Deacy, Leighton James

Substitution: Dave Roberts (for Phillips, time unknown)

Match No. 24 – Mick Mills and Brian Talbot

England 1 v 2 Scotland [0-1]

Saturday, 4 June 1977, kick-off: 3pm

Home International Championship 1976/77

Wembley Stadium, London, Att: 98,103

Scorers: England: Mick Channon (pen 87), **Scotland:** Gordon McQueen (43), Kenny Dalglish (59)

Referee: Károly Palotai (Hungary)

England (*Manager: Don Revie*)

Ray Clemence (*Liverpool*), **Phil Neal** (*Liverpool*), **Mick Mills** (*Ipswich Town*), **Brian Greenhoff** (*Manchester United*), **Dave Watson** (*Manchester City*), **Emlyn Hughes (C)** (*Liverpool*), **Trevor Francis** (*Birmingham City*), **Mick Channon** (*Southampton*), **Stuart Pearson** (*Manchester United*), **Brian Talbot** (*Ipswich Town*), **Ray Kennedy** (*Liverpool*)

Substitutions: Trevor Cherry (*Leeds United*) (for Greenhoff 57), **Dennis Tueart** (*Manchester City*) (for Kennedy 67)

Scotland (*Manager: Ally MacLeod*)

Alan Rough, Danny McGrain, Willie Donachie, Tom Forsyth, Gordon McQueen, Bruce Rioch (C), Don Masson, Kenny Dalglish, Joe Jordan, Asa Hartford, Willie Johnston

Substitutions: Lou Macari (for Jordan 43), Archie Gemmill (for Masson 83)

Match No. 25 – Brian Talbot

Brazil 0 v 0 England [0-0]

Wednesday, 8 June 1977, kick-off: 9.30pm (local)

Summer Tour of South America Match

Estádio do Maracanã, Rio de Janeiro, Att: 77,000

Scorer: None

Referee: Alberto Ducatelli (Argentina)

Brazil (*Manager: Claudio Coutinho*)

Émerson Leão, Zé Maria, Amaral, Edinho, Toninho Cerezo, José Rodrigues Neto, Gil, Zico, Roberto Dinamite, Rivellino (C), Paulo Cézar Lima

Substitution: Zé Mário (for Gil, time unknown)

England (*Manager: Don Revie*)

Ray Clemence (*Liverpool*), **Phil Neal** (*Liverpool*), **Trevor Cherry** (*Leeds United*), **Brian Greenhoff** (*Manchester United*), **Dave Watson** (*Manchester City*), **Emlyn Hughes** (*Liverpool*), **Kevin Keegan (C)** (*SV Hamburg*), **Trevor Francis** (*Birmingham City*), **Stuart Pearson** (*Manchester United*), **Ray Wilkins** (*Chelsea*), **Brian Talbot** (*Ipswich Town*)

Substitutions: Ray Kennedy (*Liverpool*) (for Pearson 70), **Mick Channon** (*Southampton*) (for Wilkins 70)

Match No. 26 – Brian Talbot

Argentina 1 v 1 England [1-1]

Sunday, 13 June 1977, kick-off: 3pm (local)

Summer Tour of South America Match

La Bombonera, Buenos Aires, Att: 60,000

Scorers: Argentina: Daniel Bertoni (15), **England:** Stuart Pearson (3)

Live on BBC (UK): **Commentator:** John Motson

Referee: Ramón Barreto Ruiz (Uruguay)

Argentina (*Manager: Cesar Luis Menotti*)

Héctor Baley, Daniel Killer, Daniel Passarella, Vicente Pernía, Alberto Tarantini, Osvaldo Ardiles, Ricardo Bochini, Américo Gallego (C), Daniel Bertoni, Leopoldo Luque, Oscar Alberto Ortiz

Substitutions: Omar Larrosa (for Bochini 55), Juan Ramón Rocha (for Ortiz 55)

England (*Manager: Don Revie*)

Ray Clemence (*Liverpool*), **Phil Neal** (*Liverpool*), **Trevor Cherry** (*Leeds United*), **Brian Greenhoff** (*Manchester United*), **Dave Watson** (*Manchester City*), **Emlyn Hughes** (*Liverpool*), **Kevin Keegan (C)** (*SV Hamburg*), **Mick Channon** (*Southampton*), **Stuart Pearson** (*Manchester United*), **Ray Wilkins** (*Chelsea*), **Brian Talbot** (*Ipswich Town*)

Substitution: Ray Kennedy (*Liverpool*) (for Greenhoff 46)

Match No. 27 – Brian Talbot

Uruguay 0 v 0 England [0-0]

Wednesday, 15 June 1977, kick-off: unknown
Summer Tour of South America Match
Estadio Centenario, Montevideo, Att: 25,000
Scorer: None
Referee: Miguel Comesana (Argentina)
Uruguay (*Manager: Juan Hohberg*)
Freddy Clavijo, Julio Rivadavia, Francisco Salomón (C), Alfredo de los Santos, Dario Pereyra, Beethoven Javier, Rudy Rodriguez, Juan Ramón Carrasco, Alberto Santelli, Ildo Maneiro, Washington Olivera
Substitution: Juan Muhlethaler (for Olivera 46)
England (*Manager: Don Revie*)
Ray Clemence (*Liverpool*), **Phil Neal** (*Liverpool*), **Trevor Cherry** (*Leeds United*), **Brian Greenhoff** (*Manchester United*), **Dave Watson** (*Manchester City*), **Emlyn Hughes** (*Liverpool*), **Kevin Keegan (C)** (*SV Hamburg*), **Mick Channon** (*Southampton*), **Stuart Pearson** (*Manchester United*), **Ray Wilkins** (*Chelsea*), **Brian Talbot** (*Ipswich Town*)

Match No. 28 – Kevin Beattie, Paul Mariner, and Trevor Whymark

Luxembourg 0 v 2 England [0-1]

Wednesday, 12 October 1977, kick-off: 7.15pm (local)
World Cup 1978 Qualifier, Group Two
Stade Municipal, Luxembourg City, Att: 10,621
Scorers: England: Paul Mariner (30), Ray Kennedy (90)
Referee: Alojzy Jarguz (Poland)
Luxembourg (*Manager: Gilbert Legrand*)
Jeannot Moes, Marcel Barthel, Roger Fandel, Léon Mond, Nico Rohmann, Paul Philipp (C), Romain Michaux, Jean Zuang, Gilbert Dussier, Nico Braun, Vinicio Monacelli
Substitutions: Marcel Di Domenico (for Braun 80), Joseph Zangerle (for Fandel 82)
England (*Manager: Ron Greenwood*)
Ray Clemence (*Liverpool*), **Trevor Cherry** (*Leeds United*), **Dave Watson** (*Manchester City*), **Emlyn Hughes (C)** (*Liverpool*), **Ray Kennedy** (*Liverpool*), **Ian Callaghan** (*Liverpool*), **Terry McDermott** (*Liverpool*), **Ray Wilkins** (*Chelsea*), **Paul Mariner** (*Ipswich Town*), **Trevor Francis** (*Birmingham City*), **Gordon Hill** (*Manchester United*)
Substitutions: Trevor Whymark (*Ipswich Town*) (for McDermott 64), **Kevin Beattie** (*Ipswich Town*) (for Watson 68)

Match No. 29 – Mick Mills

West Germany 2 v 1 England [0-1]

Wednesday, 22 February 1978, kick-off: 8.15pm (local)

International Friendly Match

Olympiastadion, Munich, Att: 77,850

Scorers: West Germany: Ronald Worm (79), Rainer Bonhof (86), **England:** Stuart Pearson (41)

Referee: Franz Wöhrer (Austria)

West Germany (*Manager: Helmut Schön*)

Sepp Maier, Bertie Vogts (C), Herbert Zimmermann, Rolf Rüssmann, Hans-George Schwarzenbeck, Rainer Bonhof, Rüdiger Abramczik, Herbert Neumann, Bernd Hölzenbein, Heinz Flohe, Karl-Heinz Rummenigge

Substitutions: Manfred Burgsmüller (for Flohe 33), Bernard Dietz (for Neumann 72), Ronald Worm (for Hölzenbein 75)

England (*Manager: Ron Greenwood*)

Ray Clemence (*Liverpool*), **Phil Neal** (*Liverpool*), **Mick Mills** (*Ipswich Town*), **Ray Wilkins** (*Chelsea*), **Dave Watson** (*Manchester City*), **Emlyn Hughes (C)** (*Liverpool*), **Kevin Keegan** (*SV Hamburg*), **Steve Coppell** (*Manchester United*), **Stuart Pearson** (*Manchester United*), **Trevor Brooking** (*West Ham United*), **Peter Barnes** (*Manchester City*)

Substitutions: Trevor Francis (*Birmingham City*) (for Keegan 80)

Match No. 30 – Mick Mills

England 1 v 1 Brazil [1-1]

Wednesday, 19 April 1978, kick-off: 7.45pm

International Friendly Match

Wembley Stadium, London, Att: 92,500

Scorers: England: Kevin Keegan (70), **Brazil:** Gil (10)

Live on BBC (UK): **Commentator:** David Coleman

Referee: Charles Corver (Netherlands)

England (*Manager: Ron Greenwood*)

Joe Corrigan (*Manchester City*), **Mick Mills** (*Ipswich Town*), **Trevor Cherry** (*Leeds United*), **Brian Greenhoff** (*Manchester United*), **Dave Watson** (*Manchester City*), **Tony Currie** (*Leeds United*), **Kevin Keegan (C)** (*SV Hamburg*), **Steve Coppell** (*Manchester United*), **Bob Latchford** (*Everton*), **Trevor Francis** (*Birmingham City*), **Peter Barnes** (*Manchester City*)

Brazil (*Manager: Claudio Coutinho*)

Émerson Leão, Zé Maria, Abel Braga, Amaral, Edinho, Toninho Cerezo, Rivellino (C), Gil, Zico, João Batista Nunes, Dirceu

Substitution: João Batista da Silva (for Nunes 61)

Match No. 31 – Paul Mariner and Mick Mills

Wales 1 v 3 England [0-1]

Saturday, 13 May 1978, kick-off: 3pm

Home International Championship 1977/78

Ninian Park, Cardiff, Att: 17,698

Scorers: Wales: Phil Dwyer (57), **England:** Bob Latchford (8), Tony Currie (81), Peter Barnes (89)

Referee: Malcolm Moffatt (Northern Ireland)

Wales (*Manager: Mike Smith*)

Dai Davies, Malcolm Page, Joey Jones, Leighton Phillips, David Jones, Terry Yorath (C), Carl Harris, Brian Flynn, Alan Curtis, Phil Dwyer, Mickey Thomas

Substitutions: John Mahoney (for Yorath 46), Gareth Davis (for D. Jones 70)

England (*Manager: Ron Greenwood*)

Peter Shilton (*Nottingham Forest*), **Mick Mills (C)** (*Ipswich Town*), **Trevor Cherry** (*Leeds United*), **Brian Greenhoff** (*Manchester United*), **Dave Watson** (*Manchester City*), **Ray Wilkins** (*Chelsea*), **Steve Coppell** (*Manchester United*), **Trevor Francis** (*Birmingham City*), **Bob Latchford** (*Everton*), **Trevor Brooking** (*West Ham United*), **Peter Barnes** (*Manchester City*)

Substitutions: Tony Currie (*Leeds United*) (for Cherry 17), **Paul Mariner** (*Ipswich Town*) (for Latchford 33)

Match No. 32 – Mick Mills

England 1 v 0 Northern Ireland [1-0]

Tuesday, 16 May 1978, kick-off: 7.45pm

Home International Championship 1977/78

Wembley Stadium, London, Att: 55,000

Scorer: England: Phil Neal (44)

Live on BBC (UK)**: Commentator:** David Coleman

Referee: John Robertson Gordon (Scotland)

England (*Manager: Ron Greenwood*)

Ray Clemence (*Liverpool*), **Phil Neal** (*Liverpool*), **Mick Mills** (*Ipswich Town*), **Emlyn Hughes (C)** (*Liverpool*), **Dave Watson** (*Manchester City*), **Ray Wilkins** (*Chelsea*), **Tony Currie** (*Leeds United*), **Brian Greenhoff** (*Manchester United*), **Steve Coppell** (*Manchester United*), **Stuart Pearson** (*Manchester United*), **Tony Woodcock** (*Nottingham Forest*)

Northern Ireland (*Manager: Danny Blanchflower*)

Jim Platt, Bryan Hamilton (C), Peter Scott, Chris Nicholl, Jimmy Nicholl, Sammy McIlroy, David McCreery, Martin O'Neill, Trevor Anderson, Gerry Armstrong, Chris McGrath

Substitution: Terry Cochrane (for McGrath, time unknown)

Match No. 33 – Paul Mariner and Mick Mills

Scotland 0 v 1 England [0-0]

Saturday, 20 May 1978, kick-off: 3pm
Home International Championship 1977/78
Hampden Park, Glasgow, Att: 88,319
Scorer: England: Steve Coppell (84)
Referee: Georges Konrath (France)
Scotland (*Manager: Ally MacLeod*)
Alan Rough, Stuart Kennedy, Willie Donachie, Tom Forsyth, Kenny Burns, Bruce Rioch (C), Don Masson, Asa Hartford, Joe Jordan, Kenny Dalglish, Willie Johnston
Substitutions: Graeme Souness (for Archibald 75), Archie Gemmill (for Masson 75)
England (*Manager: Ron Greenwood*)
Ray Clemence (*Liverpool*), **Phil Neal** (*Liverpool*), **Mick Mills** (*Ipswich Town*), **Emlyn Hughes (C)** (*Liverpool*), **Dave Watson** (*Manchester City*), **Tony Currie** (*Leeds United*), **Steve Coppell** (*Manchester United*), **Trevor Francis** (*Birmingham City*), **Ray Wilkins** (*Chelsea*), **Paul Mariner** (*Ipswich Town*), **Peter Barnes** (*Manchester City*)
Substitutions: **Brian Greenhoff** (*Manchester United*) (for Hughes 73), **Trevor Brooking** (*West Ham United*) (for Mariner 78)

Match No. 34 – Mick Mills

England 4 v 1 Hungary [3-0]

Wednesday, 24 May 1978, kick-off: 7.45pm
International Friendly Match
Wembley Stadium, London, Att: 75,000
Scorers: England: Peter Barnes (11), Phil Neal (pen 32), Trevor Francis (36), Tony Currie (82), **Hungary:** László Nagy (62)
Referee: René Vigliani (France)
England (*Manager: Ron Greenwood*)
Peter Shilton (*Nottingham Forest*), **Phil Neal** (*Liverpool*), **Mick Mills** (*Ipswich Town*), **Ray Wilkins** (*Chelsea*), **Dave Watson** (*Manchester City*), **Emlyn Hughes (C)** (*Liverpool*), **Kevin Keegan** (*SV Hamburg*), **Steve Coppell** (*Manchester United*), **Trevor Francis** (*Birmingham City*), **Trevor Brooking** (*West Ham United*), **Peter Barnes** (*Manchester City*)
Substitutions: **Brian Greenhoff** (*Manchester United*) (for Watson 46), **Tony Currie** (*Leeds United*) (for Brooking 73)
Hungary (*Manager: Lajos Baróti*)
Sándor Gujdár, Péter Török, István Kocsis, József Tóth, Sándor Zombori, Zoltán Kereki, László Fazekas (C), Tibor Nyilasi, András Törőcsik, Sándor Pintér, László Nagy
Substitution: Károly Csapó (for Fazekas 46)

Match No. 35 – Mick Mills

Denmark 3 v 4 England [2-2]

Wednesday, 20 September 1978, kick-off: 7pm (local)
European Championship 1980 Qualifier
Idrætsparken, Copenhagen, Att: 47,600
Scorers: Denmark: Allan Simonsen (pen 24), Frank Arnesen (27), Per Røntved (85),
England: Kevin Keegan (18, 23), Bob Latchford (51), Phil Neal (84)
Referee: Adolf Prokop (East Germany)
Denmark (*Manager: Kurt Nielsen*)
Birger Jensen, Flemming Nielsen, Henning Jensen, Per Røntved (C), Søren Lerby, Frank Arnesen, Flemming Lund, Carsten Nielsen, Allan Simonsen, Benny Nielsen, Jørgen Kristensen
Substitution: Allan Hansen (for B. Nielsen 46)
England (*Manager: Ron Greenwood*)
Ray Clemence (*Liverpool*), **Phil Neal** (*Liverpool*), **Mick Mills** (*Ipswich Town*), **Ray Wilkins** (*Chelsea*), **Dave Watson** (*Manchester City*), **Emlyn Hughes (C)** (*Liverpool*), **Kevin Keegan** (*SV Hamburg*), **Steve Coppell** (*Manchester United*), **Bob Latchford** (*Everton*), **Trevor Brooking** (*West Ham United*), **Peter Barnes** (*Manchester City*)

Match No. 36 – Mick Mills

Republic of Ireland 1 v 1 England [1-1]

Wednesday, 25 October 1978, kick-off: 3pm
European Championship 1980 Qualifier
Landsdowne Road, Dublin, Att: 55,000
Scorers: Republic of Ireland: Gerry Daly (28), **England:** Bob Latchford (8)
Referee: Heinz Aldinger (West Germany)
Republic of Ireland (*Manager: Johnny Giles*)
Mick Kearns, Paddy Mulligan (C), Jimmy Holmes, Mark Lawrenson, David O'Leary, Liam Brady, Gerry Daly, Tony Grealish, Paul McGee, Gerry Ryan, Don Givens
Substitutions: Frank Stapleton (for McGee 65), Eamonn Gregg (for O'Leary 74)
England (*Manager: Ron Greenwood*)
Ray Clemence (*Liverpool*), **Phil Neal** (*Liverpool*), **Mick Mills** (*Ipswich Town*), **Ray Wilkins** (*Chelsea*), **Dave Watson** (*Manchester City*), **Emlyn Hughes (C)** (*Liverpool*), **Kevin Keegan** (*SV Hamburg*), **Steve Coppell** (*Manchester United*), **Bob Latchford** (*Everton*), **Trevor Brooking** (*West Ham United*), **Peter Barnes** (*Manchester City*)
Substitutions: Phil Thompson (*Liverpool*) (for Watson 22), **Tony Woodcock** (*Nottingham Forest*) (for Barnes 85)

Match No. 37 – Mick Mills

England 4 v 0 Northern Ireland [1-0]

Wednesday, 7 February 1979, kick-off: 7.45pm

European Championship 1980 Qualifier

Wembley Stadium, London, Att: 91,224

Scorers: England: Kevin Keegan (26), Bob Latchford (46, 64), Dave Watson (50)

Referee: Ulf Eriksson (Sweden)

England (*Manager: Ron Greenwood*)

Ray Clemence (*Liverpool*), **Phil Neal** (*Liverpool*), **Mick Mills** (*Ipswich Town*), **Tony Currie** (*Leeds United*), **Dave Watson** (*Manchester City*), **Emlyn Hughes (C)** (*Liverpool*), **Kevin Keegan** (*SV Hamburg*), **Steve Coppell** (*Manchester United*), **Bob Latchford** (*Everton*), **Trevor Brooking** (*West Ham United*), **Peter Barnes** (*Manchester City*)

Northern Ireland (*Manager: Danny Blanchflower*)

Pat Jennings (C), Pat Rice, Sammy Nelson, Jimmy Nicholl, Chris Nicholl, David McCreery, Martin O'Neill, Sammy McIlroy, Gerry Armstrong, Billy Caskey, Terry Cochrane

Substitutions: Derek Spence (for Caskey 51), Chris McGrath (Cochrane 84)

Match No. 38 – Mick Mills

Northern Ireland 0 v 2 England [0-2]

Saturday, 19 May 1979, kick-off: 3pm

Home International Championship 1978/79

Windsor Park, Belfast, Att: 35,000

Scorers: England: Dave Watson (11), Steve Coppell (14)

Referee: Ian Foote (Scotland)

Northern Ireland (*Manager: Danny Blanchflower*)

Pat Jennings, Pat Rice, Sammy Nelson, Jimmy Nicholl, Chris Nicholl, Vic Moreland, Bryan Hamilton (C), Sammy McIlroy, Gerry Armstrong, Billy Caskey, Terry Cochrane

Substitutions: Chris McGrath (for Moreland 57), Derek Spence (for Cochrane 68)

England (*Manager: Ron Greenwood*)

Ray Clemence (*Liverpool*), **Phil Neal** (*Liverpool*), **Mick Mills (C)** (*Ipswich Town*), **Phil Thompson** (*Liverpool*), **Dave Watson** (*Manchester City*), **Tony Currie** (*Leeds United*), **Steve Coppell** (*Manchester United*), **Ray Wilkins** (*Chelsea*), **Bob Latchford** (*Everton*), **Terry McDermott** (*Liverpool*), **Peter Barnes** (*Manchester City*)

Match No. 39 – Mick Mills

England 3 v 1 Scotland [1-1]

Saturday, 26 May 1979, kick-off: 3pm

Home International Championship 1978/79

Wembley Stadium, London, Att: 100,000

Scorers: England: Peter Barnes (45), Steve Coppell (63), Kevin Keegan (70), **Scotland:** John Wark (21)

Live on BBC (UK): **Commentator:** David Coleman

Live on ITV (UK): **Commentator:** Brian Moore and Jackie Charlton

Referee: António Garrido (Portugal)

England (*Manager: Ron Greenwood*)

Ray Clemence (*Liverpool*), **Phil Neal** (*Liverpool*), **Mick Mills** (*Ipswich Town*), **Phil Thompson** (*Liverpool*), **Dave Watson** (*Manchester City*), **Ray Wlkins** (*Chelsea*), **Kevin Keegan (C)** (*SV Hamburg*), **Steve Coppell** (*Manchester United*), **Bob Latchford** (*Everton*), **Trevor Brooking** (*West Ham United*), **Peter Barnes** (*Manchester City*)

Scotland (*Manager: Jock Stein*)

George Wood, George Burley, Frank Gray, John Wark, Gordon McQueen, Paul Hegarty, Kenny Dalglish (C), Graeme Souness, Joe Jordan, Asa Hartford, Arthur Graham

Match No. 40 – Mick Mills

Bulgaria 0 v 3 England [0-1]

Wednesday, 6 June 1979, kick-off: 6pm (local)

Home International Championship 1978/79

Vasil Levski National Stadion, Sofia, Att: 47,500

Scorers: England: Kevin Keegan (33), Dave Watson (53), Peter Barnes (54)

Referee: Ernst Dorflinger-Buser (Switzerland)

Bulgaria (*Manager: Zvetan Iltchev*)

Yordan Filipov, Nikolai Grantcharov, Kiril Ivkov, Georgi Bonev, Ivan Iliev, Radoslav Zdravkov, Voyn Voynov, Krasimir Borisov, Andrey Zhelyazkov (C), Pavel Panov, Chavdar Tsvetkov

Substitutions: Roussi Gotchev (for Zdravkov 46), Todor Barzov (for Voynov 60)

England (*Manager: Ron Greenwood*)

Ray Clemence (*Liverpool*), **Phil Neal** (*Liverpool*), **Mick Mills** (*Ipswich Town*), **Phil Thompson** (*Liverpool*), **Dave Watson** (*SV Werder Bremen*), **Ray Wilkins** (*Chelsea*), **Kevin Keegan (C)** (*SV Hamburg*), **Steve Coppell** (*Manchester United*), **Bob Latchford** (*Everton*), **Trevor Brooking** (*West Ham United*), **Peter Barnes** (*Manchester City*)

Substitutions: Trevor Francis (*Nottingham Forest*) (for Latchford 65), **Tony Woodcock** (*Nottingham Forest*) (for Barnes 76)

Match No. 41 – Mick Mills

Austria 4 v 3 England [3-1]

Wednesday, 13 June 1979, kick-off: 7.30pm (local)

International Friendly Match

Praterstadion, Vienna, Att: 30,000

Scorers: Austria: Bruno Pezzey (17, 70), Kurt Welzl (28, 40), **England:** Kevin Keegan (29), Steve Coppell (47), Ray Wilkins (64)

Referee: Alexis Ponnet (Belgium)

Austria (*Manager: Karl Stotz*)

Friedrich Koncilia, Robert Sara (C), Erich Obermayer, Ernst Baumeister, Bruno Pezzey, Roland Hattenberger, Kurt Welzl, Herbert Prohaska, Willy Kreuz, Kurt Jara, Gernot Jurtin

Substitution: Walter Schachner (for Welzl 55)

England (*Manager: Ron Greenwood*)

Peter Shilton (*Nottingham Forest*), **Phil Neal** (*Liverpool*), **Mick Mills** (*Ipswich Town*), **Phil Thompson** (*Liverpool*), **Dave Watson** (*SV Werder Bremen*), **Ray Wilkins** (*Chelsea*), **Kevin Keegan (C)** (*SV Hamburg*), **Steve Coppell** (*Manchester United*), **Bob Latchford** (*Everton*), **Trevor Brooking** (*West Ham United*), **Peter Barnes** (*Manchester City*)

Substitutions: Ray Clemence (*Liverpool*) (for Shilton 46), **Trevor Francis** (*Nottingham Forest*) (for Latchford 46), **Laurie Cunningham** (*West Bromwich Albion*) (for Barnes 81)

Match No. 42 – Mick Mills

England 1 v 0 Denmark [1-0]

Wednesday, 12 September 1979, kick-off: 7.45pm

European Championship 1980 Qualifier

Wembley Stadium, London, Att: 85,000

Scorer: England: Kevin Keegan (17)

Referee: Cesar Dias Correira (Portugal)

England (*Manager: Ron Greenwood*)

Ray Clemence (*Liverpool*), **Phil Neal** (*Liverpool*), **Mick Mills** (*Ipswich Town*), **Phil Thompson** (*Liverpool*), **Dave Watson** (*SV Werder Bremen*), **Ray Wlkins** (*Manchester United*), **Kevin Keegan (C)** (*SV Hamburg*), **Steve Coppell** (*Manchester United*), **Terry McDermott** (*Liverpool*), **Trevor Brooking** (*West Ham United*), **Peter Barnes** (*West Bromwich Albion*)

Denmark (*Manager: Sepp Piontek*)

Birger Jensen, Ole Højgaard, Søren Busk, Sten Ziegler (C), Morten Olsen, Søren Lerby, Frank Arnesen, Benny Nielsen, Henning Jensen, Allan Simonsen, Preben Elkjær

Substitutions: Jens Jørn Bertelsen (for Nielsen 67), Ove Flindt Bjerg (for Elkjær 80)

Match No. 43 – Mick Mills
Northern Ireland 1 v 5 England [0-2]
Wednesday, 17 October 1979, kick-off: 3pm
European Championship 1980 Qualifier
Windsor Park, Belfast, Att: 25,000
Scorers: Northern Ireland: Vic Moreland (49 pen), **England:** Trevor Francis (18, 29), Tony Woodcock (34, 71), Jimmy Nicholl (og 74)
Referee: Alexis Ponnet (Belgium)
Northern Ireland (*Manager: Danny Blanchflower*)
Pat Jennings (C), Pat Rice, Sammy Nelson, Jimmy Nicholl, Allan Hunter, David McCreery, Tommy Cassidy, Sammy McIlroy, Gerry Armstrong, Tommy Finney, Vic Moreland
Substitutions: Peter Rafferty (for Hunter 46), Billy Caskey (for Finney 70)
England (*Manager: Ron Greenwood*)
Peter Shilton (*Nottingham Forest*), **Phil Neal** (*Liverpool*), **Mick Mills** (*Ipswich Town*), **Phil Thompson** (*Liverpool*), **Dave Watson** (*Southampton*), **Ray Wilkins** (*Manchester United*), **Kevin Keegan (C)** (*SV Hamburg*), **Steve Coppell** (*Manchester United*), **Trevor Francis** (*Nottingham Forest*), **Trevor Brooking** (*West Ham United*), **Tony Woodcock** (*Nottingham Forest*)
Substitutions: **Terry McDermott** (*Liverpool*) (for Brooking 83)

Match No. 44 – Mick Mills

Spain 0 v 2 England [0-1]

Wednesday, 26 March 1980, kick-off: 8.30pm (local)
International Friendly Match
Camp Nou, Barcelona, Att: 50,000
Scorers: England: Tony Woodcock (16), Trevor Francis (65)
Referee: Volker Roth (West Germany)
Spain (*Manager: Ladislao Kubala*)
Luis Arconada, Santiago Urquiaga, Migueli, Rafael Gordillo, José Ramón Alexanko, Agustín Guisasola, Dani (C), Enrique Saura, Jesús María Satrústegui, Francisco Javier Uría, Juanito
Substitutions: José Diego Álvarez (for Saura 46), Francisco José Carrasco (for Juanito 46), Antonio Olmo (for Alexanko 66)
England (*Manager: Ron Greenwood*)
Peter Shilton (*Nottingham Forest*), **Phil Neal** (*Liverpool*), **Mick Mills** (*Ipswich Town*), **Phil Thompson** (*Liverpool*), **Dave Watson** (*Southampton*), **Ray Wilkins** (*Manchester United*), **Kevin Keegan (C)** (*SV Hamburg*), **Steve Coppell** (*Manchester United*), **Trevor Francis** (*Nottingham Forest*), **Ray Kennedy** (*Liverpool*), **Tony Woodcock** (*FC Cologne*)
Substitutions: **Laurie Cunningham** (*Real Madrid*) (for Francis 80), **Emlyn Hughes** (*Wolverhampton Wanderers*) (for Neal 84)

Match No. 45 – Paul Mariner

Wales 4 v 1 England [2-1]

Saturday, 17 May 1980, kick-off: 3pm
Home International Championship 1979/80
Racecourse Ground, Wrexham, Att: 24,358
Scorers: Wales: Mickey Thomas (19), Ian Walsh (31), Leighton James (61), Phil Thompson (og 66), **England:** Paul Mariner (16)
Referee: Ian Foote (Scotland)
Wales (*Manager: Mike England*)
Dai Davies, Paul Price, Joey Jones, Peter Nicholas, David Jones, Terry Yorath (C), Brian Flynn, Leighton James, Ian Walsh, David Giles, Mickey Thomas
Substitution: Keith Pontin (for D. Jones 46)
England (*Manager: Ron Greenwood*)
Ray Clemence (*Liverpool*), **Phil Neal** (*Liverpool*), **Trevor Cherry** (*Leeds United*), **Phil Thompson (C)** (*Liverpool*), **Larry Lloyd** (*Nottingham Forest*), **Ray Kennedy** (*Liverpool*), **Steve Coppell** (*Manchester United*), **Glenn Hoddle** (*Tottenham Hotspur*), **Paul Mariner** (*Ipswich Town*), **Trevor Brooking** (*West Ham United*), **Peter Barnes** (*West Bromwich Albion*)
Substitutions: Kenny Sansom (*Crystal Palace*) (for Neal 20), **Ray Wilkins** (*Manchester United*) (for Lloyd 81)

Match No. 46 – Paul Mariner

England 1 v 1 Northern Ireland [0-0]

Tuesday, 20 May 1980, kick-off: 7.45pm
Home International Championship 1979/80
Wembley Stadium, London, Att: 33,676
Scorers: England: David Johnson (81), **Northern Ireland:** Terry Cochrane (82)
Referee: Gwyn Owen (Wales)
England (*Manager: Ron Greenwood*)
Joe Corrigan (*Manchester City*), **Trevor Cherry** (*Leeds United*), **Kenny Sansom** (*Crystal Palace*), **Emlyn Hughes (C)** (*Wolverhampton Wanderers*), **Dave Watson** (*Southampton*), **Ray Wilkins** (*Manchester United*), **Kevin Reeves** (*Manchester City*), **Terry McDermott** (*Liverpool*), **David Johnson** (*Liverpool*), **Trevor Brooking** (*West Ham United*), **Alan Devonshire** (*West Ham United*)
Substitution: Paul Mariner (*Ipswich Town*) (for Reeves 70)
Northern Ireland (*Manager: Billy Bingham*)
Jim Platt, Jimmy Nicholl, Mal Donaghy, Tommy Cassidy, Chris Nicholl, John O'Neill, Noel Brotherston, Sammy McIlroy (C), Gerry Armstrong, Billy Hamilton, Tommy Finney
Substitutions: David McCreery (for Hamilton 73), Terry Cochrane (for Cassidy 73)

Match No. 47 – Paul Mariner

Scotland 0 v 2 England [0-1]

Saturday, 24 May 1980, kick-off: 3pm
Home International Championship 1979/80
Hampden Park, Glasgow, Att: 85,500
Scorers: England: Trevor Brooking (8), Steve Coppell (75)
Live on BBC (UK): **Commentator:** Barry Davies
Live on ITV (UK): **Commentator:** Brian Moore
Referee: António Garrido (Portugal)
Scotland (*Manager: Jock Stein*)
Alan Rough, Danny McGrain, Iain Munro, Willie Miller, Paul Hegarty, Alex McLeish, Gordon Strachan, Archie Gemmill (C), Joe Jordan, Kenny Dalglish, Roy Aitken
Substitutions: Andy Gray (for Aitken 53), George Burley (for Munro 62)
England (*Manager: Ron Greenwood*)
Ray Clemence (*Liverpool*), **Trevor Cherry** (*Leeds United*), **Kenny Sansom** (*Crystal Palace*), **Phil Thompson (C)** (*Liverpool*), **Dave Watson** (*Southampton*), **Ray Wilkins** (*Manchester United*), **Steve Coppell** (*Manchester United*), **Terry McDermott** (*Liverpool*), **David Johnson** (*Liverpool*), **Paul Mariner** (*Ipswich Town*), **Trevor Brooking** (*West Ham United*)
Substitution: Emlyn Hughes (*Wolverhampton Wanderers*) (for Mariner 70)

Match No. 48 – Terry Butcher, Paul Mariner, and Russell Osman

Australia 1 v 2 England [0-2]

Saturday, 31 May 1980, kick-off: unknown
The Winfield Cup
Sydney Cricket Ground, Sydney, Att: 30,084
Scorers: Australia: Gary Cole (88 pen), **England:** Glenn Hoddle (10), Paul Mariner (25)
Referee: Tony Boskovic (Australia)
Australia (*Manager: Rudi Gutendorf*)
Greg Woodhouse, Steve Perry, Jim Tansey, Jim Muir, Ivo Prskalo, Tony Henderson, John Yzendoorn, Jimmy Rooney (C), Mark Jankovics, Gary Cole, Ken Boden
Substitutions: Peter Sharne (for Boden 46), Theo Selemidis (for Rooney 62)
England (*Manager: Ron Greenwood*)
Joe Corrigan (*Manchester City*), **Trevor Cherry (C)** (*Leeds United*), **Frank Lampard** (*West Ham United*), **Russell Osman** (*Ipswich Town*), **Terry Butcher** (*Ipswich Town*), **Glenn Hoddle** (*Tottenham Hotspur*), **Bryan Robson** (*West Bromwich Albion*), **Brian Talbot** (*Arsenal*), **David Armstrong** (*Middlesbrough*), **Alan Sunderland** (*Arsenal*), **Paul Mariner** (*Ipswich Town*)
Substitutions: Alan Devonshire (*West Ham United*) (for Armstrong 62), **Peter Ward** (*Brighton & Hove Albion*) (for Sunderland 82), **Brian Greenhoff** (*Leeds United*) (for Robson 88)

Match No. 49 – Paul Mariner

Italy 1 v 0 England [0-0]

Sunday, 15 June 1980, kick-off: 8.30pm (local)
Euro 80 Group 2, Game 2
Stadio Comunale di Torino, Turin, Att: 59,649
Scorer: Italy: Marco Tardelli (78)
Live on ITV (UK): **Commentators:** Brian Moore and Ron Atkinson
Referee: Nicolae Rainea (Portugal)
Italy (*Manager: Enzo Bearzot*)
Dino Zoff (C), Claudio Gentile, Gabriele Oriali, Romeo Benetti, Fulvio Collovati, Gaetano Scirea, Franco Causio, Marco Tardelli, Francesco Graziani, Giancarlo Antognoni, Roberto Bettega
Substitution: Giuseppe Baresi (for Causio 88)
England (*Manager: Ron Greenwood*)
Peter Shilton (*Nottingham Forest*), **Phil Neal** (*Liverpool*), **Kenny Sansom** (*Crystal Palace*), **Phil Thompson** (*Liverpool*), **Dave Watson** (*Southampton*), **Ray Wilkins** (*Manchester United*), **Kevin Keegan (C)** (*SV Hamburg*), **Steve Coppell** (*Manchester United*), **Garry Birtles** (*Nottingham Forest*), **Ray Kennedy** (*Liverpool*), **Tony Woodcock** (*FC Cologne*)
Substitution: Paul Mariner (*Ipswich Town*) (for Birtles 75)

Match No. 50 – Paul Mariner and Mick Mills

Spain 1 v 2 England [0-1]

Wednesday, 18 June 1980, kick-off: 5.45pm (local)
Euro 80, Group 2, Game 3
Stadio San Paolo, Naples, Att: 14,000
Scorers: Spain: Dani (48 pen), **England:** Trevor Brooking (19), Tony Woodcock (61)
Live on ITV (UK): **Commentators:** Brian Moore and Ron Atkinson
Referee: Erick Linemayr (Austria)
Spain (*Manager: Ladislao Kubala*)
Luis Arconada, Cundi, Antonio Olmo, Rafael Gordillo, José Ramón Alexanko, Francisco Uria, Juanito, Enrique Saura, Santillana (C), Jesús María Zamora, Julio Cardeñosa
Substitutions: Dani (for Cardeñosa 46), Francisco Carrasco (for Juanito 46)
England (*Manager: Ron Greenwood*)
Ray Clemence (*Liverpool*), **Viv Anderson** (*Nottingham Forest*), **Mick Mills** (*Ipswich Town*), **Phil Thompson** (*Liverpool*), **Dave Watson** (*Southampton*), **Ray Wilkins** (*Manchester United*), **Kevin Keegan (C)** (*SV Hamburg*), **Terry McDermott** (*Liverpool*), **Glenn Hoddle** (*Tottenham Hotspur*), **Trevor Brooking** (*West Ham United*), **Tony Woodcock** (*FC Cologne*)
Substitutions: Paul Mariner (*Ipswich Town*) (for Hoddle 76), **Trevor Cherry** (*Leeds United*) (for Mills 83)

Match No. 51 – Eric Gates and Paul Mariner

England 4 v 0 Norway [1-0]

Wednesday, 10 September 1980, kick-off: 7.45pm
World Cup 1982 Qualifier, Group Four
Wembley Stadium, London, Att: 48,200
Scorers: England: Terry McDermott (37, pen 78), Tony Woodcock (69), Paul Mariner (87)
Referee: Marcel van Langenhove (Belgium)
England (*Manager: Ron Greenwood*)
Peter Shilton (*Nottingham Forest*), **Viv Anderson** (*Nottingham Forest*), **Kenny Sansom** (*Arsenal*), **Phil Thompson (C)** (*Liverpool*), **Dave Watson** (*Southampton*), **Bryan Robson** (*West Bromwich Albion*), **Eric Gates** (*Ipswich Town*), **Terry McDermott** (*Liverpool*), **Paul Mariner** (*Ipswich Town*), **Tony Woodcock** (*FC Cologne*), **Graham Rix** (*Arsenal*)
Norway (*Manager: Tor Røste Fossen*)
Tom Rüsz Jacobsen, Bjarne Berntsen, Tore Kordahl, Einar Aas, Svein Grøndalen (C), Roger Albertsen, Åge Hareide, Arne Dokken, Arne Larsen Økland, Pål Jacobsen, Arne Erlandsen
Substitution: Rune Ottesen (for Erlandsen 83)

Match No. 52 – Eric Gates

Romania 2 v 1 England [1-0]

Wednesday, 15 October 1980, kick-off: 3pm (local)
World Cup 1982 Qualifier, Group Four
Stadionul 23 August, Bucharest, Att: 80,000
Scorers: Romania: Marcel Răducanuani (36), Anghel Iordănescu (75 pen), **England:** Tony Woodcock (66)
Referee: Ulf Eriksson (Sweden)
Romania (*Manager: Valentin Stanescu*)
Vasile Iordache, Nicolae Negrilă, Ion Munteanu, Ştefan Sameş, Costică Ştefănescu (C), Aurel Beldeanu, Zoltan Crićan, Anghel Iordănescu, Rodion Cămătaru, Aurel Ţicleanu, Marcel Răducanu
Substitution: Ion Dumitru (for Ţicleanu 71)
England (*Manager: Ron Greenwood*)
Ray Clemence (*Liverpool*), **Phil Neal** (*Liverpool*), **Kenny Sansom** (*Arsenal*), **Phil Thompson (C)** (*Liverpool*), **Dave Watson** (*Southampton*), **Bryan Robson** (*West Bromwich Albion*), **Graham Rix** (*Arsenal*), **Terry McDermott** (*Liverpool*), **Garry Birtles** (*Nottingham Forest*), **Tony Woodcock** (*FC Cologne*), **Eric Gates** (*Ipswich Town*)
Substitutions: Steve Coppell (*Manchester United*) (for Gates 46), **Laurie Cunningham** (*Real Madrid*) (for Birtles 65)

Match No. 53 – Paul Mariner and Mick Mills

England 2 v 1 Switzerland [2-0]

Wednesday, 19 November 1980, kick-off: 7.45pm
World Cup 1982 Qualifier, Group Four
Wembley Stadium, London, Att: 70,000
Scorers: England: Markus Tanner (og 22), Paul Mariner (31), **Switzerland:** Hans-Jörg Pfister (76)
Referee: Jan Keizer (Netherlands)
England (*Manager: Ron Greenwood*)
Peter Shilton (*Nottingham Forest*), **Phil Neal** (*Liverpool*), **Kenny Sansom** (*Arsenal*), **Bryan Robson** (*West Bromwich Albion*), **Dave Watson** (*Southampton*), **Mick Mills (C)** (*Ipswich Town*), **Steve Coppell** (*Manchester United*), **Terry McDermott** (*Liverpool*), **Paul Mariner** (*Ipswich Town*), **Trevor Brooking** (*West Ham United*), **Tony Woodcock** (*FC Cologne*)
Substitution: Graham Rix (*Arsenal*) (for Brooking 82)
Switzerland (*Manager: Leo Walker*)
Erich Burgener, Roger Wehrli, Heinz Hermann, Heinz Lüdi, Alain Geiger, Umberto Barberi, Hans-Jörg Pfister, Markus Tanner, Roland Schönenberger, Rudolf Elsener, Bobo Botteron (C)
Substitutions: Peter Marti (for Schönenberger 37), André Egli (for Tanner 46)

Match No. 54 – Terry Butcher, Paul Mariner, and Russell Osman

England 1 v 2 Spain [1-2]

Wednesday, 25 March 1981, kick-off: 7.45pm
International Friendly Match
Wembley Stadium, London, Att: 71,840
Scorers: England: Glenn Hoddle (27), **Spain:** Jesús Satrústegui (4), Jesús María Zamora (32)
Referee: Walter Eschweiler (West Germany)
England (*Manager: Ron Greenwood*)
Ray Clemence (*Liverpool*), **Phil Neal** (*Liverpool*), **Kenny Sansom** (*Arsenal*), **Bryan Robson** (*West Bromwich Albion*), **Russell Osman** (*Ipswich Town*), **Terry Butcher** (*Ipswich Town*), **Kevin Keegan (C)** (*Southampton*), **Trevor Francis** (*Nottingham Forest*), **Paul Mariner** (*Ipswich Town*), **Trevor Brooking** (*West Ham United*), **Glenn Hoddle** (*Tottenham Hotspur*)
Substitutions: Ray Wilkins (*Manchester United*) (for Brooking 70), **Peter Barnes** (*West Bromwich Albion*) (for Francis 81)
Spain (*Manager: José Santamaría*)
Luis Arconada (C), José Antonio Camacho, Rafael Gordillo, Antonio Maceda, Miguel Tendillo, Víctor Muñoz, Juanito, Joaquín, Jesús María Satrústegui, Jesús María Zamora, Marcos Alonso
Substitutions: Enrique Montero (for Muñoz 68), Dani (for Juanito 84)

Match No. 55 – Russell Osman

England 0 v 0 Romania [0-0]

Wednesday, 29 April 1981, kick-off: 7.45pm
World Cup 1982 Qualifier, Group Four
Wembley Stadium, London, Att: 62,500
Scorer: None
Referee: Alexis Ponnet (Belgium)
England (*Manager: Ron Greenwood*)
Peter Shilton (*Nottingham Forest*), Viv Anderson (*Nottingham Forest*), Kenny Sansom (*Arsenal*), Bryan Robson (*West Bromwich Albion*), Dave Watson (C) (*Southampton*), Russell Osman (*Ipswich Town*), Ray Wilkins (*Manchester United*), Steve Coppell (*Manchester United*), Trevor Francis (*Nottingham Forest*), Trevor Brooking (*West Ham United*), Tony Woodcock (*FC Cologne*)
Substitution: Terry McDermott (*Liverpool*) (for Brooking 70)
Romania (*Manager: Valentin Stanescu*)
Vasile Iordache, Nicolae Negrilă, Ion Munteanu, Ştefan Sameş, Costică Ştefănescu (C), Aurel Beldeanu, Zoltan Crićan, Anghel Iordănescu, Rodion Cămătaru, Tudorel Stoica, Ilie Balaci

Match No. 56 – Paul Mariner, Mick Mills, and Russell Osman

Switzerland 2 v 1 England [2-0]

Saturday, 30 May 1981, kick-off: 8pm (local)
World Cup 1982 Qualifier, Group Four
St Jakob Stadium, Basle, Att: 40,000
Scorers: Switzerland: Fredy Scheiwiler (28), Claudio Sulser (30), England: Terry McDermott (55)
Live on BBC (UK): Commentator: John Motson
Referee: Adolf Prokop (East Germany)
Switzerland (*Manager: Leo Walker*)
Erich Burgener, Herbert Hermann, Heinz Lüdi, André Egli, Gianpietro Zappa, Roger Wehrli, Fredy Scheiwiler, Bobo Botteron (C), Claudio Sulser, Umberto Barberis, Rudolf Elsener
Substitutions: Erni Maissen (for Elsener 85), Martin Weber (for Hermann 88)
England (*Manager: Ron Greenwood*)
Ray Clemence (*Liverpool*), Mick Mills (*Ipswich Town*), Kenny Sansom (*Arsenal*), Ray Wilkins (*Manchester United*), Dave Watson (*Southampton*), Russell Osman (*Ipswich Town*), Kevin Keegan (C) (*Southampton*), Bryan Robson (*West Bromwich Albion*), Steve Coppell (*Manchester United*), Paul Mariner (*Ipswich Town*), Trevor Francis (*Nottingham Forest*)
Substitutions: Terry McDermott (*Liverpool*) (for Francis 46), Peter Barnes (*West Bromwich Albion*) (for Watson 80)

Match No. 57 – Paul Mariner and Mick Mills

Hungary 1 v 3 England [1-1]

Saturday, 6 June 1981, kick-off: 8pm (local)
World Cup 1982 Qualifier, Group Four
Népstadion, Budapest, Att: 65,000
Scorers: Hungary: Imre Garaba (45), **England:** Trevor Brooking (18, 60), Kevin Keegan pen 73)
Live on ITV (UK): **Commentators:** Brian Moore and John Bond
Referee: Paulo Casarin (Italy)
Hungary (*Manager: Kálmán Mészöly*)
Béla Katzirz, Győző Martos, László Bálint, József Varga, Sándor Müller, Imre Garaba, László Fazekas, Tibor Nyilasi (C), László Kiss, József Mucha, András Törőcsik
Substitutions: András Komjáti (for Müller 55), Béla Bodonyi (for Fazekas 62)
England (*Manager: Ron Greenwood*)
Ray Clemence (*Liverpool*), Phil Neal (*Liverpool*), Mick Mills (*Ipswich Town*), Phil Thompson (*Liverpool*), **Dave Watson** (*Southampton*), **Bryan Robson** (*West Bromwich Albion*), **Kevin Keegan (C)** (*Southampton*), **Steve Coppell** (*Manchester United*), **Paul Mariner** (*Ipswich Town*), **Trevor Brooking** (*West Ham United*), **Terry McDermott** (*Liverpool*)
Substitution: Ray Wilkins (*Manchester United*) (for Brooking 72)

Match No. 58 – Paul Mariner, Mick Mills, and Russell Osman

Norway 2 v 1 England [2-1]

Wednesday, 9 September 1981, kick-off: 7pm (local)
World Cup 1982 Qualifier, Group Four
Ullevål Stadion, Oslo, Att: 28,500
Scorers: Norway: Roger Albertsen (34), Hallvar Thoresen (44), **England:** Bryan Robson (14)
Live on ITV (UK): **Commentators:** Brian Moore and Ron Atkinson
Referee: Jerzy Kacprzak (Poland)
Norway (*Manager: Tor Røste Fossen*)
Tore Antonsen, Bjarne Berntsen, Åge Hareide, Einar Aas, Svein Grøndalen, Roger Albertsen, Anders Giske, Hallvar Thoresen (C), Arne Larsen Økland, Pål Jacobsen, Tom Lund
Substitutions: Arne Dokken (for Lund 75), Trond Pedersen (for Økland 87)
England (*Manager: Ron Greenwood*)
Ray Clemence (*Tottenham Hotspur*), **Phil Neal** (*Liverpool*), **Mick Mills** (*Ipswich Town*), **Phil Thompson** (*Liverpool*), **Russell Osman** (*Ipswich Town*), **Bryan Robson** (*West Bromwich Albion*), **Kevin Keegan (C)** (*Southampton*), **Trevor Francis** (*Manchester City*), **Paul Mariner** (*Ipswich Town*), **Glenn Hoddle** (*Tottenham Hotspur*), **Terry McDermott** (*Liverpool*)
Substitutions: Peter Barnes (*Leeds United*) (for Hoddle 65), **Peter Withe** (*Aston Villa*) (for Mariner 75)

Match No. 59 – Paul Mariner and Mick Mills

England 1 v 0 Hungary [1-0]

Wednesday, 18 November 1981, kick-off: 7.45pm
World Cup 1982 Qualifier, Group Four
Wembley Stadium, London, Att: 92,000
Scorer: England: Paul Mariner (16)
Live on BBC (UK): **Commentator:** John Motson
Referee: Georges Konrath (France)
England (*Manager: Ron Greenwood*)

Peter Shilton (*Nottingham Forest*), **Phil Neal** (*Liverpool*), **Mick Mills** (*Ipswich Town*), **Phil Thompson** (*Liverpool*), **Alvin Martin** (*West Ham United*), **Bryan Robson** (*Manchester United*), **Kevin Keegan (C)** (*Southampton*), **Steve Coppell** (*Manchester United*), **Paul Mariner** (*Ipswich Town*), **Trevor Brooking** (*West Ham United*), **Terry McDermott** (*Liverpool*)

Substitution: Tony Morley (*Aston Villa*) (for Coppell 65)

Hungary (*Manager: Kálmán Mészöly*)

Béla Katzirz, Győző Martos, László Bálint, József Tóth (C), Sándor Müller, Imre Garaba, László Fazekas, Károly Csapó, László Kiss, András Törőcsik, Sándor Sallai
Substitutions: Attila Kerekes (for Fazekas 46), Gábor Szántó (for Csapó 80)

Match No. 60 – Terry Butcher

Wales 0 v 1 England [0-0]

Tuesday, 27 April 1982, kick-off: 7.30pm
World Cup 1982 Qualifier, Group Four
Ulleväl Stadion, Oslo, Att: 28,500
Scorer: England: Trevor Francis (74)
Referee: Thomas Donnelly (Northern Ireland)
Wales (*Manager: Mike England*)
Dai Davies, Chris Marustik, Kevin Ratcliffe, Peter Nicholas, Nigel Stevenson, Joey Jones, Alan Curtis, Brian Flynn (C), Ian Rush, Mickey Thomas, Robbie James
Substitutions: Leighton James (for Thomas 46), Carl Harris (for Flynn 77)
England (*Manager: Ron Greenwood*)
Joe Corrigan (*Manchester City*), **Phil Neal** (*Liverpool*), **Kenny Sansom** (*Arsenal*), **Phil Thompson (C)** (*Liverpool*), **Terry Butcher** (*Ipswich Town*), **Bryan Robson** (*Manchester United*), **Trevor Francis** (*Manchester City*), **Peter Withe** (*Aston Villa*), **Glenn Hoddle** (*Tottenham Hotspur*), **Tony Morley** (*Aston Villa*)
Substitutions: Terry McDermott (*Liverpool*) (for Hoddle 52), **Cyrille Regis** (*West Bromwich Albion*) (for Francis 80)

Match No. 61 – Paul Mariner

England 2 v 0 Netherlands [0-0]

Tuesday, 25 May 1982, kick-off: 7.45pm
International Friendly Match
Wembley Stadium, London, Att: 69,000
Scorers: England: Tony Woodcock (48), Paul Mariner (53)
Referee: Paulo Bergamo (Italy)
England (*Manager: Ron Greenwood*)
Peter Shilton (C) (*Nottingham Forest*), **Phil Neal** (*Liverpool*), **Kenny Sansom** (*Arsenal*), **Phil Thompson** (*Liverpool*), **Steve Foster** (*Brighton & Hove Albion*), **Bryan Robson** (*Manchester United*), **Ray Wilkins** (*Manchester United*), **Alan Devonshire** (*West Ham United*), **Paul Mariner** (*Ipswich Town*), **Terry McDermott** (*Liverpool*), **Tony Woodcock** (*FC Cologne*)
Substitutions: Graham Rix (*Arsenal*) (for Devonshire 46), **Peter Barnes** (*Leeds United*) (for Mariner 82)
Netherlands (*Manager: Kees Rijvers*)
Hans van Breukelen, Michel van de Korput, John Metgod, Edo Ophof, Ruud Krol (C), Peter Boeve, Tschen La Ling, Jan Peters, Wim Kieft, Arnold Mühren, Simon Tahamata
Substitutions: René van de Kerkhof (for Peters 63), Frank Rijkaard (for La Ling 71), Cees van Kooten (for Metgod 71)

Match No. 62 – Terry Butcher, Paul Mariner, and Mick Mills

Scotland 0 v 1 England [0-1]

Saturday, 29 May 1982, kick-off: 3pm
Home International Championship 1981/82
Hampden Park, Glasgow, Att: 80,529
Scorer: England: Paul Mariner (13)
Live on BBC (UK): **Commentator:** Barry Davies
Live on ITV (UK): **Commentators:** Brian Moore and Jack Charlton
Referee: Jen Redelfs (West Germany)
Scotland (*Manager: Jock Stein*)
Alan Rough, George Burley, Danny McGrain (C), Alan Hansen, Allan Evans, Dave Narey, Kenny Dalglish, Graeme Souness, Joe Jordan, Asa Hartford, Alan Brazil
Substitutions: John Robertson (for Hartford 46), Paul Sturrock (for Jordan 63)
England (*Manager: Ron Greenwood*)
Peter Shilton (*Nottingham Forest*), **Mick Mills** (*Ipswich Town*), **Kenny Sansom** (*Arsenal*), **Phil Thompson** (*Liverpool*), **Terry Butcher** (*Ipswich Town*), **Bryan Robson** (*Manchester United*), **Kevin Keegan (C)** (*Southampton*), **Steve Coppell** (*Manchester United*), **Paul Mariner** (*Ipswich Town*), **Trevor Brooking** (*West Ham United*), **Ray Wilkins** (*Manchester United*)
Substitutions: Trevor Francis (*Manchester City*) (for Mariner 46), **Terry McDermott** (*Liverpool*) (for Keegan 56)

Match No. 63 – Russell Osman

Iceland 1 v 1 England [1-0]

Wednesday, 2 June 1982, kick-off: 7pm (local)
World Cup warm-up tour match
Laugardalsvöllur, Reykjavík, Att: 10,814
Scorers: Iceland: Arnór Guðjohnsen (23), **England:** Paul Goddard (69)
Referee: Ib Nielsen (Denmark)
Iceland (*Manager: Jóhannes Atlason*)
Guðmundur Baldursson, Örn Óskarsson, Trausti Haraldsson, Atli Eðvaldsson, Marteinn Geirsson (C), Sævar Jónsson, Janus Guðlaugsson, Arnór Guðjohnsen, Teitur Thordarson, Lárus Guðmundsson, Karl Thórdarson
Substitution: Pétur Ormslev (for Guðlaugsson 82)
England (*Manager: Ron Greenwood*)
Joe Corrigan (*Manchester City*), **Viv Anderson** (*Nottingham Forest*), **Phil Neal (C)** (*Liverpool*), **Dave Watson** (*Stoke City*), **Russell Osman** (*Ipswich Town*), **Terry McDermott** (*Liverpool*), **Glenn Hoddle** (*Tottenham Hotspur*), **Alan Devonshire** (*West Ham United*), **Peter Withe** (*Aston Villa*), **Cyrille Regis** (*West Bromwich Albion*), **Tony Morley** (*Aston Villa*)
Substitutions: Paul Goddard (*West Ham United*) (for Regis 40), **Steve Perryman** (*Tottenham Hotspur*) (for Devonshire 70)

Match No. 64 – Paul Mariner and Mick Mills

Finland 1 v 4 England [0-2]

Thursday, 3 June 1982, kick-off: 7pm (local)
International Friendly Match
Olympiastadion, Helsinki, Att: 21,421
Scorers: Finland: Kai Haaskivi (pen 83), **England:** Paul Mariner (13, 62), Bryan Robson (27, 58)
Referee: Romualdas Juška (USSR)
Finland (*Manager: Martti Kuusela*)
Pertti Alaja, Aki Lahtinen, Jukka Ikäläinen (C), Mikail Granskog, Esa Pekonen, Hannu Turunen, Kai Haaskivi, Pasi Rautiainen, Juhani Himanka, Atik Ismail, Jyrki Nieminen
Substitutions: Ari Valvee (for Nieminen 55), Pauno Kymäläinen (for Turunen 63), Olli Huttunen (for Alaja 68)
England (*Manager: Ron Greenwood*)
Ray Clemence (*Tottenham Hotspur*), **Mick Mills** (*Ipswich Town*), **Kenny Sansom** (*Arsenal*), **Phil Thompson** (*Liverpool*), **Alvin Martin** (*West Ham United*), **Bryan Robson** (*Manchester United*), **Kevin Keegan (C)** (*Southampton*), **Steve Coppell** (*Manchester United*), **Paul Mariner** (*Ipswich Town*), **Trevor Brooking** (*West Ham United*), **Ray Wilkins** (*Manchester United*)
Substitutions: Graham Rix (*Arsenal*) (for Robson 65), **Trevor Francis** (*Manchester City*) (for Coppell 65), **Tony Woodcock** (*FC Cologne*) (for Brooking 68)

Match No. 65 – Terry Butcher, Paul Mariner, and Mick Mills

England 3 v 1 France [1-1]

Wednesday, 16 June 1982, kick-off: 5.15pm (local)
1982 World Cup, First Phase, Group Four
Estadio San Mamés, Bilbao, Att: 44,172
Scorers: **England:** Bryan Robson (1, 67), Paul Mariner (83), **France:** Gérard Soler (25)
Live on BBC (World Cup Grandstand): **Commentators:** John Motson and Jimmy Hill
Referee: António Garrido (Portugal)
England (*Manager: Ron Greenwood*)

Peter Shilton (*Nottingham Forest*), **Mick Mills (C)** (*Ipswich Town*), **Kenny Sansom** (*Arsenal*), **Phil Thompson** (*Liverpool*), **Terry Butcher** (*Ipswich Town*), **Bryan Robson** (*Manchester United*), **Ray Wilkins** (*Manchester United*), **Graham Rix** (*Arsenal*), **Paul Mariner** (*Ipswich Town*), **Trevor Francis** (*Manchester City*), **Steve Coppell** (*Manchester United*)

Substitution: Phil Neal (*Liverpool*) (for Sansom 90+1)
France (*Manager: Michel Hidalgo*)

Jean-Luc Ettori, Patrick Battiston, Maxime Bossis, Christian Lopez, Marius Trésor, René Girard, Dominique Rocheteau, Alain Giresse, Jean-François Larios, Michel Platini (C), Gérard Soler
Substitutions: Didier Six (for Rocheteau 71), Jean Tigana (for Larios 74)

Match No. 66 – Terry Butcher, Paul Mariner, and Mick Mills

England 2 v 0 Czechoslovakia [0-0]

Sunday, 20 June 1982, kick-off: 5.15pm (local)
1982 World Cup, First Phase, Group Four
Estadio San Mamés, Bilbao, Att: 44,182
Scorers: **England:** Trevor Francis (62), Jozef Barmoš (og 67)
Live on ITV (World Cup '82): **Commentators:** Martin Tyler and Jack Charlton
Referee: Charles Corver (Netherlands)
England (*Manager: Ron Greenwood*)

Peter Shilton (*Nottingham Forest*), **Mick Mills (C)** (*Ipswich Town*), **Kenny Sansom** (*Arsenal*), **Phil Thompson** (*Liverpool*), **Terry Butcher** (*Ipswich Town*), **Bryan Robson** (*Manchester United*), **Ray Wilkins** (*Manchester United*), **Graham Rix** (*Arsenal*), **Paul Mariner** (*Ipswich Town*), **Trevor Francis** (*Manchester City*), **Steve Coppell** (*Manchester United*)

Substitution: Glenn Hoddle (*Tottenham Hotspur*) (for Robson 46)
Czechoslovakia (*Manager: Jozef Venglos*)

Stanislav Seman, Jan Fiala, Rostislav Vojáček, Ladislav Jurkemik, Jozef Barmoš, Libor Radimec, Pavel Chaloupka, Jan Berger, Ladislav Vízek, Petr Janečka, Zdeněk Nehoda (C)
Substitutions: Karel Stromšík (for Seman 76), Marián Masný (for Janečka 78)

Match No. 67 – Paul Mariner, and Mick Mills

England 1 v 0 Kuwait [0-0]

Friday, 25 June 1982, kick-off: 5.15pm (local)

1982 World Cup, First Phase, Group Four

Estadio San Mamés, Bilbao, Att: 39,700

Scorer: England: Trevor Francis (28)

Live on ITV (World Cup '82): **Commentators:** Martin Tyler and Jack Charlton

Referee: Gilberto Aristizabal (Colombia)

England (*Manager: Ron Greenwood*)

Peter Shilton (*Nottingham Forest*), **Mick Mills (C)** (*Ipswich Town*), **Phil Neal** (*Liverpool*), **Phil Thompson** (*Liverpool*), **Stephen Foster** (*Brighton & Hove Albion*), **Glenn Hoddle** (*Tottenham Hotspur*), **Ray Wilkins** (*Manchester United*), **Graham Rix** (*Arsenal*), **Paul Mariner** (*Ipswich Town*), **Trevor Francis** (*Manchester City*), **Steve Coppell** (*Manchester United*)

Kuwait (*Manager: Carlos Alberto Parreira*)

Ahmed Al-Tarabulsi, Naeem Saad, Mahboub Juma'a, Abdullah Mayouf, Waleed Al-Jasem, Sa'ad Al-Houti (C), Fathi Kameel, Abdullah Al-Buloushi, Yousef Al-Suwayed, Abdulaziz Al-Anberi, Faisal Al-Dakhil

Substitution: Hamoud Al-Shemmari (for Al-Jasem 76)

Match No. 68 – Terry Butcher, Paul Mariner, and Mick Mills

England 0 v 0 West Germany [0-0]

Tuesday, 29 June 1982, kick-off: 9pm (local)

1982 World Cup, Second Phase, Group B

Estadio Santiago Bernabéu, Madrid, Att: 90,089

Scorers: None

Live on BBC1 (World Cup Grandstand): **Commentators:** John Motson and Jimmy Hill

Referee: Arnaldo David César Coelho (Brazil)

England (*Manager: Ron Greenwood*)

Peter Shilton (*Nottingham Forest*), **Mick Mills (C)** (*Ipswich Town*), **Kenny Sansom** (*Arsenal*), **Phil Thompson** (*Liverpool*), **Terry Butcher** (*Ipswich Town*), **Bryan Robson** (*Manchester United*), **Ray Wilkins** (*Manchester United*), **Graham Rix** (*Arsenal*), **Paul Mariner** (*Ipswich Town*), **Trevor Francis** (*Manchester City*), **Steve Coppell** (*Manchester United*)

Substitution: Tony Woodcock (*Arsenal*) (for Francis 78)

West Germany (*Manager: Jupp Derwall*)

Harald Schumacher, Manfred Kaltz, Uli Stielike, Karlheinz Förster, Bernd Förster, Wolfgang Dremmler, Hans-Peter Briegel, Paul Breitner, Uwe Reinders, Hansi Müller, Karl-Heinz Rummenigge (C)

Substitutions: Pierre Littbarski (for Reinders 62), Klaus Fischer (for Müller 73)

Match No. 69 – Terry Butcher, Paul Mariner, and Mick Mills

England 0 v 0 Spain [0-0]

Monday, 5 July 1982, kick-off: 9pm (local)
1982 World Cup, Second Phase, Group B
Estadio Santiago Bernabéu, Madrid, Att: 75,000
Scorers: None
Live on ITV (World Cup '82): **Commentators:** Martin Tyler and Jack Charlton
Referee: Alexis Ponnet Coelho (Belgium)
England (*Manager: Ron Greenwood*)
Peter Shilton (*Nottingham Forest*), **Mick Mills (C)** (*Ipswich Town*), **Kenny Sansom** (*Arsenal*), **Phil Thompson** (*Liverpool*), **Terry Butcher** (*Ipswich Town*), **Bryan Robson** (*Manchester United*), **Ray Wilkins** (*Manchester United*), **Graham Rix** (*Arsenal*), **Paul Mariner** (*Ipswich Town*), **Trevor Francis** (*Manchester City*), **Tony Woodcock** (*Arsenal*)
Substitutions: Trevor Brooking (*West Ham United*) (for Rix 63), **Kevin Keegan** (*Southampton*) (for Woodcock 64)
Spain (*Manager: José Santamaría*)
Luis Arconada (C), José Antonio Camacho, Rafael Gordillo, Miguel Ángel Alonso, Miguel Tendillo, José Ramón Alexanko, Santiago Urquiaga, Enrique Saura, Jesús María Satrústegui, Jesús María Zamora, Santillana
Substitutions: Pedro Uralde (for Saura 67), Antonio Maceda (for Tendillo 73)

Match No. 70 – Terry Butcher, Paul Mariner, and Russell Osman

Denmark 2 v 2 England [0-1]

Wednesday, 22 June 1982, kick-off: 7pm (local)
European Championship 1984 Qualifier
Idrætsparken, Copenhagen, Att: 44,300
Scorers: Denmark: Allan Hansen (pen 68), Jesper Olsen (89), **England:** Trevor Francis (8, 82)
Referee: Charles Corver (Netherlands)
Denmark (*Manager: Sepp Piontek*)
Troels Rasmussen, Ivan Nielsen, Søren Busk, Per Røntved (C), Ole Rasmussen, Søren Lerby, Jens Jørn Bertelsen, Jesper Olsen, Allan Hansen, Preben Elkjær, Lars Bastrup
England (*Manager: Bobby Robson*)
Peter Shilton (*Southampton*), **Phil Neal** (*Liverpool*), **Kenny Sansom** (*Arsenal*), **Russell Osman** (*Ipswich Town*), **Terry Butcher** (*Ipswich Town*), **Bryan Robson** (*Manchester United*), **Ray Wilkins (C)** (*Manchester United*), **Tony Morley** (*Aston Villa*), **Paul Mariner** (*Ipswich Town*), **Trevor Francis** (*Sampdoria*), **Graham Rix** (*Arsenal*)
Substitution: Ricky Hill (*Luton Town*) (for Morley 83)

Match No. 71 – Terry Butcher and Paul Mariner

England 1 v 2 West Germany [0-0]

Wednesday, 13 October 1982, kick-off: 7.45pm
International Friendly Match
Wembley Stadium, London, Att: 68,000
Scorers: England: Tony Woodcock (86), **West Germany:** Karl-Heinz Rummenigge (72, 76)
Referee: Károly Palotai (Hungary)
England (*Manager: Bobby Robson*)
Peter Shilton (*Southampton*), **Gary Mabbutt** (*Tottenham Hotspur*), **Kenny Sansom** (*Arsenal*), **Phil Thompson** (*Liverpool*), **Terry Butcher** (*Ipswich Town*), **Ray Wilkins (C)** (*Manchester United*), **Ricky Hill** (*Luton Town*), **Paul Mariner** (*Ipswich Town*), **Cyrille Regis** (*West Bromwich Albion*), **David Armstrong** (*Southampton*), **Alan Devonshire** (*West Ham United*)
Substitutions: Tony Woodcock (*Arsenal*) (for Mariner 80), **Graham Rix** (*Arsenal*) (for Armstrong 80), **Luther Blissett** (*Watford*) (for Regis 80)
West Germany (*Manager: Jupp Derwall*)
Harald Schumacher, Manfred Kaltz, Gerd Strack, Karlheinz Förster, Bernd Förster, Wolfgang Dremmler, Hans-Peter Briegel, Norbert Meier, Klaus Allofs, Lothar Matthäus, Karl-Heinz Rummenigge (C)
Substitutions: Holger Hieronymus (for K. Förster 5), Pierre Littbarski (for Meier 69), Stephan Engels (for Allofs 89)

Match No. 72 – Paul Mariner

Greece 0 v 3 England [0-1]

Wednesday, 17 November 1982, kick-off: 2pm (local)
European Championship 1984 Qualifier
Kaftanzoglio Stadio, Thessaloniki, Att: 41,554
Scorers: England: Tony Woodcock (2, 64), Sammy Lee (68)
Referee: Adolf Prokop (East Germany)
Greece (*Manager: Christos Archontidis*)
Nikos Sarganis, Ioannis Gounaris, Konstantinos Iosifidis, Giorgos Foiros, Anthimos Kapsis (C), Spiros Livathinos, Petros Michos, Tasos Mitropoulos, Nikos Anastopoulos, Christos Ardizoglou, Thomas Mavros
Substitutions: Georgios Kostikos (for Ardizoglou 41), Savvas Kofidis (for Mavros 78)
England (*Manager: Bobby Robson*)
Peter Shilton (*Southampton*), **Phil Neal** (*Liverpool*), **Kenny Sansom** (*Arsenal*), **Phil Thompson** (*Liverpool*), **Alvin Martin** (*West Ham United*), **Bryan Robson (C)** (*Manchester United*), **Sammy Lee** (*Liverpool*), **Tony Morley** (*Aston Villa*), **Paul Mariner** (*Ipswich Town*), **Tony Woodcock** (*Arsenal*), **Gary Mabbutt** (*Tottenham Hotspur*)

Match No. 73 – Terry Butcher

England 9 v 0 Luxembourg [4-0]

Wednesday, 15 December 1982, kick-off: 7.45pm
European Championship 1984 Qualifier
Wembley Stadium, London, Att: 33,980
Scorers: England: Jeannot Moes (og 18), Steve Coppell (22), Tony Woodcock (34), Luther Blissett (44, 62, 86), Mark Chamberlain (71), Glenn Hoddle (87), Phil Neal (89)
Referee: Hreidar Jonsson (Iceland)
England (*Manager: Bobby Robson*)
Ray Clemence (*Tottenham Hotspur*), **Phil Neal** (*Liverpool*), **Kenny Sansom** (*Arsenal*), **Terry Butcher** (*Ipswich Town*), **Alvin Martin** (*West Ham United*), **Bryan Robson (C)** (*Manchester United*), **Sammy Lee** (*Liverpool*), **Steve Coppell** (*Manchester United*), **Luther Blissett** (*Watford*), **Tony Woodcock** (*Arsenal*), **Gary Mabbutt** (*Tottenham Hotspur*)
Substitutions: Mark Chamberlain (*Stoke City*) (for Coppell 66), **Glenn Hoddle** (*Tottenham Hotspur*) (for Mabbutt 74)
Luxembourg (*Manager: Louis Pilot*)
Jeannot Moes (C), Jean-Paul Girres, Hubert Meunier, Marcel Bossi, Nico Rohmann, Johny Clemens, Guy Hellers, Carlo Weis, Gilbert Dresch, Jeannot Hoffmann, Marcel Di Domenico
Substitution: Alain Nurenberg (for Di Domenico 46)

Match No. 74 – Terry Butcher and Paul Mariner

England 2 v 1 Wales [1-1]

Wednesday, 23 February 1983, kick-off: 7.45pm
Home International Championship 1982/83
Wembley Stadium, London, Att: 23,600
Scorers: England: Terry Butcher (39), Phil Neal (pen 78), **Wales:** Ian Rush (14)
Referee: Bob Valentine (Scotland)
England (*Manager: Bobby Robson*)
Peter Shilton (C) (*Southampton*), **Phil Neal** (*Liverpool*), **Derek Statham** (*West Bromwich Albion*), **Sammy Lee** (*Liverpool*), **Alvin Martin** (*West Ham United*), **Terry Butcher** (*Ipswich Town*), **Gary Mabbutt** (*Tottenham Hotspur*), **Luther Blissett** (*Watford*), **Paul Mariner** (*Ipswich Town*), **Gordon Cowans** (*Aston Villa*), **Alan Devonshire** (*West Ham United*)
Wales (*Manager: Mike England*)
Neville Southall, Joey Jones, Kevin Ratcliffe, John Mahoney, Paul Price (C), Kenny Jackett, Robbie James, Brian Flynn, Ian Rush, Gordon Davies, Mickey Thomas
Substitutions: George Berry (for Jones 44), Leighton James (for Mahoney 80)

Match No. 75 – Terry Butcher

England 0 v 0 Greece [0-0]

Wednesday, 30 March 1983, kick-off: 7.45pm

European Championship 1984 Qualifier

Wembley Stadium, London, Att: 68,000

Scorer: None

Referee: Dusan Krisznak (Czechoslovakia)

England (*Manager: Bobby Robson*)

Peter Shilton (C) (*Southampton*), Phil Neal (*Liverpool*), Kenny Sansom (*Arsenal*), Sammy Lee (*Liverpool*), Alvin Martin (*West Ham United*), Terry Butcher (*Ipswich Town*), Steve Coppell (*Manchester United*), Gary Mabbutt (*Tottenham Hotspur*), Trevor Francis (*Sampdoria*), Tony Woodcock (*Arsenal*), Alan Devonshire (*West Ham United*)

Greece (*Manager: Christos Archontidis*)

Nikos Sarganis, Ioannis Gounaris (C), Nikos Karoulias, Giannis Galitsios, Petros Michos, Charalambos Xanthopoulos, Vangelis Kousoulakis, Dinos Kouis, Nikos Anastopoulos, Tasos Mitropoulos, Georgios Kostikos

Substitutions: Christos Ardizoglou (for Mitropoulos 78), Giannis Dontas (for Anastopoulos 87)

Match No. 76 – Terry Butcher

England 2 v 0 Hungary [1-0]

Wednesday, 27 April 1983, kick-off: 7.45pm

European Championship 1984 Qualifier

Wembley Stadium, London, Att: 55,000

Scorers: England: Trevor Francis (31), Peter Withe (70)

Referee: Pietro D'Elia (Italy)

England (*Manager: Bobby Robson*)

Peter Shilton (C) (*Southampton*), Phil Neal (*Liverpool*), Kenny Sansom (*Arsenal*), Sammy Lee (*Liverpool*), Alvin Martin (*West Ham United*), Terry Butcher (*Ipswich Town*), Gary Mabbutt (*Tottenham Hotspur*), Trevor Francis (*Sampdoria*), Peter Withe (*Aston Villa*), Luther Blissett (*Watford*), Gordon Cowans (*Aston Villa*)

Hungary (*Manager: Kálmán Mészöly*)

Béla Katzirz (C), Győző Martos, István Kocsis, József Tóth, Péter Hannich, Imre Garaba, József Varga, Tibor Nyilasi, László Kiss, József Kardos, Gyula Hajszán

Substitutions: Győző Burcsa (for Martos 68), András Törőcsik (for Kiss 68)

Match No. 77 – Terry Butcher

Northern Ireland 0 v 0 England [0-0]

Saturday, 28 May 1983, kick-off: 7.45pm
Home International Championship 1982/83
Windsor Park, Belfast, Att: 22,000
Scorer: None
Live on ITV (UK): **Commentators:** Martin Tyler and Ron Atkinson
Referee: Howard King (Wales)
Northern Ireland (*Manager: Billy Bingham*)
Pat Jennings, Jimmy Nicholl, Mal Donaghy, Chris Nicholl, John McClelland, Martin O'Neill (C), Gerry Mullan, Sammy McIlroy, Gerry Armstrong, Billy Hamilton, Ian Stewart
Substitutions: Noel Brotherston (for Mullan 80)
England (*Manager: Bobby Robson*)
Peter Shilton (C) (*Southampton*), **Phil Neal** (*Liverpool*), **Kenny Sansom** (*Arsenal*), **Glenn Hoddle** (*Tottenham Hotspur*), **Graham Roberts** (*Tottenham Hotspur*), **Terry Butcher** (*Ipswich Town*), **Gary Mabbutt** (*Tottenham Hotspur*), **Trevor Francis** (*Sampdoria*), **Peter Withe** (*Aston Villa*), **Luther Blissett** (*Watford*), **Gordon Cowans** (*Aston Villa*)
Substitution: John Barnes (*Watford*) (for Blissett 69)

Match No. 78 – Terry Butcher

England 2 v 0 Scotland [0-0]

Wednesday, 1 June 1983, kick-off: 7.45pm
Home International Championship 1982/83
Wembley Stadium, London, Att: 84,000
Scorers: England: Bryan Robson (13), Gordon Cowans (52)
Live on BBC (England & Wales): **Commentator:** John Motson
Live on BBC (Scotland): **Commentator:** Archie McPherson and Alex Ferguson
Referee: Erik Fredriksson (Sweden)
England (*Manager: Bobby Robson*)
Peter Shilton (*Southampton*), **Phil Neal** (*Liverpool*), **Kenny Sansom** (*Arsenal*), **Sammy Lee** (*Liverpool*), **Graham Roberts** (*Tottenham Hotspur*), **Terry Butcher** (*Ipswich Town*), **Bryan Robson (C)** (*Manchester United*), **Trevor Francis** (*Sampdoria*), **Peter Withe** (*Aston Villa*), **Glenn Hoddle** (*Tottenham Hotspur*), **Gordon Cowans** (*Aston Villa*)
Substitutions: Gary Mabbutt (*Tottenham Hotspur*) (for Robson 23), **Luther Blissett** (*Watford*) (for Withe 46)
Scotland (*Manager: Jock Stein*)
Jim Leighton, Richard Gough, Frank Gray, Dave Narey, Alex McLeish, Willie Miller, Gordon Strachan, Graeme Souness (C), Andy Gray, Charlie Nicholas, Eamonn Bannon
Substitutions: Alan Brazil (for Bannon 55), John Wark (for Nicholas 67)

Match No. 79 – Terry Butcher and Russell Osman

Australia 0 v 0 England [0-0]

Sunday, 12 June 1983, kick-off: unknown
Tour of Australia Friendly
Sydney Cricket Ground, Sydney, Att: 28,000
Scorer: None
Referee: Tony Boskovic (Australia)
Australia (*Manager: Frank Arok*)

Terry Greedy, Alan Davidson, Charlie Yankos, David Ratcliffe, Steve O'Connor, Graham Jennings, Joe Watson, Jimmy Cant, Peter Katholos, John Kosmina (C), Phil O'Connor
Substitutions: Dave Mitchell (for O'Connor 65), Peter Stone (for Watson 80)
England (*Manager: Bobby Robson*)

Peter Shilton (C) (*Southampton*), **Danny Thomas** (*Coventry City*), **Derek Statham** (*West Bromwich Albion*), **Steve Williams** (*Southampton*), **Russell Osman** (*Ipswich Town*), **Terry Butcher** (*Ipswich Town*), **Mark Barham** (*Norwich City*), **John Gregory** (*Queens Park Rangers*), **Luther Blissett** (*Watford*), **Trevor Francis** (*Sampdoria*), **Gordon Cowans** (*Aston Villa*)
Substitutions: **Paul Walsh** (*Luton Town*) (for Blissett 59), **John Barnes** (*Watford*) (for Statham 69)

Match No. 80 – Terry Butcher and Russell Osman

Australia 0 v 1 England [0-0]

Wednesday, 15 June 1983, kick-off: unknown
Tour of Australia Friendly
Lang Park, Brisbane, Att: 16,000
Scorer: England: Paul Walsh (57)
Referee: Peter Rampley (Australia)
Australia (*Manager: Frank Arok*)

Terry Greedy, Alan Davidson, Charlie Yankos, David Ratcliffe, Steve O'Connor, Graham Jennings, Joe Watson, Jimmy Cant, Peter Katholos, John Kosmina (C), Phil O'Connor
Substitutions: Kenny Murphy (for Katholos 69), Dave Mitchell (for O'Connor 75)
England (*Manager: Bobby Robson*)

Peter Shilton (C) (*Southampton*), **Phil Neal** (*Liverpool*), **Derek Statham** (*West Bromwich Albion*), **Mark Barham** (*Norwich City*), **Russell Osman** (*Ipswich Town*), **Terry Butcher** (*Ipswich Town*), **John Gregory** (*Queens Park Rangers*), **Paul Walsh** (*Luton Town*), **Trevor Francis** (*Sampdoria*), **Gordon Cowans** (*Aston Villa*), **John Barnes** (*Watford*)
Substitution: Steve Williams (*Southampton*) (for Statham 21)

Match No. 81 – Terry Butcher and Russell Osman

Australia 0 v 1 England [0-0]

Sunday, 19 June 1983, kick-off: unknown
Tour of Australia Friendly
Olympic Park, Melbourne, Att: 20,000
Scorers: Australia: Phil Neal (og 27), **England:** Trevor Francis (19)
Referee: Jack Johnston (Australia)
Australia (*Manager: Frank Arok*)
Terry Greedy, Alan Davidson, Charlie Yankos, David Ratcliffe, Steve O'Connor, Graham Jennings, Joe Watson, Jimmy Cant, Kenny Murphy, John Kosmina (C), Phil O'Connor
England (*Manager: Bobby Robson*)
Peter Shilton (C) (*Southampton*), **Phil Neal** (*Liverpool*), **Nick Pickering** (*Sunderland*), **Sammy Lee** (*Liverpool*), **Russell Osman** (*Ipswich Town*), **Terry Butcher** (*Ipswich Town*), **John Gregory** (*Queens Park Rangers*), **Paul Walsh** (*Luton Town*), **Trevor Francis** (*Sampdoria*), **Gordon Cowans** (*Aston Villa*), **John Barnes** (*Watford*)
Substitution: Nigel Spink (*Aston Villa*) (for Shilton 46), **Danny Thomas** (*Coventry City*) (for Neal 46), **Luther Blissett** (*Watford*) (for Walsh 69)

Match No. 82 – Terry Butcher, Paul Mariner, and Russell Osman

England 0 v 1 Denmark [0-1]

Wednesday, 21 September 1983, kick-off: 7.45pm
European Championship 1984 Qualifier
Wembley Stadium, London, Att: 79,323
Scorer: Denmark: Allan Simonsen (pen 36)
Live on ITV (UK): **Commentators:** Brian Moore and Brian Clough
Referee: Alexis Ponnet (Belgium)
England (*Manager: Bobby Robson*)
Peter Shilton (*Southampton*), **Phil Neal** (*Liverpool*), **Kenny Sansom** (*Arsenal*), **Sammy Lee** (*Liverpool*), **Russell Osman** (*Ipswich Town*), **Terry Butcher** (*Ipswich Town*), **Ray Wilkins (C)** (*Manchester United*), **John Gregory** (*Queens Park Rangers*), **Paul Mariner** (*Ipswich Town*), **Trevor Francis** (*Sampdoria*), **John Barnes** (*Watford*)
Substitutions: Mark Chamberlain (*Stoke City*) (for Barnes 70), **Luther Blissett** (*AC Milan*) (for Lee 77)
Denmark (*Manager: Sepp Piontek*)
Ole Kjær, Ole Rasmussen, Ivan Nielsen, Morten Olsen (C), Søren Busk, Søren Lerby, Jens Jørn Bertelsen, Jesper Olsen, Allan Simonsen, Michael Laudrup, Klaus Berggreen
Substitutions: Preben Elkjær (for Laudrup 46), Jan Mølby (for M. Olsen 85)

Match No. 83 – Terry Butcher and Paul Mariner

Hungary 0 v 3 England [0-3]

Wednesday, 12 October 1983, kick-off: 6pm (local)
European Championship 1984 Qualifier
Nepstadion, Budapest, Att: 19,956
Scorers: England: Glenn Hoddle (13), Sammy Lee (19), Paul Mariner (42)
Live on BBC (UK): **Commentator:** John Motson
Referee: Bruno Galler (Switzerland)
Hungary (*Manager: György Mezey*)
Attila Kovacs, Gyula Csonka, József Kardos, József Varga, Péter Hannich, Imre Garaba, László Dajka, Ferenc Csongrádi, Tibor Nyilasi (C), Győző Burcsa, Gyula Hajszán
Substitutions: Antal Nagy (for Burcsa 46), László Szokolai (for Hannich 64)
England (*Manager: Bobby Robson*)
Peter Shilton (*Southampton*), **John Gregory** (*Queens Park Rangers*), **Kenny Sansom** (*Arsenal*), **Sammy Lee** (*Liverpool*), **Alvin Martin** (*West Ham United*), **Terry Butcher** (*Ipswich Town*), **Bryan Robson (C)** (*Manchester United*), **Glenn Hoddle** (*Tottenham Hotspur*), **Paul Mariner** (*Ipswich Town*), **Luther Blissett** (*AC Milan*), **Gary Mabbutt** (*Tottenham Hotspur*)
Substitution: Peter Withe (*Aston Villa*) (for Blissett 74)

Match No. 84 – Terry Butcher and Paul Mariner

Luxembourg 0 v 4 England [0-2]

Wednesday, 16 November 1983, kick-off: 7.15pm (local)
European Championship 1984 Qualifier
Stade Municipal, Luxembourg, Att: 5,418
Scorers: England: Bryan Robson (10, 56), Paul Mariner (38), Terry Butcher (50)
Live on ITV (UK): **Commentators:** Brian Moore and Brian Clough
Referee: Cornelius Bakker (Netherlands)
Luxembourg (*Manager: Louis Pilot*)
Jean-Paul Defrang, Romain Michaux, Hubert Meunier, Gilbert Dresch (C), Marcel Bossi, Nico Wagner, Guy Hellers, Théo Malget, Jean-Pierre Barboni, Jeannot Hoffmann, Roby Langers
Substitutions: Jean-Paul Girres (for Malget 56), Gérard Jeitz (for Barboni 71)
England (*Manager: Bobby Robson*)
Ray Clemence (*Tottenham Hotspur*), **Mike Duxbury** (*Manchester United*), **Kenny Sansom** (*Arsenal*), **Sammy Lee** (*Liverpool*), **Alvin Martin** (*West Ham United*), **Terry Butcher** (*Ipswich Town*), **Bryan Robson (C)** (*Manchester United*), **Glenn Hoddle** (*Tottenham Hotspur*), **Paul Mariner** (*Ipswich Town*), **Tony Woodcock** (*Arsenal*), **Alan Devonshire** (*West Ham United*)
Substitution: John Barnes (*Watford*) (for Woodcock 24)

Match No. 85 – Terry Butcher

France 2 v 0 England [0-0]

Wednesday, 29 February 1984, kick-off: 8.30pm (local)

International Friendly Match

Parc des Princes, Paris, Att: 45,554

Scorer: France: Michel Platini (58, 71)

Referee: Marcel Van Langenhove (Belgium)

France (*Manager: Michel Hidalgo*)

Joël Bats, Patrick Battiston, Manuel Amoros, Yvon Le Roux, Maxime Bossis, Jean Tigana, Luis Fernandez, Alain Giresse, José Touré, Michel Platini (C), Bruno Bellone

Substitutions: Thierry Tusseau (for Battiston 72), Dominique Rocheteau (for Bellone 83)

England (*Manager: Bobby Robson*)

Peter Shilton (*Southampton*), **Mike Duxbury** (*Manchester United*), **Kenny Sansom** (*Arsenal*), **Sammy Lee** (*Liverpool*), **Graham Roberts** (*Tottenham Hotspur*), **Terry Butcher** (*Ipswich Town*), **Bryan Robson (C)** (*Manchester United*), **Brian Stein** (*Luton Town*), **Paul Walsh** (*Luton Town*), **Glenn Hoddle** (*Tottenham Hotspur*), **Steve Williams** (*Southampton*)

Substitutions: John Barnes (*Watford*) (for Lee 78), **Tony Woodcock** (*Arsenal*) (for Stein 78)

Match No. 86 – Terry Butcher

England 1 v 0 Northern Ireland [1-0]

Wednesday, 4 April 1984, kick-off: 7.45pm

Home International Championship 1983/84

Wembley Stadium, London, Att: 24,000

Scorer: England: Tony Woodcock (49)

Referee: Ron Bridges (Wales)

England (*Manager: Bobby Robson*)

Peter Shilton (*Southampton*), **Viv Anderson** (*Nottingham Forest*), **Alan Kennedy** (*Liverpool*), **Sammy Lee** (*Liverpool*), **Graham Roberts** (*Tottenham Hotspur*), **Terry Butcher** (*Ipswich Town*), **Bryan Robson (C)** (*Manchester United*), **Ray Wilkins** (*Manchester United*), **Tony Woodcock** (*Arsenal*), **Trevor Francis** (*Sampdoria*), **Graham Rix** (*Arsenal*)

Northern Ireland (*Manager: Billy Bingham*)

Jim Platt, Jimmy Nicholl, Mal Donaghy, John McClelland, Gerry McElhinney, Martin O'Neill (C), Gerry Armstrong, Sammy McIlroy, Billy Hamilton, Norman Whiteside, Ian Stewart

Match No. 87 – Terry Butcher

England 1 v 0 East Germany [0-0]

Wednesday, 12 September 1984, kick-off: 7.45pm
International Friendly Match
Wembley Stadium, London, Att: 23,951
Scorer: England: Bryan Robson (82)
Referee: Albert Thomas (Netherlands)
England (*Manager: Bobby Robson*)
Peter Shilton (*Southampton*), **Mike Duxbury** (*Manchester United*), **Kenny Sansom** (*Arsenal*), **Steve Williams** (*Southampton*), **Mark Wright** (*Southampton*), **Terry Butcher** (*Ipswich Town*), **Bryan Robson (C)** (*Manchester United*), **Ray Wilkins** (*AC Milan*), **Paul Mariner** (*Arsenal*), **Tony Woodcock** (*Arsenal*), **John Barnes** (*Watford*)
Substitutions: Mark Hateley (*AC Milan*) (for Mariner 80), **Trevor Francis** (*Sampdoria*) (for Woodcock 80)
East Germany (*Manager: Bernd Stange*)
René Müller, Ronald Kreer, Hans-Jürgen Dörner (C), Dirk Stahmann, Uwe Zötzsche, Rainer Troppa, Matthias Liebers, Wolfgang Steinbach, Joachim Streich, Rainer Ernst, Ralf Minge
Substitutions: Hans Richter (for Streich 76), Jürgen Raab (for Ernst 89)

Match No. 88 – Terry Butcher

England 5 v 0 Finland [2-0]

Wednesday, 17 October 1984, kick-off: 7.45pm
World Cup 1986 Qualifier, Group Three
Wembley Stadium, London, Att: 47,234
Scorers: England: Mark Hateley (29, 49), Tony Woodcock (40), Bryan Robson (71), Kenny Sansom (85)
Referee: Aleksander Suchanek (Poland)
England (*Manager: Bobby Robson*)
Peter Shilton (*Southampton*), **Mike Duxbury** (*Manchester United*), **Kenny Sansom** (*Arsenal*), **Steve Williams** (*Southampton*), **Mark Wright** (*Southampton*), **Terry Butcher** (*Ipswich Town*), **Bryan Robson (C)** (*Manchester United*), **Ray Wilkins** (*AC Milan*), **Mark Hateley** (*AC Milan*), **Tony Woodcock** (*Arsenal*), **John Barnes** (*Watford*)
Substitutions: Gary Stevens (*Tottenham Hotspur*) (for Duxbury 46), **Mark Chamberlain** (*Stoke City*) (for Robson 75)
Finland (*Manager: Martti Kuusela*)
Olli Huttunen, Esa Pekonen, Pauno Kymäläinen (C), Aki Lahtinen, Erkka Petäjä. Kai Haaskivi, Leo Houtsonen, Kari Ukkonen, Jukka Ikäläinen, Pasi Rautiainen, Ari Valvee
Substitutions: Hannu Turunen (for Haaskivi 46), Ari Hjelm (for Valvee 70)

Match No. 89 – Terry Butcher

Turkey 0 v 8 England [0-3]

Wednesday, 14 November 1984,
kick-off: 2pm (local)
World Cup 1986 Qualifier, Group Three
Besiktas Ismet Inönü Stadyumu, Istanbul, Att: 26,494
Scorers: England: Bryan Robson (13, 44, 59), Tony Woodcock (17, 61), John Barnes (47, 53), Viv Anderson (86)
Referee: Vojteck Christian (Czechoslovakia)
Turkey (*Manager: Candan Tarhan*)

Yaşar Duran, İsmail Kartal, Yusuf Altıntaş, Kemal Serdar, Cem Pamiroğlu (C), Raşit Çetiner, Müjdat Yetkiner, Rıdvan Dilmen, Ahmet Keloglu, İlyas Tüfekçi, Erdal Keser
Substitutions: Tuncay Soyak (for Tüfekçi 46)
England (*Manager: Bobby Robson*)

Peter Shilton (*Southampton*), **Viv Anderson** (*Arsenal*), **Kenny Sansom** (*Arsenal*), **Steve Williams** (*Southampton*), **Mark Wright** (*Southampton*), **Terry Butcher** (*Ipswich Town*), **Bryan Robson (C)** (*Manchester United*), **Ray Wilkins** (*AC Milan*), **Peter Withe** (*AC Milan*), **Tony Woodcock** (*Arsenal*), **John Barnes** (*Watford*)
Substitutions: **Trevor Francis** (*Sampdoria*) (for Woodcock 66), **Gary Stevens** (*Tottenham Hotspur*) (for Williams 67)

Match No. 90 – Terry Butcher

Northern Ireland 0 v 1 England [0-0]

Wednesday, 27 February 1985, kick-off: 7.30pm
World Cup 1986 Qualifier, Group Three
Windsor Park, Belfast, Att: 28,500
Scorer: England: Mark Hateley (76)
Live on BBC (UK): **Commentators:** John Motson and Trevor Brooking
Referee: Volker Roth (West Germany)
Northern Ireland (*Manager: Billy Bingham*)

Pat Jennings, Jimmy Nicholl, Mal Donaghy, John O'Neill, John McClelland, Paul Ramsey, Gerry Armstrong, Sammy McIlroy, Jimmy Quinn, Norman Whiteside, Ian Stewart
England (*Manager: Bobby Robson*)

Peter Shilton (*Southampton*), **Viv Anderson** (*Arsenal*), **Kenny Sansom** (*Arsenal*), **Gary Stevens** (*Tottenham Hotspur*), **Alvin Martin** (*West Ham United*), **Terry Butcher** (*Ipswich Town*), **Trevor Steven** (*Everton*), **Ray Wilkins (C)** (*AC Milan*), **Mark Hateley** (*AC Milan*), **Tony Woodcock** (*Arsenal*), **John Barnes** (*Watford*)
Substitution: **Trevor Francis** (*Sampdoria*) (for Woodcock 78)

Match No. 91 – Terry Butcher

England 2 v 1 Republic of Ireland [1-0]

Tuesday, 26 March 1985, kick-off: 7.45pm
International Friendly Match
Wembley Stadium, London, Att: 34,793
Scorers: England: Trevor Steven (45), Gary Lineker (76), **Republic of Ireland:** Liam Brady (88)
Referee: George Smith (Scotland)
England (*Manager: Bobby Robson*)
Gary Bailey (*Manchester United*), **Viv Anderson** (*Arsenal*), **Kenny Sansom** (*Arsenal*), **Trevor Steven** (*Everton*), **Mark Wright** (*Southampton*), **Terry Butcher** (*Ipswich Town*), **Bryan Robson (C)** (*Manchester United*), **Ray Wilkins** (*AC Milan*), **Mark Hateley** (*AC Milan*), **Gary Lineker** (*Leicester City*), **Chris Waddle** (*Newcastle United*)
Substitutions: Peter Davenport (*Nottingham Forest*) (for Hateley 73), **Glenn Hoddle** (*Tottenham Hotspur*) (for Robson 82)
Republic of Ireland (*Manager: Eoin Hand*)
Pat Bonner, Chris Hughton, Jim Beglin, Mark Lawrenson, Mick McCarthy, Liam Brady, Ronnie Whelan, Gary Waddock, Eamonn O'Keefe, Frank Stapleton (C), Paul McGrath
Substitutions: David O'Leary (for McGrath 46), Kevin O'Callaghan (for Whelan 70), John Byrne (for O'Keefe 79)

Match No. 92 – Terry Butcher

Romania 0 v 0 England [0-0]

Wednesday, 1 May 1985, kick-off: 6pm (local)
World Cup 1986 Qualifier, Group Three
Stadionul 23 August, Bucharest, Att: 70,000
Scorer: None
Live on BBC (UK): **Commentators:** John Motson and Bobby Charlton
Referee: Emilio Guruceta (Spain)
Romania (*Manager: Mircea Lucescu*)
Silviu Lung, Nicolae Negrilă, Costică Ştefănescu (C), Nicolae Ungureanu, Mircea Rednic, Gino Iorgulescu, Marcel Coraş, Michael Klein, Rodion Cămătaru, Ladislau Bölöni, Gheorghe Hagi
Substitutions: Ştefan Iovan (for Iorgulescu 40), Marius Lăcătuş (for Coraş 78)
England (*Manager: Bobby Robson*)
Peter Shilton (*Southampton*), **Viv Anderson** (*Arsenal*), **Kenny Sansom** (*Arsenal*), **Trevor Steven** (*Everton*), **Mark Wright** (*Southampton*), **Terry Butcher** (*Ipswich Town*), **Bryan Robson (C)** (*Manchester United*), **Ray Wilkins** (*AC Milan*), **Paul Mariner** (*Arsenal*), **Trevor Francis** (*Sampdoria*), **John Barnes** (*Watford*)
Substitutions: Chris Waddle (*Newcastle United*) (for Barnes 73), **Gary Lineker** (*Leicester City*) (for Mariner 83)

Match No. 93 – Terry Butcher

Finland 1 v 1 England [1-0]

Wednesday, 22 May 1985, kick-off: 6pm (local)
World Cup 1986 Qualifier, Group Three
Olympiastadion, Helsinki, Att: 30,311
Scorers: Finland: Jari Rantanen (5), **England:** Mark Hateley (50)
Live on ITV (UK): **Commentators:** Brian Moore and Mick Channon
Referee: Siegfried Kirschen (East Germany)
Finland (*Manager: Martti Kuusela*)

Olli Huttunen, Aki Lahtinen, Pauno Kymäläinen (C), Jukka Ikäläinen, Jyrki Nieminen, Hannu Turunen, Leo Houtsonen, Kari Ukkonen, Mika Lipponen, Pasi Rautiainen, Jari Rantanen

Substitutions: Ari Hjelm (for Ukkonen 79), Erkka Petäjä (for Lahtinen 86)
England (*Manager: Bobby Robson*)

Peter Shilton (*Southampton*), **Viv Anderson** (*Arsenal*), **Kenny Sansom** (*Arsenal*), **Trevor Steven** (*Everton*), **Terry Fenwick** (*Queens Park Rangers*), **Terry Butcher** (*Ipswich Town*), **Bryan Robson (C)** (*Manchester United*), **Ray Wilkins** (*AC Milan*), **Mark Hateley** (*AC Milan*), **Trevor Francis** (*Sampdoria*), **John Barnes** (*Watford*)

Substitution: Chris Waddle (*Newcastle United*) (for Steven 78)

Match No. 94 – Terry Butcher

Scotland 1 v 0 England [0-0]

Saturday, 25 May 1985, kick-off: 3pm
Rous Cup 1985
Hampden Park, Glasgow, Att: 66,439
Scorer: Scotland: Richard Gough (68)
Live on BBC (England & Wales): **Commentators:** John Motson and Jimmy Hill
Live on BBC (Scotland): **Commentator:** Archie McPherson
Referee: Michel Vautrot (France)
Scotland (*Manager: Jock Stein*)

Jim Leighton, Richard Gough, Maurice Malpas, Roy Aitken, Alex McLeish, Willie Miller, Gordon Strachan, Graeme Souness (C), Steve Archibald, Jim Bett, David Speedie

Substitution: Murdo MacLeod (for Strachan 71)
England (*Manager: Bobby Robson*)

Peter Shilton (*Southampton*), **Viv Anderson** (*Arsenal*), **Kenny Sansom** (*Arsenal*), **Glenn Hoddle** (*Tottenham Hotspur*), **Terry Fenwick** (*Queens Park Rangers*), **Terry Butcher** (*Ipswich Town*), **Bryan Robson (C)** (*Manchester United*), **Ray Wilkins** (*AC Milan*), **Mark Hateley** (*AC Milan*), **Trevor Francis** (*Sampdoria*), **John Barnes** (*Watford*)

Substitutions: Chris Waddle (*Newcastle United*) (for Barnes 63), **Gary Lineker** (*Leicester City*) (for Hoddle 78)

Match No. 95 – Terry Butcher

Italy 2 v 1 England [0-0]

Thursday, 6 June 1985, kick-off: 2pm (local)
Ciudad de México Cup
Estadio Azteca, Mexico City, Att: 8,000
Scorers: Italy: Salvatore Bagni (73), Alessandro Altobelli (pen 90+1), **England:** Mark Hateley (75)
Live on ITV (UK): **Commentators:** In Mexico: Brian Moore and Mick Channon. In the UK: Martin Tyler with Ian St John and Jimmy Greaves from the fifth to 19th minutes.
Referee: Antonio Ramirez Márquez (Mexico)
Italy (*Manager: Enzo Bearzot*)
Giovanni Galli, Giuseppe Bergomi, Pietro Vierchowod, Giuseppe Baresi, Fulvio Collovati (C), Roberto Tricella, Bruno Conti, Salvatore Bagni, Giuseppe Galderisi, Antonio Di Gennaro, Alessandro Altobelli
Substitutions: Franco Tancredi (for Galli 76), Antonio Cabrini (for Collovati 46), Pietro Fanna (for Conti 46), Marco Tardelli (for Galderisi 85)
England (*Manager: Bobby Robson*)
Peter Shilton (*Southampton*), **Gary Stevens** (*Everton*), **Kenny Sansom** (*Arsenal*), **Trevor Steven** (*Everton*), **Mark Wright** (*Southampton*), **Terry Butcher** (*Ipswich Town*), **Bryan Robson (C)** (*Manchester United*), **Ray Wilkins** (*AC Milan*), **Mark Hateley** (*AC Milan*), **Trevor Francis** (*Sampdoria*), **Chris Waddle** (*Newcastle United*)
Substitutions: Glenn Hoddle (*Tottenham Hotspur*) (for Steven 64), **John Barnes** (*Watford*) (for Waddle 70), **Gary Lineker** (*Leicester City*) (for Francis 78)

Match No. 96 – Terry Butcher

West Germany 0 v 3 England [0-1]

Wednesday, 12 June 1985, kick-off: 2pm (local)
Azteca 2000 Tournament
Estadio Azteca, Mexico City, Att: 8,000
Scorers: England: Bryan Robson (34), Kerry Dixon (54, 67)
Live on ITV (UK): **Commentators:** Brian Moore and Mick Channon
Referee: Jorge Leanza Sansonen (Mexico)
West Germany (*Manager: Franz Beckenbauer*)
Harald Schumacher (C), Thomas Berthold, Andreas Brehme, Ditmar Jakobs, Matthias Herget, Klaus Augenthaler, Pierre Littbarski, Lothar Matthäus, Frank Mill, Felix Magath, Uwe Rahn
Substitutions: Olaf Thon (for Magath 60), Herbert Waas (for Littbarski 73)
England (*Manager: Bobby Robson*)
Peter Shilton (*Southampton*), **Gary Stevens** (*Everton*), **Kenny Sansom** (*Arsenal*), **Glenn Hoddle** (*Tottenham Hotspur*), **Mark Wright** (*Southampton*), **Terry Butcher** (*Ipswich Town*), **Bryan Robson (C)** (*Manchester United*), **Peter Reid** (*Everton*), **Kerry Dixon** (*Chelsea*), **Gary Lineker** (*Leicester City*), **Chris Waddle** (*Newcastle United*)
Substitutions: John Barnes (*Watford*) (for Lineker 60), **Paul Bracewell** (*Everton*) (for Robson 73)

Match No. 97 – Terry Butcher

USA 0 v 5 England [0-2]

Sunday, 16 June 1985, kick-off: 5pm (local)
International Friendly Match presented by Paramark
Memorial Coliseum, Los Angeles, Att: 10,145
Scorers: England: Gary Lineker (13, 47), Kerry Dixon (30, 73), Trevor Steven (81)
Referee: Edgardo Codesal Méndez (Mexico)
USA (*Manager: Alkis Panagoulias*)
Arnie Mausser, Perry Van der Beck, Mike Windischmann, Dan Canter, Paul Caligiuri, Ed Radwanski, Kevin Crow, John Kerr, Hugo Pérez, Rick Davis (C), Bruce Murray
Substitutions: Tim Harris (for Mausser 46), Jacques LaDouceur (for Murray 46), Jeff Hooker (for Kerr 46), Michael Brady (for Canter 54), Troy Snyder (for Radwanski 79)
England (*Manager: Bobby Robson*)
Chris Woods (*Norwich City*), **Viv Anderson** (*Arsenal*), **Kenny Sansom** (*Arsenal*), **Glenn Hoddle** (*Tottenham Hotspur*), **Terry Fenwick** (*Queens Park Rangers*), **Terry Butcher** (*Ipswich Town*), **Bryan Robson (C)** (*Manchester United*), **Paul Bracewell** (*Everton*), **Kerry Dixon** (*Chelsea*), **Gary Lineker** (*Leicester City*), **Chris Waddle** (*Newcastle United*)
Substitutions: Dave Watson (*Norwich City*) (for Sansom 55), **Peter Reid** (*Everton*) (for Robson 63), **Trevor Steven** (*Everton*) (for Hoddle 63), **John Barnes** (*Watford*) (for Waddle 75)

Match No. 98 – Terry Butcher

Israel 1 v 2 England [1-0]

Wednesday, 26 February 1986,
kick-off: 4.45pm (local)
International Friendly Match
Ramat Gan Stadium, Tel Aviv, Att: 30,000
Scorers: Israel: Eli Ohana (7), **England:** Bryan Robson (51, pen 86)
Live on BBC (UK): **Commentator:** Barry Davies
Referee: Philippe Mercier (Switzerland)
Israel (*Manager: Yosef Mirmorvich*)
Avi Ran, Eitan Aharoni, Efraim Davidi, Motti Ivanir, Avi Cohen (C), Menashe Shimonov, Rifaat Turk, Uri Malmilian, Zahi Armeli, Moshe Sinai, Eli Ohana
Substitutions: Moshe Alu (for Davidi 42), Eli Cohen (for Turk 62), Ronny Rosenthal (for Ohana 62)
England (*Manager: Bobby Robson*)
Peter Shilton (*Southampton*), **Gary Stevens** (*Everton*), **Kenny Sansom** (*Arsenal*), **Glenn Hoddle** (*Tottenham Hotspur*), **Alvin Martin** (*West Ham United*), **Terry Butcher** (*Ipswich Town*), **Bryan Robson (C)** (*Manchester United*), **Ray Wilkins** (*AC Milan*), **Kerry Dixon** (*Chelsea*), **Peter Beardsley** (*Newcastle United*), **Chris Waddle** (*Tottenham Hotspur*)
Substitutions: Tony Woodcock (*Arsenal*) (for Dixon 53), **John Barnes** (*Watford*) (for Waddle 80), **Chris Woods** (*Norwich City*) (for Shilton 81)

Match No. 99 – Terry Butcher

USSR 0 v 1 England [0-0]

Wednesday, 26 March 1986, kick-off: 8pm (local)
International Friendly Match
Dinamo Stadium, Tbilisi, Att: 62,000
Scorer: England: Chris Waddle (67)
Live on ITV (UK): **Commentators:** Martyn Tyler and David Pleat
Referee: Velitchko Tzonchev (Bulgaria)
USSR (*Manager: Eduard Malofeyev*)
Rinat Dasayev (C), Volodymyr Bezsonov, Aleksandre Chivadze, Anatoliy Demyanenko, Aleksandr Bubnov, Oleh Kuznetsov, Sergey Gotsmanov, Oleksandr Zavarov, Sergei Aleinikov, Georgi Kondratiev, Sergei Rodionov
Substitutions: Hennadiy Lytovchenko (for Bezsonov 57), Oleg Blokhin (for Rodionov 57), Igor Dobrovolski (for Zavarov 75)
England (*Manager: Bobby Robson*)
Peter Shilton (*Southampton*), **Viv Anderson** (*Arsenal*), **Kenny Sansom** (*Arsenal*), **Glenn Hoddle** (*Tottenham Hotspur*), **Mark Wright** (*Southampton*), **Terry Butcher** (*Ipswich Town*), **Gordon Cowans** (*AS Bari*), **Ray Wilkins (C)** (*AC Milan*), **Peter Beardsley** (*Newcastle United*), **Gary Lineker** (*Everton*), **Chris Waddle** (*Tottenham Hotspur*)
Substitutions: Steve Hodge (*Aston Villa*) (for Cowans 52), **Trevor Steven** (*Everton*) (for Waddle 75)

Match No. 100 – Terry Butcher

England 2 v 1 Scotland [2-0]

Wednesday, 23 April 1986, kick-off: 7.45pm
Rous Cup 1986
Wembley Stadium, London, Att: 68,357
Scorers: England: Terry Butcher (27), Glenn Hoddle (43), **Scotland:** Graeme Souness (pen 56)
Live on ITV (England): **Commentator:** Martyn Tyler
Live on ITV (Scotland & Grampian): **Commentators:** Jock Brown and Lou Macari
Referee: Michel Vautrot (France)
England (*Manager: Bobby Robson*)
Peter Shilton (*Southampton*), **Gary Stevens** (*Everton*), **Kenny Sansom** (*Arsenal*), **Glenn Hoddle** (*Tottenham Hotspur*), **Dave Watson** (*Norwich City*), **Terry Butcher** (*Ipswich Town*), **Steve Hodge** (*Aston Villa*), **Ray Wilkins (C)** (*AC Milan*), **Mark Hateley** (*AC Milan*), **Trevor Francis** (*Sampdoria*), **Chris Waddle** (*Tottenham Hotspur*)
Substitutions: Peter Reid (*Everton*) (for Wilkins 46), **Gary Stevens** (*Tottenham Hotspur*) (for Hodge 75)
Scotland (*Manager: Alex Ferguson*)
Alan Rough, Richard Gough, Maurice Malpas, Graeme Souness (C), Alex McLeish, Willie Miller, Steve Nicol, David Speedie, Charlie Nicholas, Roy Aitken, Eamonn Bannon
Substitution: Pat Nevin (for Nicholas 58)

Match No. 101 – Terry Butcher

Mexico 0 v 3 England [0-3]

Saturday, 17 May 1986, kick-off: 3pm (local)
World Cup warm-up match
Memorial Coliseum, Los Angeles, Att: 63,770
Scorers: England: Mark Hateley (22, 30), Peter Beardsley (37)
Referee: Vincent Mauro (USA)
Mexico (*Manager: Bora Miluntinovic*)
Pablo Larios, Mario Trejo, Félix Cruz, Armando Manzo, Raúl Servín, Carlos Muñoz, Miguel España, Manuel Negrete, Javier Aguirre (C), Carlos Hermosillo, Luis Flores
Substitutions: Francisco Javier Cruz (for Manzo 46), Fernando Quirarte (for Hermosillo 46), Alejandro Dominguez (for España 75)

England (*Manager: Bobby Robson*)
Peter Shilton (*Southampton*), **Viv Anderson** (*Arsenal*), **Kenny Sansom** (*Arsenal*), **Glenn Hoddle** (*Tottenham Hotspur*), **Terry Fenwick** (*Queens Park Rangers*), **Terry Butcher** (*Ipswich Town*), **Bryan Robson (C)** (*Manchester United*), **Ray Wilkins** (*AC Milan*), **Mark Hateley** (*AC Milan*), **Peter Beardsley** (*Newcastle United*), **Chris Waddle** (*Tottenham Hotspur*)
Substitutions: Kerry Dixon (*Chelsea*) (for Hateley 71), **John Barnes** (*Watford*) (for Waddle 71), **Gary Stevens** (*Tottenham Hotspur*) (for Robson 71), **Trevor Steven** (*Everton*) (for Wilkins 80)

Match No. 102 – Terry Butcher

Canada 0 v 1 England [0-0]

Saturday, 24 May 1986, kick-off: midday (local)
World Cup warm-up match
Swangard Stadium, Vancouver, Att: 8,150
Scorer: England: Mark Hateley (61)
Referee: John Meachin (Canada)
Canada (*Manager: Tony Waiters*)
Paul Dolan, Bob Lenarduzzi, Bruce Wilson (C), Randy Ragan, Terry Moore, Randy Samuel, Carl Valentine, Gerry Gray, Paul James, Igor Vrablic, Mike Sweeney
Substitutions: Dale Mitchell (for Valentine '76), Jamie Lowery (for Gray 80)
England (*Manager: Bobby Robson*)
Peter Shilton (*Southampton*), **Gary Stevens** (*Everton*), **Kenny Sansom** (*Arsenal*), **Glenn Hoddle** (*Tottenham Hotspur*), **Alvin Martin** (*West Ham United*), **Terry Butcher** (*Ipswich Town*), **Steve Hodge** (*Aston Villa*), **Ray Wilkins (C)** (*AC Milan*), **Mark Hateley** (*AC Milan*), **Gary Lineker** (*Everton*), **Chris Waddle** (*Tottenham Hotspur*)
Substitutions: Chris Woods (*Norwich City*) (for Shilton 46), **Peter Reid** (*Everton*) (for Wilkins 73), **Peter Beardsley** (*Newcastle United*) (for Lineker 74), **John Barnes** (*Watford*) (for Waddle 74)

Match No. 103 – Terry Butcher

Portugal 1 v 0 England [0-0]

Tuesday, 3 June 1986, kick-off: 4pm (local)
1986 World Cup, First Phase, Group F
Estadio Tecnológico, Monterrey, Att: 19,998
Scorer: Portugal: Carlos Manuel (75)
Live on BBC1 (World Cup Grandstand): **Commentators:** John Motson and Jimmy Hill
Referee: Volker Roth (West Germany)
Portugal (*Manager: José Torres*)
Manuel Bento (C), Augusto Inácio, António Sousa, António Oliveira, Álvaro Magalhães, Diamantino Miranda, Jaime Pacheco, Frederico Rosa, Fernando Gomes, Carlos Manuel, António André
Substitutions: Paulo Futre (for Gomes 74), José António (for Diamantino 83)
England (*Manager: Bobby Robson*)
Peter Shilton (*Southampton*), **Gary Stevens** (*Everton*), **Kenny Sansom** (*Arsenal*), **Glenn Hoddle** (*Tottenham Hotspur*), **Terry Fenwick** (*Queens Park Rangers*), **Terry Butcher** (*Ipswich Town*), **Bryan Robson (C)** (*Manchester United*), **Ray Wilkins** (*AC Milan*), **Mark Hateley** (*AC Milan*), **Gary Lineker** (*Everton*), **Chris Waddle** (*Tottenham Hotspur*)
Substitutions: Steve Hodge (*Aston Villa*) (for Robson 79), **Peter Beardsley** (*Newcastle United*) (for Waddle 79)

Match No. 104 – Terry Butcher

Morocco 0 v 0 England [0-0]

Friday, 6 June 1986, kick-off: 4pm (local)
1986 World Cup, First Phase, Group F
Estadio Tecnológico, Monterrey, Att: 19,998
Scorer: None
Live on ITV (World Cup '86): **Commentators:** Martin Tyler and David Pleat
Referee: Gabriel Gonzales Roa (Paraguay)
Morocco (*Manager: José Faria*)
Ezzaki Badou (C), Labid Khalifa, Abdelmajid Lamriss, Mustapha El Biyaz, Noureddine Bouyahyaoui, Abdelmajid Dolmy, Abderrazak Khairi, Aziz Bouderbala, Abdelkrim Merry, Mohamed Timoumi, Mustafa Merry
Substitutions: Lahcen Ouadani (for Lamriss 74), Abdelaziz Souleimani (for Merry 88)
England (*Manager: Bobby Robson*)
Peter Shilton (*Southampton*), **Gary Stevens** (*Everton*), **Kenny Sansom** (*Arsenal*), **Glenn Hoddle** (*Tottenham Hotspur*), **Terry Fenwick** (*Queens Park Rangers*), **Terry Butcher** (*Ipswich Town*), **Bryan Robson (C)** (*Manchester United*), **Ray Wilkins** (*AC Milan*), **Mark Hateley** (*AC Milan*), **Gary Lineker** (*Everton*), **Chris Waddle** (*Tottenham Hotspur*)
Substitutions: Steve Hodge (*Aston Villa*) (for Robson 42), **Gary Stevens** (*Tottenham Hotspur*) (for Hateley 76)

Match No. 105 – Terry Butcher

Poland 0 v 3 England [0-3]

Wednesday, 11 June 1986, kick-off: 4pm (local)
1986 World Cup, First Phase, Group F
Estadio Universitario de Nuevo León, Monterrey,
Att: 22,700
Scorer: England: Gary Lineker (8, 14, 36)
Live on BBC1 (World Cup Grandstand): **Commentators:** Barry Davies and Jimmy Hill
Referee: André Daina (Switzerland)
Poland (*Manager: Antoni Piechniczek*)
Józef Młynarczyk, Krzysztof Pawlak, Stefan Majewski, Marek Ostrowski, Roman Wójcicki, Waldemar Matysik, Ryszard Komornicki, Jan Urban, Zbigniew Boniek (C), Dariusz Dziekanowski, Włodzimierz Smolarek
Substitutions: Jan Karaś (for Komornicki 23), Andrzej Buncol (for Matysik 46)
England (*Manager: Bobby Robson*)
Peter Shilton (C) (*Southampton*), **Gary Stevens** (*Everton*), **Kenny Sansom** (*Arsenal*), **Glenn Hoddle** (*Tottenham Hotspur*), **Terry Fenwick** (*Queens Park Rangers*), **Terry Butcher** (*Ipswich Town*), **Trevor Steven** (*Everton*), **Peter Reid** (*Everton*), **Steve Hodge** (*Aston Villa*), **Gary Lineker** (*Everton*), **Peter Beardsley** (*Newcastle United*)
Substitutions: Chris Waddle (*Tottenham Hotspur*) (for Beardsley 75), **Kerry Dixon** (*Chelsea*) (for Lineker 86)

Match No. 106 – Terry Butcher

Paraguay 0 v 3 England [0-1]

Wednesday, 18 June 1986, kick-off: midday (local)
1986 World Cup, Round of 16
Estadio Azteca, Mexico City, Att: 98,728
Scorers: England: Gary Lineker (32, 73), Peter Beardsley (56)
Live on BBC1 (World Cup Grandstand): **Commentators:** John Motson and Jimmy Hill
Live on ITV (World Cup '86): **Commentators:** Martin Tyler and David Pleat
Referee: Jamal Al Sharif (Syria)
Paraguay (*Manager: Cayetano Ré*)
Roberto Fernández, Juan Torales, César Zabala, Vladimiro Schetina, Rogelio Delgado (C), Jorge Nunes, Buenaventura Ferreira, Julio César Romero, Roberto Cabañas, Adolfino Cañete, Alfredo Mendoza
Substitution: Jorge Guasch (for Torales 64)
England (*Manager: Bobby Robson*)
Peter Shilton (C) (*Southampton*), **Gary Stevens** (*Everton*), **Kenny Sansom** (*Arsenal*), **Glenn Hoddle** (*Tottenham Hotspur*), **Alvin Martin** (*West Ham United*), **Terry Butcher** (*Ipswich Town*), **Trevor Steven** (*Everton*), **Peter Reid** (*Everton*), **Steve Hodge** (*Aston Villa*), **Gary Lineker** (*Everton*), **Peter Beardsley** (*Newcastle United*)
Substitutions: **Gary Stevens** (*Tottenham Hotspur*) (for Reid 58), **Mark Hateley** (*AC Milan*) (for Beardsley 82)

Match No. 107 – Terry Butcher

Argentina 2 v 1 England [0-0]

Sunday, 22 June 1986, kick-off: midday (local)
1986 World Cup, Quarter-Final
Estadio Azteca, Mexico City, Att: 114,580
Scorers: Argentina: Diego Maradona (51, 55), **England:** Gary Lineker (81)
Live on BBC1 (World Cup Grandstand): **Commentators:** Barry Davies and Jimmy Hill
Live on ITV (World Cup 86): **Commentators:** Martin Tyler and David Pleat
Referee: Ali Bennaceur (Tunisia)
Argentina (*Manager: Carlos Bilardo*)
Nery Pumpido, José Luis Cuciuffo, José Luis Brown, Oscar Ruggeri, Julio Olarticoechea, Sergio Batista, Jorge Burruchaga, Ricardo Giusti, Héctor Enrique, Diego Maradona (C), Jorge Valdano
Substitution: Carlos Tapia (for Burruchaga 77)
England (*Manager: Bobby Robson*)
Peter Shilton (C) (*Southampton*), **Gary Stevens** (*Everton*), **Kenny Sansom** (*Arsenal*), **Glenn Hoddle** (*Tottenham Hotspur*), **Terry Fenwick** (*Queens Park Rangers*), **Terry Butcher** (*Ipswich Town*), **Trevor Steven** (*Everton*), **Peter Reid** (*Everton*), **Steve Hodge** (*Aston Villa*), **Gary Lineker** (*Everton*), **Peter Beardsley** (*Newcastle United*)
Substitutions: Chris Waddle (*Tottenham Hotspur*) (for Reid 66), **John Barnes** (*Watford*) (for Steven 76)

Match No. 108 – Richard Wright

Malta 1 v 2 England [1-1]

Saturday, 3 June 2000, kick-off: 4pm (local)
Malta FA Centenary Celebration Match
Ta'Qali National Stadium, Valletta, Att: 10,023
Scorers: Malta: Richard Wright (og 28), **England:** Martin Keown (22), Emile Heskey (75)
Referee: Stefano Braschi (Italy)
Malta (*Manager: Josif Ilić*)
Ernest Barry, Brian Said, Michael Spiteri, Silvo Vella, Darren Debono, John Buttigieg, Carmel Busuttil (C), David Carabott, Noel Turner, Joe Brincat, Gilbert Agius
Substitutions: David Camilleri (for Debono 33), Daniel Theuma (for Vella 40), Chucks Nwoko (for Busuttil 46), Jeffrey Chetcuti (for Buttigieg 54), George Mallia (for Agius 60), Digger Okonkwo (for Said 77), Luke Dimech (for Spiteri 77), Jonathan Holland (for Brincat 82), Nenad Vaselji (for Turner 86), Mario Muscat (for Barry 90), Adrian Ciantar (for Carabott 90+1)
England (*Manager: Kevin Keegan*)
Richard Wright (*Ipswich Town*), **Gary Neville** (*Manchester United*), **Phil Neville** (*Manchester United*), **Dennis Wise** (*Chelsea*), **Sol Campbell** (*Tottenham Hotspur*), **Martin Keown** (*Arsenal*), **David Beckham** (*Manchester United*), **Paul Scholes** (*Manchester United*), **Alan Shearer (C)** (*Newcastle United*), **Kevin Phillips** (*Sunderland*), **Nicky Barmby** (*Everton*)
Substitutions: Emile Heskey (*Liverpool*) (for Shearer 50), **Gareth Southgate** (*Aston Villa*) (for Keown 57), **Robbie Fowler** (*Liverpool*) (for Phillips 68), **Paul Ince** (*Middlesbrough*) (for Scholes 68), **Steve McManaman** (*Real Madrid*) (for Wise 68), **Gareth Barry** (*Aston Villa*) (for Beckham 79)

STATISTICS SECTION

APPEARANCES & GOALS

England games and goals while a player with Ipswich

Appearances	ITFC	Total
Terry Butcher	45	77
Mick Mills	42	42
Paul Mariner	33	35
Russell Osman	11	11
Kevin Beattie	9	9
Brian Talbot	5	6
David Johnson	3	8
Ray Crawford	2	2
Eric Gates	2	2
Colin Viljoen	2	2
Trevor Whymark	1	1
Richard Wright	1	2

Goals	ITFC	Total
Paul Mariner	13	13
David Johnson	3	5
Terry Butcher	3	3
Kevin Beattie	1	1
Ray Crawford	1	1

Key: *ITFC: Caps/goals while at Ipswich*

Total: Total number of caps/goals

175

PLAYER SUMMARIES

	P	W	D	L	F	A	GS
Beattie, Kevin							
World Cup Qualifiers	3	2	0	1	4	3	0
Euro Qualifiers	3	2	1	0	7	1	0
Home Championship	1	1	0	0	5	1	1
Friendlies	2	1	0	1	2	3	0
Totals	9	6	1	2	18	8	1
Butcher, Terry							
World Cup	9	4	3	2	12	4	0
World Cup Qualifiers	5	4	2	0	15	1	0
Euro Qualifiers	7	4	2	1	20	3	1
Home Championship	6	4	1	0	7	1	1
Friendlies	18	11	2	5	27	14	1
Totals	45	27	10	8	81	23	3
Crawford, Ray							
Home Championship	1	0	1	0	1	1	0
Friendlies	1	1	0	0	3	1	1
Totals	2	1	1	0	4	2	1
Gates, Eric							
World Cup Qualifiers	2	1	0	1	5	2	0
Totals	2	1	0	1	5	2	0
Johnson, David							
Home Championship	2	1	1	0	7	3	3
Friendlies	1	1	0	0	2	1	0
Totals	3	2	1	0	9	4	3
Mariner, Paul							
World Cup	5	3	2	0	6	1	1
World Cup Qualifiers	8	6	0	2	19	6	4
Euros	2	1	0	1	2	2	0
Euro Qualifiers	5	3	1	1	12	3	2
Home Championship	8	6	1	1	13	8	2
Friendlies	5	3	0	2	10	6	4
Totals	33	22	4	7	62	26	13

	P	W	D	L	F	A	GS
Mills, Mick							
World Cup	5	3	2	0	6	1	0
World Cup Qualifiers	8	5	0	3	14	10	0
Euros	1	1	0	0	2	1	0
Euro Qualifiers	6	5	1	0	18	5	0
Home Championship	12	9	0	3	20	8	0
Friendlies	10	5	2	3	21	14	0
Totals	42	28	5	9	81	39	0
Osman, Russell							
World Cup Qualifiers	3	0	1	2	2	4	0
Euro Qualifiers	2	0	1	1	2	3	0
Friendlies	6	2	3	1	6	5	0
Totals	11	2	5	4	10	12	0
Talbot, Brian							
Home Championship	2	1	0	1	3	3	0
Friendlies	3	0	3	0	1	1	0
Totals	5	1	3	1	4	4	0
Viljoen, Colin							
Home Championship	2	0	2	0	2	2	0
Totals	2	0	2	0	2	2	0
Whymark, Trevor							
World Cup Qualifiers	1	1	0	0	2	0	0
Totals	1	1	0	0	2	0	0
Wright, Richard							
Friendlies	1	1	0	0	2	1	0
Totals	1	1	0	0	2	1	0
Totals	156	92	32	32	280	123	21

Old Wembley Stadium just days before it was demolished

OPPONENTS RECORD

Full lists of opposition faced

Kevin Beattie

Team	Comp	P	W	D	L	F	A	Gls
Cyprus	Euros Q	2	2	0	0	6	0	
Finland	World Cup Q	1	1	0	0	2	1	
Italy	World Cup Q	1	0	0	1	0	2	
Luxembourg	World Cup Q	1	1	0	0	2	0	
Netherlands	Friendly	1	0	0	1	0	2	
Portugal	Euros Q.	1	0	1	0	1	1	
Scotland	Home Champs	1	1	0	0	5	1	1
Switzerland	Friendly	1	1	0	0	2	1	
	Totals	9	6	1	2	18	8	1

Terry Butcher

Team	Comp	P	W	D	L	F	A	Gls
Argentina	World Cup	1	0	0	1	1	2	
Australia	Friendlies	4	2	2	0	4	2	
Canada	Friendly	1	1	0	0	1	0	
Czechoslovakia	World Cup	1	1	0	0	2	0	
Denmark	Euros Q	2	0	1	1	2	3	
East Germany	Friendly	1	1	0	0	1	0	
Finland	World Cup Q	2	1	1	0	6	1	
France	World Cup	1	1	0	0	3	1	
	Friendly	1	0	0	1	0	2	
Greece	Euros Q	1	0	1	0	0	0	
Hungary	Euros Q	2	2	0	0	5	0	
Israel	Friendly	1	1	0	0	2	1	
Italy	Friendly	1	0	0	1	1	2	
Luxembourg	Euros Q	2	2	0	0	13	0	1
Mexico	Friendly	1	1	0	0	3	0	
Morocco	World Cup	1	0	1	0	0	0	
Northern Ireland	World Cup Q	1	1	0	0	1	0	
	Home Champs	2	1	1	0	1	0	

Paraguay	World Cup	1	1	0	0	3	0	
Poland	World Cup	1	1	0	0	3	0	
Portugal	World Cup	1	0	0	1	0	1	
Rep of Ireland	Friendly	1	1	0	0	2	1	
Romania	World Cup Q	1	0	1	0	0	0	
Scotland	Home Champs	2	2	0	0	3	0	
	Friendlies	2	1	0	1	2	2	1
Spain	World Cup	1	0	1	0	0	0	
	Friendly	1	0	0	1	1	2	
Turkey	World Cup Q	1	1	0	0	8	0	
USA	Friendly	1	1	0	0	5	0	
USSR	Friendly	1	1	0	0	1	0	
Wales	Home Champs	2	2	0	0	3	1	1
West Germany	World Cup	1	0	1	0	0	0	
	Friendlies	2	1	0	1	4	2	
	Totals	45	27	10	8	81	23	3

Ray Crawford

Team	Comp	P	W	D	L	F	A	Gls
Austria	Friendly	1	1	0	0	3	1	1
Northern Ireland	Euros Q	1	0	1	0	1	1	0
	Totals	2	1	1	0	4	2	1

Eric Gates

Team	Comp	P	W	D	L	F	A	Gls
Norway	World Cup Q	1	1	0	0	4	0	0
Romania	World Cup Q	1	0	0	1	1	2	0
	Totals	2	1	0	1	5	2	0

David Johnson

Team	Comp	P	W	D	L	F	A	Gls
Scotland	Home Champs	1	1	0	0	5	1	1
Switzerland	Friendly	1	1	0	0	2	1	0
Wales	Home Champs	1	0	1	0	2	2	2
	Totals	3	2	1	0	9	4	3

Old Wembley Stadium just days before it was demolished

Paul Mariner

Team	Comp	P	W	D	L	F	A	Gls
Australia	Friendly	1	1	0	0	2	1	1
Czechoslovakia	World Cup	1	1	0	0	2	0	
Denmark	Euros Q	2	0	1	1	2	3	
Finland	Friendly	1	1	0	0	4	1	2
France	World Cup	1	1	0	0	3	1	1
Greece	Euros Q	1	1	0	0	3	0	
Hungary	World Cup Q	2	2	0	0	4	1	1
	Euros Q	1	1	0	0	3	0	1
Italy	Euros	1	0	0	1	0	1	
Kuwait	World Cup	1	1	0	0	1	0	
Luxembourg	World Cup Q	2	2	0	0	7	0	1
	Euros Q	1	1	0	0	4	0	1
Netherlands	Friendly	1	1	0	0	2	0	1
Northern Ireland	Home Champs	2	1	1	0	3	2	
Norway	World Cup Q	2	1	0	1	5	2	1
Scotland	Home Champs	3	3	0	0	4	0	1
Spain	World Cup	1	0	1	0	0	0	
	Euros	1	1	0	0	2	1	1
	Friendly	1	0	0	1	1	2	
Switzerland	World Cup Q	2	1	0	1	3	3	1
Wales	Home Champs	3	2	0	1	6	6	1
West Germany	World Cup	1	0	1	0	0	0	
	Friendly	1	0	0	1	1	2	
	Totals	33	22	4	7	62	26	13

Mick Mills

Team	Comp	P	W	D	L	F	A
Austria	Friendly	1	0	0	1	3	4
Brazil -	Friendlies	2	0	1	1	1	2
Bulgaria	Euros Q	1	1	0	0	3	0
Czechoslovakia	World Cup	1	1	0	0	2	0
Denmark	Euros Q	2	2	0	0	5	3
Finland	World Cup Q	2	2	0	0	6	2
	Friendly	1	1	0	0	4	1

France	World Cup	1	1	0	0	3	1
Hungary	World Cup Q	2	2	0	0	4	1
	Friendly	1	1	0	0	4	1
Italy	World Cup Q	1	0	0	1	0	2
	Friendly	1	1	0	0	3	2
Kuwait	World Cup	1	1	0	0	1	0
Northern Ireland	Euros Q	2	2	0	0	9	1
	Home Champs	4	4	0	0	9	1
Norway	World Cup Q	1	0	0	1	1	2
Rep of Ireland	Euros Q	1	0	1	0	1	1
Scotland	Home Champs	5	3	0	2	7	5
Spain	World Cup	1	0	1	0	0	0
	Euros	1	1	0	0	2	1
	Friendly	1	1	0	0	2	0
Switzerland	World Cup Q	2	1	0	1	3	3
Wales	Home Champs	3	2	0	1	4	2
	Friendly	1	1	0	0	2	1
West Germany	World Cup	1	0	1	0	0	0
	Friendly	1	0	0	1	1	2
Yugoslavia	Friendly	1	0	1	0	1	1
	Totals	42	28	5	9	81	39

Russell Osman

Team	Comp	P	W	D	L	F	A
Australia	Friendlies	4	2	2	0	4	2
Denmark	Euros Q	2	0	1	1	2	3
Iceland	Friendly	1	0	1	0	1	1
Norway	World Cup Q	1	0	0	1	1	2
Romania	World Cup Q	1	0	1	0	0	0
Spain	Friendly	1	0	0	1	1	2
Switzerland	World Cup Q	1	0	0	1	1	2
	Totals	11	2	5	4	10	12

Old Wembley Stadium just days before it was demolished

Brian Talbot

Team	Comp	P	W	D	L	F	A
Argentina	Friendly	1	0	1	0	1	1
Brazil	Friendly	1	0	1	0	0	0
Northern Ireland	Home Champs	1	1	0	0	2	1
Scotland	Home Champs	1	0	0	1	1	2
Uruguay	Friendly	1	0	1	0	0	0
	Totals	5	1	3	1	4	4

Colin Viljoen

Team	Comp	P	W	D	L	F	A
Northern Ireland	Home Champs	1	0	1	0	0	0
Wales	Home Champs	1	0	1	0	2	2
	Totals	2	0	2	0	2	2

Trevor Whymark

Team	Comp	P	W	D	L	F	A
Luxembourg	World Cup Q	1	1	0	0	2	0
	Totals	1	1	0	0	2	0

Richard Wright

Team	Comp	P	W	D	L	F	A
Malta	Friendly	1	1	0	0	2	1
	Totals	1	1	0	0	2	1

ACKNOWLEDGEMENTS

RESEARCHING and writing this book would not have been possible had it not been for the permission and help of several people.

First and foremost, my heartfelt thanks go to Chris Goodwin of England Football Online for allowing me use of match reports and statistical information from his excellent website which can be found at: www.englandfootballonline.com.

The information available on this website is phenomenal and has just about everything you ever need to know about those players who have represented England over the years.

For the purpose of this book, I am grateful for the use of match reports supplied on Chris's website by Norman Giller for matches one to 106, and to Mike Payne for matches 107 and 108. Thank you so much, Chris.

For the fourth time of writing an Ipswich Town-related book, huge thanks to Brad Lloyd of Glory Days Artwork. Brad is an amazing illustrator who has now provided the artwork for all four of my books. Not only does that keep a consistent look to them all, but it is also a testament to the consistent work of Brad who continues to illustrate such masterpieces. Take a look at his work at: www.glorydaysartwork.co.uk. Thank you so much as always, Brad. I would be lost without you.

I would also like to thank Michael Smart for sending me photos of the old Wembley Stadium that he took just days before its demolishment. That historic stadium not only saw Ipswich win the FA Cup in 1978, and play-off final in 2000, but also, those many England games that featured Ipswich players. Thank you, Michael.

It has been an absolute honour and a privilege to interview some of those players to have represented both Ipswich Town and England. At some point in my time of supporting the club, they have all been heroes of mine.

To talk to them personally was a massive moment on each occasion. All were so very helpful and afforded me all the time I needed to chat away about their Town and country careers.

I had interviewed Kevin Beattie many years ago and luckily retained those recordings to refer to. What a lovely man 'Beat' was, and always good for a story.

I am indebted to my friend Julian Rose for putting me in touch with ESPN's Mark Donaldson, the author of Paul Mariner's *My Rock and Roll Football Story*. Mark was able to provide me with some stories of Paul's international career and kindly gave me permission to use material from his book. Thank you so much, Julian and Mark.

In turn, Mark also gave me contact details for Joe Corrigan. Not previously an Ipswich player of course, but a man who had a strong connection to those Ipswich players that he lined up alongside while on England duty. Joe spoke with passion and glowingly about those Ipswich players of the time and was, again, a lovely man to talk to. Thank you for your help, Joe.

The first of those players I spoke to in early 2024 was Ray Crawford – the first Ipswich player to play for England. What an honour that was. Ray was an absolute pleasure to talk to and even arranged for his wife Carol to send me some photos for the book, which I am very grateful for. Thank you to you both.

In February 2024, it was a thrill to interview Terry Butcher before a recording of the current Ipswich Town YouTube show *Life's a Pitch* and then Russell Osman after the recording. They formed a formidable partnership for Town and country, and it is great to see them still paired together on the show after all these years. They too were insightful to sit and listen to.

It was also an honour when Terry agreed to write the foreword to this book. I am so grateful for this act of generosity. Thank you, Terry, and Russell, They also assisted with putting me in contact with two more legends in Brian Talbot and Eric Gates.

Again, two fantastic interviews, although I was apparently very lucky to get hold of Eric who does not have a mobile phone and is never at home! Thank you, Brian and Eric, for giving up your time to talk with me.

Lastly, my final interview was with Richard Wright who gave up some time to speak to me over Easter when he was busy in his current employment with Manchester City. Another hero of mine and the only Ipswich and England player who I have seen play live at Wembley. Thank you for your time, Richard.

I must also thank my regular helper Matt Holland, who arranged for me to speak with Richard. Without your help, Matt, that would not have been possible. Thank you as always.

And as they did with my first Ipswich book, *Town on the Telly*, what another great job Steve Caron and his team at JMD Media have done in putting this book together for me. I thank you all for your work and patience with me to publish yet another excellent book.

Thank you to all those involved in helping another dream of mine to materialise in seeing *For Town and Country* in print.

Printed in Great Britain
by Amazon

52760725R00108